The Scarecrow's Legion

or

Smuggling in the South East

The Scarecrow's Legion

or

Smuggling in the South East

by

Geoffrey Hufton and **Elaine Baird**

ROCHESTER PRESS
1983

First Published 1983

ISBN 0 946379 181

Geoffrey Hufton is a solicitor living and practising in the Medway towns. Besides writing, his interests include church architecture and playing squash. He is married with two children.

Elaine Baird was formerly a librarian at the Brighton Library. She retired recently, however, and has since been elected as a local councillor. She lives at Worthing and is interested in all aspects of Sussex history.

Published by Rochester Press Ltd, PO Box SX19, Upchurch, Sittingbourne, Kent ME9 7HU
Printed in Great Britain by Clark Constable (1982) Ltd, Edinburgh

Contents

Introduction

There is a legend down on Romney Marsh that back in the days when smuggling was rife one unfortunate participant in that business fell under suspicion of passing information to the authorities. Such was the desperate nature of his associates that he was summarily beaten to death in the most brutal manner and his body dismembered, the parts being scattered around the marsh as a grim warning to those who might be ill-advised enough to follow his example. It is further said that on dark moonless nights when the sea mist rolls over the marsh and it is even more eerie than usual the ghost of the murdered man can be seen wandering across the fields searching vainly for the parts of his body; and that until he finds them he will know no rest.

A little fanciful perhaps? Maybe, but such stories are often founded on actual events and the existence of this gruesome tale gives a clue to the true nature of the smuggling trade which flourished in Kent and Sussex from the Middle Ages until the nineteenth century.

The figure of the smuggler has ever fascinated authors and provided material for innumerable tales of intrigue and high adventure. The events which actually occurred during the heyday of the smuggling trade, which lasted from the mid seventeenth to the mid nineteenth century, for once provide us with stories which are every bit as wild as may be dreamed in the fiction writer's imagination. In an island nation like Britain it is perhaps inevitable that over the centuries many of the people should have made their living from this highly profitable business. Almost every county (even those inland like, for instance, Wiltshire with its moonrakers) can tell its stories of the free traders. In Kent and Sussex however a degree of lawlessness has, in the past, been achieved by the inhabitants which is perhaps unparalleled anywhere else in the country, with the possible exception of Cornwall.

Ideas as to the character of the smuggler vary considerably. On the one hand, he has been elevated to the status of a hero and on the other denigrated as a murdering ruffian. Richard Harris Barham included a poem entitled 'The Smuggler's Leap' in his *Ingoldsby Legends*. The tale is based on a Thanet Legend concerning a disused chalkpit where a revenue officer named Anthony Gill of Sandwich is alleged to have died whilst in pursuit of a smuggler and has as its hero one 'Smuggler Bill' who is described by Barham as follows:

> Smuggler Bill is six feet high,
> He has curling locks and a roving eye,
> He has a tongue and he has a smile
> Trained the female heart to beguile, . . .

A dashing romantic figure indeed and, of course, Barham should have known. He was Rector of Snargate and Warehorn, deep in smuggling territory, in 1817, and his churches are known to have been used for storing contraband. Barham himself refers to meetings with smugglers whilst out at night on the lonely Marsh roads. There is nonetheless ample evidence to support the opposite view with numerous stories of the violent measures which were adopted from time to time to escape capture and safeguard illegal cargoes. The truth of the matter is that two very distinct categories of smuggler existed. Many people were involved to some degree or another. Most were small operators, running the odd cargo and perhaps regarding the whole thing as a profitable sport. Others however, as we shall see, adopted an altogether more ruthless approach.

It would be a great mistake, however, to judge the smuggler by the standards of the late twentieth century when a wide range of luxury goods are available to all and the treatment of criminals, by comparison at least, fairly lenient. Firstly it should be remembered that those involved in smuggling were not, in the main, thieves. The cargoes which were brought ashore would have been bought and paid for on the other side of the Channel in perfectly legitimate business deals. Endeavours to evade the harsh customs duties imposed at the time were hardly more reprehensible in the eyes of those involved than modern attempts to avoid income tax liability. Secondly the law was harsh to the point of savagery in criminal matters, with flogging being the punishment for the most minor of offences and hanging reserved for crimes which were hardly more serious. Charles Dickens wrote his *Barnaby Rudge* partly as a protest against the criminal laws of the eighteenth and nineteenth centuries in general and public execution in particular. He relates a story in the preface, one that is to be woven into the tale much later, which is completely true and brings home to us the cruelty of the times in the most poignant way. It happened in 1777:

> Under this Act [the Shop-lifting Act] One Mary Jones was executed, whose case I shall just mention; it was at the time when press warrants were issued on the alarm about Falkland Islands. The woman's husband was pressed, their goods seized for some debts of his and she, with two small children turned into the streets a-begging. It is a circumstance not to be forgotten, that she was very young (under nineteen) and most remarkably handsome. She went to a linen draper's shop, took some course linen off the counter an slipped it under her cloak; the shopman saw her and she laid it down; for this she was hanged. . . . Her defence was that she had lived in credit and wanted for nothing, till a press gang stole her husband from her but since then she had no bed to lie on; nothing to give her children to eat; and they were almost naked; . . . . When brought to

receive sentence, she behaved in such a frantic manner, as proved her mind to be in a distracted and disponding state; and the child was suckling at her breast when she set out for Tyburn.

Such was the England of the smuggling era. It is of particular interest to our story that this unfortunate woman's tradegy arose as a direct result of the activities of the press gang. The coastal counties suffered much at the hands of that institution.

Whatever the nature of the smugglers, two things are certain; that the 'trade' was as highly organised as any legitimate business and that they generally had the sympathy and support of the population at large. To quote Barham again:

> there is not a farmer there but he still
> buys gin and tobacco from Smuggler Bill

Likewise Rudyard Kipling in his *Smugglers Song* wrote of:

> Five and twenty ponies,
> Trotting through the dark,
> Brandy for the Parson,
> 'Baccy for the Clerk

Kent is, of course, the part of England which lies closest to the mainland of Europe from which most of the luxury contraband goods came. The great expanse of Romney Marsh with its secluded inlets and concealing mists was a smuggler's paradise. The people of this and other coastal areas in the country were frequently visited by the Royal Navy press gangs and it is hardly surprising therefore that such communities, frequently deprived of able-bodied bread-winners should turn to the trade as a means of bringing in additional money, supporting 'fatherless' families and, no doubt, getting some revenge on the establishment which, after all, gave them precious little.

Increasing urbanisation and the commercial development of seaside towns on the South East coast have in many places destroyed the atmosphere and romance of those old halcyon smuggling days. In the Romney Marsh however much of this atmosphere and romance still survives. Barham wrote that 'the world is divided into five parts, namely Europe, Asia, Africa, America and Romney Marsh'. The visitor can still see what he meant. An air of loneliness still surrounds the area and many of its small towns and villages remain little changed by the twentieth century. It is not difficult here to conjure up pictures in the imagination of moonless, misty nights with flat-bottomed boats gliding silently into remote creeks; of men toiling in the darkness and of revenue officers lying in ambush.

All of what follows is true. The authors have, however, succumbed on occasion to the temptation to refer in passing to the exploits of the notorious Doctor Syn (alias 'The Scarecrow'). Visitors who search for the name of this good parson on the roll at Dymchurch do so in vain. The character is entirely the product of the imagination of Russell Thorndike. The Syn stories are, however, woven against a factual backcloth and the devil riders of the Scarecrow's legion, who fought so many battles with the forces of law and order and who struck terror into the hearts of those who fell foul of them, do indeed typify the ruthlessness and ingenuity of the most notorious smugglers.

It is in their memory, though certainly not their honour, that this history is written.

CHAPTER I

Beginnings of the trade

William Lambarde, the Kentish historian writing in the late sixteenth century, refers to a mighty inundation of the sea which occurred in the Low Countries around the end of the reign of William the Second. The calamity resulted in a massive influx to Britain of refugees seeking new homes. These unfortunates were welcomed readily, being, as they were, skilled weavers and clothiers. It is to their descendants that the 'honour' of developing the smuggling trade into a large scale industry is accorded.

English wool being of a quality unparalleled elsewhere in Europe, a brisk and thriving legitimate trade in textiles was for many years carried on between the Flemish settlers in Kent who had established themselves successfully as wool merchants and their kinsmen in Flanders. The prosperity of this business was hindered however by the conflict of interests of the wool merchants and the native English weavers. The weavers, who desired to restrict the export of wool in order that their own supplies could be safeguarded and maintained at lower prices, were, on the whole, the more sucessful in their endeavours. As a result high taxes were imposed on exports of wool and restrictions placed upon the ports from which it could be despatched.

The imposition of import and export taxes was nothing new. In 1275 the 'New Custom' was enacted, but this really did nothing more than legalise a very ancient method of raising revenue for the Crown. What was new was the scale of the taxation. Export duty on wool was imposed at £3 a bag, this being increased to £6 in 1298. English wool was worth only 1s. 6d. a pound.

Wool was the most important export of the country in medieval times (the Lord Chancellor himself sits on the 'woolsack' in Parliament, as a symbol of our source of wealth). It was this fact that led to smuggling on so huge a scale that it was estimated that as much, and very probably more, wool was exported illegally than legally. Much of this wool came from Kent and Sussex. Huge flocks grazed Romney Marsh, the coastal areas of Worthing and Brighton and the country round Chichester. In Tudor times, for example, records exist of a landowner at Hove being fined for keeping more than the statutory allowance of 2,000 sheep.

In 1274 an inquiry into the illegal export of wool from Shoreham is noted in the hundred rolls. We can suppose this was no isolated event. In one year, 1287, the following amounts of wool were legally exported from Sussex ports:

Chichester	104 sacks	4 cloves	7,272 fells
Shoreham	238 sacks	31 cloves	5,476 fells
Seaford	113 sacks	25 cloves	3,127 fells

A sack was 364 lbs, a clove 7 lbs, and a fell was a whole skin. Therefore it is clear that a considerable legal trade in wool existed in Kent and Sussex, and in this early period, the west part of Sussex exported more wool than the east part. If the later, Stuart, estimates are to be believed, and hold good also for the early period, even more wool would have been exported illegally.

In the following century the innumerable wars with France, and several outbreaks of plague, affected the legal export of wool and records are sparse. In 1353 several English ports were selected as Staples, the one for Sussex being Chichester. Here the wool had to be taken, weighed and the tax paid before it could be exported. In 1364–5 The Chichester Customers attended on occasions at Lewes, so that wool could be evaluated there, due to complaints about the inconvenience of the system. Before 1353, the Mayors of Winchelsea and Chichester had been directed not to allow the export of wool until the duty had been paid. In 1343 an Act was passed to fix the price of wool, the fixing being done by officials. In 1341 the duty was fifty shillings a sack, an enormous amount in those days.

The wool growers were gradually squeezed out of their livelihood and turned to smuggling. Initially the chief object of the trade was the export of wool as those involved sought only to continue their old business. These medieval forerunners of the later, more notorious smugglers were a tough breed; in general more so than their counterparts of the eighteenth and nineteenth centuries who dealt in tobacco, tea, silk and spirits. The wool smugglers became known as owlers possibly as a result of the warning signal they used whilst in pursuit of their business. The work was arduous and, for those who undertook the labour and danger, not very lucrative. They were employed by the wool producers and by the seventeenth century were only being paid one shilling for a night's work.

It does not need much imagination to see that this mixture of inconvenience, price fixing and heavy duty was an open invitation to smuggling. Although the references to illegal export are sparse until late Tudor and Stuart times, it is fair assumption that it flourished in the Medieval period. There are a few tantalising references on record.

In 1394 there was issued a

> Pardon to John Russell of Lewes, for, with others, shipping over sea at night on the feast of St. Margaret in the 17th year, 3 sacks of wools, uncustomed and uncoketted, in Kyngeston Havene at Goring, co. Sussex, in the boat of Laurence Blake, a denizen and in like manner exporting on Friday night in the first week of August from Kyngeston four sacks in sixteen pockets in the vessel of John Paynot.

Laurence Blake, 'denizen', was roughly the equivalent of what in modern times we would call a naturalised Briton. The good flat beach at Goring remained a favourite place for the later import smugglers, as well as being constantly used by 'the owlers'.

And three years later, in February, a complicated situation occurred in which all the parties were pardoned on the supplication of Edmond, duke of York, to William Roubein who, when Thomas Kytte and Richard Bernard the elder on Tuesday night after Michaelmas in the seventeenth year had brought about four sacks of wool on horses to the sea which the said Thomas and one Laurence Hildere had sold previously to a foreigner — with Robert Smyth of Offyngton, Henry Elot, William Kytte, John Mechelgrove, John Clerk of Worthing, William Otham and Adam Gravat was indicted for that night in the highway at Worthing, near the sea, opposite the port of Kyngeston [the original document, which was in Latin as was the custom at that time, reads citra mare ex opposito], lying in hiding, seizing them with their horses and wool, and keeping them until they made a fine with them of 8 marks and promised to keep their counsel. The like to the said Robert, William Otham and Adam.

One of the earliest records of smuggling in Kent appears in the Patent Rolls dated April 18th, 1341:

> Commission to Roger Power, King's Sergeant at Arms, John Condy of Sandwich and William Forestall of Faversham to make investigation in the County of Kent touching wool and other merchandise which as is said, have been put in ships and boats on the coast by Reculver and sent beyond as the seas uncocheted and certify the King, whose were such wool and merchandise and the said ships and boats, of the value of the said merchandise and of the names of the masters of the said ships and boats.

It was the practice during the Middle Ages to 'farm out' the collection of customs to financiers (who accordingly became known as 'farmers'). The 'farmers' paid substantial amounts to the Crown and in return were granted the right to collect the import and export duties. It was a system which was riddled with corruption and there can be little doubt that the 'farmers' contributed as much to the losses of the Revenue as did the 'owlers'. It is interesting to note that Geoffrey Chaucer was appointed Controller of Customs and Subsidy of wools, skins and hides for the Port of London in 1374 and enjoyed a period of considerable prosperity in the ensuing period. Chaucer's description of the wool merchant who 'His resons he spak full solempnely' in the prologue to the *Canterbury Tales* is rather less than complimentary. The farming system was abandoned in 1671 when the first board of Commissions of Customs was appointed by Charles II.

In the mid fifteenth century the price of wool fell below the price it had held a hundred years earlier, and there were official complaints of 'abundance of wools, as well by stealth as by license, uttered into the parts beyond the sea'. Throughout the Tudor period, particularly the reign of Elizabeth, legislation flowed plentifully regulating the sale of wool, and the Queen particularly favoured the enlargement of the English wool industry by encouraging the immigration of foreign weavers, with their great skills. We can clearly see from all these facts the two basic causes of the smuggling of great quantities of tea, a few centuries later, existed as in this period with regard to wool: that is, a monopoly which enabled external forces to fix the price, and heavy taxes and licence fees. Throughout the late Tudor and the Stuart period there were a series of enactments and proclamations forbidding the export of wool, yet still the authorities granted a few licences to export, at a high price. W. S. Gent, in his *Golden Fleece*, published in 1656, complained in terms that were to become depressingly familiar in the eighteenth century when brandy and tea were being smuggled! 'So many were the evasions, such combination and interests in the officers who ought to punish; such favour had they in the courts of justice, that those most interested in trade dared not to prevent that mischief which their eyes beheld.' In 1660 an act expressly forbade the export of wool and in 1662 smuggling wool became a felony; but with little effect as the illegal export of wool along the southern coast and Romney Marsh continued as before. William Carter in *England's Interest in Trade Asserted*, published in 1671, tells us that the smugglers of Romney Marsh not only exported their own wool, but bought wool from ten and twenty miles inland and shipped that off too. He said the smuggled wool was taken to the ships, guarded with bands of about twenty armed men, and that in two years forty thousand packs of wool from Sussex and Kent had been sent to one town alone — Calais. Carter appears to have had some authority in customs matters and of him more will be heard shortly. Joseph Trevers writing four years later, said that smugglers 'are not of meanest persons in the places where they dwell, but have often times great interest with the magistrates: and, being purse proud, do not value what they spend to ingratiate themselves with persons of authority. To distrust all such as discover their fraudulent dealings, or else by bribes to stop their mouths . . . (they) are well acquainted with some attorneys and clerks . . . make good interest with the undersheriffs . . . and these have strange tricks and delays in their returns, in which some of them will take part with the offenders, instead of executing the law against them.'

Throughout the 1670's a stream of official proclamations and partisan propaganda was issued on the subject: government officials were concerned with their loss of revenue and the various companies of cloth makers were concerned with their loss of cheap wool. The 'State Papers Domestic' for May 1673 contain a very strict injunction:

> The King to the Earl of Dorset, Lord Lieutenant of Sussex. Directing him to use his utmost endeavours to discover persons transporting combed wool to France, and to search for and seize all such wool as it is probably designed to be transported, and to apprehend the owners thereof, if they cannot give a sufficient account of the same.

The government was being pushed by pressure groups on behalf of the clothmakers into further action: the State Papers contain a petition made in the following month which was typical of the utterances made by the cloth trade, which was in serious competition with weaving industries of France and the Low Countries. The clothiers had a strong lobby, were well organised in guilds, and were naturally incensed to see English wool being sold for a fair price to their competitors, instead of a fixed price to the monopoly for their own use. The wool growers, whether large landowners or small farmers, do not seem to have made their case so convincingly. The smugglers said nothing: they just went on illegally exporting wool to their own profit. The petition went as follows:

> Francis Monet and several others in behalf of themselves, the clothiers, cloth workers, dyers, and many of those poor manufacturers of the once flourishing drapery of England to the King. Petition for a commission under the Great Seal empowering them to put in execution the laws prohibiting the transportation of sheep, wool, woollen yarn, fuller's earth, and stuffs of the new drapery made of wool undyed, undressed and unfinished, as by the exportation thereof his Majesty's dominions are extremely impoverished and unpeopled, and rents decayed, and neighbouring nations augmented in wealth and populace, for his poor subjects chose to follow the materials of this manufacture, and to teach it to foreigners and enemies, rather than to starve at home.

This effusion, calculated to wring the withers of the reader, is particularly interesting in that it indicates an exodus of skilled craftsmen from this country, in addition to a diminution of profits of the clothing industry, as one of the results of smuggling activities. One of the smuggled goods mentioned, Fuller's earth, was mined at Nutley in Sussex, and there is a record of an inquiry into the export of a consignment of it, which was dropped when it was discovered that the material was in fact some other substance. Fuller's earth was used for cleansing and de-oiling the wool, and its export was forbidden under an ordnance of 1647.

The indefatigable William Carter also was active again:

> William Carter to the King and Privy Council. June 1673. Petition showing that he, finding an additional Act for preventing the transportation of wool to have passed the House of Commons the last Session and to have miscarried in the House of Lords ... and further showing that the petitioner has heard from Capt. Steele of Dover employed by His Majesty at sea to prevent the transportation of wool, that wool has been shipped in some French vessels, which pretend to be privateers, and who, having thereby safe conduct on the English Coast under pretence of their commission from the Most Christian King, will abuse their privilege and continue this mischievous practice, and therefore as the season draws near for shearing, beseeching His Majesty to issue out this Proclamation or such other orders for the more effectual execution of the laws that are in force as he shall think meet.

A note attached stated that the proclamation should be issued, by the advice of the Privy Council.

The smuggler's co-operation with their French counterparts mentioned here was to be a recurring theme throughout the history of smuggling, as indeed was the clever plan to outwit authorities by pretending to be privateers — private vessels who had special licence to stop and search vessels, and therefore were supposed to be the gamekeepers, not the poachers. Also noteworthy in this proclamation is the note of panic sounded at the oncoming of sheep shearing time. This can be seen in several official documents of the time, and the responsible officials were clearly very apprehensive at the thought of the numerous bands of men in Romney Marsh and the other coastal parts of Sussex silently and efficiently despatching their wool. In 1697 the Supervisor of Customs in Kent and Sussex wrote that in a few weeks 160,000 sheep would be shorn in Romney Marsh and the greater part of the fleece would be sent 'hot into France'.

Not everyone, however, was satisfied with words and moral strictures: William Carter converted his convictions into action. Taking out the appropriate warrants, he took a small party of men and captured about ten smugglers on Romney Marsh whom he discovered transporting wool on horseback. The amazement and incredulity of the smugglers, who had been quietly carrying on with their business, as they had done for years, can be imagined. He took his captives to the Mayor of Romney, and demanded that they be put on trial. The Mayor, probably embarrassed by this action against a trade that included practically every other person on the Marsh, let them out on bail. Carter and his company were somewhat shaken by this, and prudently retired to Lydd. Now, however, the dark side of smuggling became apparent. He was pursued by angry smugglers, who made an attack at night, so on the advice of the son of the Mayor of Lydd (it is noticeable how eagerly all the officials tried to get rid of so troublesome a right-doer) he set out the following day at speed for Rye. He and his party were chased by some fifty armed men — a terrifying experience — and at Camber Point were forced to abandon their horses as they had no time to wait for the ferry, but leapt into some nearby boats which came to their rescue and took them over to Rye. The contemporary account — 'An abstract of the proceedings of William Carter', 1694 says with splendid understatement, 'had they not got into the boats, Mr. Carter would have received some hurt, for many of the exporters were desperate fellows, not caring what mischief they did.'

There is no record of the prosecutions being proceeded with.

This incident provides a graphic illustration of the degree of violence and lawlessness which was being achieved by the smugglers. A most reprehensible crime had occurred some years earlier when in 1644 a Spanish vessel, the *Alfresia* was lured aground at Dungeness in order that its cargo of spirits could be looted and brought ashore, the crew having first been brutally murdered.

Another violent incident is contained in the Kent Quarter Sessions Records which include a deposition made by one Robert Jull of Folkestone in 1657. Jull states that in the evening of the October 9th, he was walking (patrolling one assumes) with a man named William Sneed at Shornecliff near Hythe when he saw a sloop pulled up on the shore and several bags of goods in the process of being unlawfully unloaded. He challenged the smugglers and was immediately assaulted. His assailants were armed with staves and he was knocked down, beaten and eventually forced to flee with his companion.

The unequal struggle to protect the wool cloth trade from all assaults took a truly bizarre turn in 1678 when an act ordered that the dead should be buried only in woollen shrouds, that registers and affidavits guaranteeing the material of the shrouds should be kept and be open to inspection. The words of the act have a final biblical ring, saying witnesses to the affidavit had to swear that the body, 'was not put in wrapt or wound up or buried in any shirt, shift, sheet or shroud made or mingled with flax, hempe, silke, haire, gold or silver or other than what is made of sheeps wool only'.

Ardent bibliographers have tried to argue that the purpose of this act was to save linen rags for papermaking, as paper which at that time was made mainly of linen rags was of poor quality and in short supply. This is not so, its purpose was to protect the cloth trade which was so sorely beleaguered by the activities of the wool smugglers. This act, ridiculous as it may seem, was more easily put into action than any of the legislation against armed smugglers: some affidavits and registers still exist, and there is one in the Parish Registers for Sedlescombe in 1745. Also in these registers is the chilling entry, in 1710, 'Joan Diamond, a traveller, was buried on July 2nd, and because not buried in wool, then taken up again and reburied'.

The authorities, however, were apparently satisfied that in this respect at least they were protecting the wool trade, and combating 'the misery of England' by the 'wool stolen out of the Kentish, Essex and Sussex Coasts' and the consequent unemployment bemoaned by William Carter, and we learn from the *Gazette* in 1688 that widow Amy Potter, 'has made of woollen only decent and fashionable laced dresses for the dead, as well as other plainer, for burying in woollen will be much quieted, and many hundreds of subjects employed'.

After the dizzy success of the 'Burial in Woollen Act', the authorities continued to address themselves to limiting the activities of the smugglers. Both private individuals and officials gained a monetary reward for any seizures of wool that they made. A letter in the Sate Papers, July 1676 says:

> since my last about the frigates coming in from cruising, and the *Greyhound*'s bringing in a vessal with wool commonly called an owle, I have only to acquaint you that yesterday went to sea the *Rose*, *Drake* and *Greyhound* to cruise between Dover and Beachy Head for eight days for securing trade . . . and seizing such privateers as they meet, belonging either to France or Spain . . . one third of the vessel with wool and all, comes to the King, and will come to about 25 [i.e. £25].

In fact by the beginning of the eighteenth century the situation was completely out of hand so far as the authorities were concerned. In 1705 a Treasury warrant was issued for the sum of £200 to supply a regiment with new boots and stockings, the usual allowance having been 'worn out in the pursuit of smugglers'. Daniel Defoe writing in his *Tour through the Whole Island of Great Britain* (published 1824–6) made two references to smuggling in Kent. Of Faversham Defoe wrote that it was remarkable for its notorious smuggling trade and that the local people were 'grown monstrous rich' as a result. It is notable that a local historian Edward Jacob who published his *History of Faversham* in 1774 appears to have taken great exception to such allegations:

> It would require little pains, he wrote, to satisfy persons who know the site and course of our creek, which runs not less than 3 miles within land, before it reaches its mouth or entrance to the Swale, to convince them of the ridiculousness of the repeated assertion of this town being notorious for smuggling;

Jacob suggests that the fact that smuggled goods were brought from other places to the customs house at Faversham and later advertised for sale was responsible for this reputation. Petty sessions records however do not support Jacob's view. Defoe's second reference to smuggling deals with observations made in the vicinity of Hythe:

> As I rode along this coast, I perceived several dragoons riding officers and others armed and on horseback, riding always about as if they were huntsmen, beating up their game; upon enquiring I found their diligence was employed in quest of the owlers, as they call them, and sometimes they catch some of them; but when I came to enquire further I found too, that often times those are attacked in the night, with such numbers that they dare not resist, or if they do, they are wounded and beaten and sometimes killed; and at other times are obliged as it were to stand still and see the wool carried off before their faces, not daring to meddle.

Defoe concludes by saying that notwithstanding such violence smuggling was on the decrease and the 'knots . . . very much broken'. Such a view was clearly born out of optimism rather than assessment of the true state of affairs. In truth smuggling was on the increase and the smugglers slowly turning their attentions away from the export of wool and towards the import of luxury goods where profit margins were higher and the work less arduous. It is worth noting however that owling continued, although on a gradually decreasing scale until the early years of the nineteenth century.

Some people think that the word 'owlers' is derived from a corruption of 'woollers', but this is not very likely on philological grounds. A more probable explanation of the term is the obvious one — the smugglers worked mainly by night and are said to have used an owl hoot as a signal. The term 'owlers' was always applied specifically to the illegal exporters of wool, never to the importers of brandy and luxury goods.

One of the earliest uses of the word smugglers is a proclamation of August 1661, which complained of, 'A sort of lewd people called Smuckellors, never heard of before the late disordered times, who make it their trade . . . to steal and defraud His Majesty of his Customs'.

Ships have been employed for many years to patrol the Channel for smugglers — in August 1670 John Steele was commissioned 'to be employed in a small sloop . . . to prevent the transportation of wool'.

> though there is a very Strict Act against the transportation of wool, yet great quantities arrive at Calais, where there are hundreds of wool combers, and that complaint is made by a buyer of great quantities for his own use in England, who, though the Act empowers him sufficiently to seize the same, desires further countenance by a more particular warrant.
>
> State Papers, Undated, pre 1677.

In 1696 some of the harsh punishments for smuggling wool were repealed, and it was made an offence for anyone living in Kent or Sussex within fifteen miles of the sea to buy wool without signing a bond guaranteeing that such wool should not be resold within the area. Also farmers living within ten miles of the sea had to register their fleeces at shearing time and say where they were stored. It was foolishly thought that this legislation would stop smuggling, and a false air of security was apparent in official documents of the time. The facts were otherwise: in the year of the act only 91 packs of wool were seized in Sussex and Kent, and of these only twenty could be proved to be illegal! Wool, in fact, continued to be exported illegally until the Napoleonic Wars: it is mentioned in the 1739 and 1787 Parliamentary Bills, and there are accounts in local newspapers of such exports.

For the moment, however, official quarters were well pleased with the state of affairs. Henry Baker, who was the Supervisor of Customs in Kent and Sussex wrote an official letter in 1703 advising the Contracting of the Customs service:

> May it please your Honours:
>
> In obedience to your Honours, commending me to consider how the charge of the ryding-officers appointed for the guard of the coasts of Kent and Sussex may, in some measure, be reduced without prejudice to his Majestie's service, in preventing the exportation of wool etc, from these coasts. Upon consideration thereof, and from observations I have made of that and the smuggling trade, as they have been carried on since the present warr, I have observed and do believe that the neck of the owling trade, as well as the spirit of the owlers, is, in a great measure, broke, particularly in Romney Marsh — there are not now many visable signs of any quantites being transported. But for the fine goods, as they call them (viz. silks, lace, etc.), I am well assured that the trade goes on through both counties, though not in such vast quantities as have been formerly brought in — I mean in those days when (as a gentleman of estate in one of the counties has, within this twelve months, told me) he had been at once, besides at other times, at the loading of a wagon with silks, lace, till six oxen could hardly move it out of place: I do not think that trade is now so carried on as 'twas then. Therefore, upon consideration of the whole matter, since your Honours are of opinion that it is for his Majestie's service to lessen the charge, I humbly propose: That whereas there are now, for the security of those coasts, fifty officers appointed from the Isle of Sheppey, in Kent, to Emsworth, in Hampshire, which is coastwise more than two hundred miles, at 60 li per annum, with an allowance to each of them of 30 li per annum for a servant and horse, to assist them upon their duty in the night, the whole amounting to about 4,500 li per annum . . . my opinion is . . . that the said allowance of 30 li to each of them . . . may be taken off . . . which will reduce one third part of the whole, and leave it then at about 3,000 li per anum: and for some kind of supply in their nightly duty, instead of their servants, that the course of that may not be broken, especially in Romney Marsh where the mischief has most prevailed, I further propose that the dragoons now quartered in Kent . . . be detached into severall parts of the Marsh, to assist the officer in the exportation of wool . . . If your Honours can obtain the guard of cruisers . . . for these coasts from the North Foreland to the Isle of Wight, and shall be pleased to remove your weak and superannuated officers, as soon as you can provide otherwise for them, and for the future, resolve to admit none into the service; but that the officers be kept to a strict and diligent discipline in the performance of their duties . . . I am humbly of the opinion both coasts may be ventured with a single guard . . .

The hopes expressed in this letter proved to be sadly misjudged.

Wool continued to be exported and the incoming luxury trade soon grew into an overwhelming flood. Lord Macaulay, in his *History of England*, describes large runs of Lyons silks, and Valenciennes lace in 1696, loaded onto 30 pack horses and transported inland, which he associated with Jacobite interests. These two references are among the earliest to draw attention to the trade in the import smuggling of luxuries. However, the next few years were still concerned mainly with the protection of the English wool trade. As a result of a 1638 proclamation, hats were among the goods prohibited for import into England. John Wilkinson of Hastings reported that he had

> lately seized fyve dozen and 3 hatts so prohibited which he found in the house of one John Spy of Hastings in Sussex: but the said Spy would not obey his Majestie's aucthoritie so given unto your petitioner. Likewise the officer of whome your petitioner required ayd (being the said Spy's neighbour and friend) refused to assist him. So the said Spy by force took the said hatts away, saying they were all fooles to let their goods goe upon such terms or auctority

In addition to refusing to give up the hats, Spy compounded his offence by offering bribes, 'the said Spy in bribeing way hath since byn offered gould, But he altogether desireth the offence may be punished, it being to the evill example of others'.

Spy became a freeman of Hastings a few years afterwards. The offering of bribes to the officials became common practice in the following years.

Hats were the occasion of another trouble at Hastings, when Thomas Carman of Fairlight and Thomas

Harwood of Guestling were returning from Lewes in Hastings in 1695. At Bulverhythe they noticed a ship anchored, which appeared to them to be French. They therefore kept watch, and as dark fell a boat came ashore, to be met by five men, one of whom was a well known smuggler, John Young, and Thomas Pope of Bexhill, a Customs officer. The five men went for a drink at an inn called Bulverhythe House, whose landlord, Roberts, was a member of the party. Meetings at inns and arrangements made over a drink featured in a great many smuggling ventures. Later 16 packs, a pack of hats and a 'large pacquet of letters' were handed by the Frenchman to Pope, the customs officer. This was an event that became increasingly a by-product of smuggling — the carrying of intelligence to and from the enemy. The goods were reputedly lodged in the house of Edward Hall, customs officer of Hastings. Yet another point that comes from this event is that it is indicative of the fact that many people laid what was possibly false evidence against customs officers, either from natural malevolence or in collusion with the smugglers. This was possibly such an occasion, as it seems strange that two distant observers should see such great detail, and highly unlikely that a customs officer would openly store smuggled goods in his own house. A few years later both Hall and Pope were still on duty, and sharing in prizes for goods they had legally confiscated, so it would appear that this was a false charge.

Perhaps the most important conclusion one can draw from these events is that it is small wonder that goods were smuggled, in the face of the stupidity of successive governments, which on the one hand passed foolish edicts forbidding the living to wear good French hats and the dead to wear linen and placed harsh conditions on the legal export of wool, while on the other hand they backed a parsimonious plan to patrol the coasts of Kent and Sussex with a hopelessly inadequate preventive force. While the emphasis from this time onwards was on the import smuggling of luxury goods, the export smuggling of wool continued to some degree until the era of the Napoleonic Wars.

It will perhaps be instructive to finish this chapter by considering one incident which nicely illustrates the transition of emphasis from import smuggling to export smuggling, which took place on November 14, 1713 in Fairlight Cove, 'a place famous for shipping of wool to France ... riding over Fairlight Down about one mile from the coast, observed five men crossing the down on foot . . . observed by their discourse to be four Frenchmen and one Englishman'.

The group told the customs officer to stand, or otherwise they would fire, but he came on. In the ensuing scuffle the Englishman ran off, but the four Frenchmen, 'kept close together in a posture of defence and presented their peeces at the Officer and particularly one of them snapped his fusee ... and in all probability would have murdered him but fotunately happed not to go of but only flas'd in the pan'.

The customs officer fired back and the Frenchmen submitted. These four men — Nicholas Maison, Louis Rondell, Andrew Carpentier, and Frances Pollet were smuggling goods into the country in exchange for the wool which they were taking out. This report is contained in a collection of correspondence to John Collier, Surveyor General of the Customs of Kent and Sussex, contained in the East Sussex County Record Office, which will be referred to as the Sayer Manuscripts. These manuscripts are a rich mine of information about smugglers. The Englishman, it will be noted, ran off and evaded capture, and in many accounts of encounters between smugglers and customs officers on the Romney Marsh, the smugglers, who knew every inch of the land, escaped by scattering, darting in all directions, plunging into the ditches which intersected the marsh and disappearing.

In the preceding pages we have seen that for five centuries the export smuggling of wool was done on such a considerable scale that it threatened the profitability of the legitimate wool trade — England's most important export. We have seen that successive governments were alive to the problems, and passed a never ending stream of legislation that enacted harsh punishments that were almost impossible to impose, as at the same time all governments were too mean to spend the necessary amount of money on a good preventive force. We have seen the development of a hardy race of smugglers who had the courage and means to collect wool, arrange transport, ship it under guard and find foreign buyers. We have learnt that a number of civic officials turned a blind eye to their proceedings, and that legal officers could be bribed. We have learnt that, if pushed, the smugglers would not shrink at great violence, and also that noblemen and tradesmen openly admitted associating with them. In short, the machinery, the routines, the public attitudes existed already that made the great escalation of import smuggling in the next century, when duties on luxuries rose sharply, almost inevitable.

As William Cooper wrote in 1858:

> The habit of export smuggling, then, has been, for some hundreds of years at least, part of the system under which the middle and lower classes in Kent and Sussex have been trained. Large fortunes were made by it in East Sussex, and it came to an end only during the last war with France.

The change in smuggled goods stemmed directly from the Glorious Revolution of 1688 which had involved Britain in an expensive war with the Netherlands and for which finance had to be raised. To meet this emergency import duty on tea and spirits were raised sharply, the trend being followed shortly by other luxury items. The natural result was to increase greatly the profits to be made from large-scale smuggling.

In an age where lawlessness was getting worse and social unrest escalating the smuggler was entering into his 'golden age'.

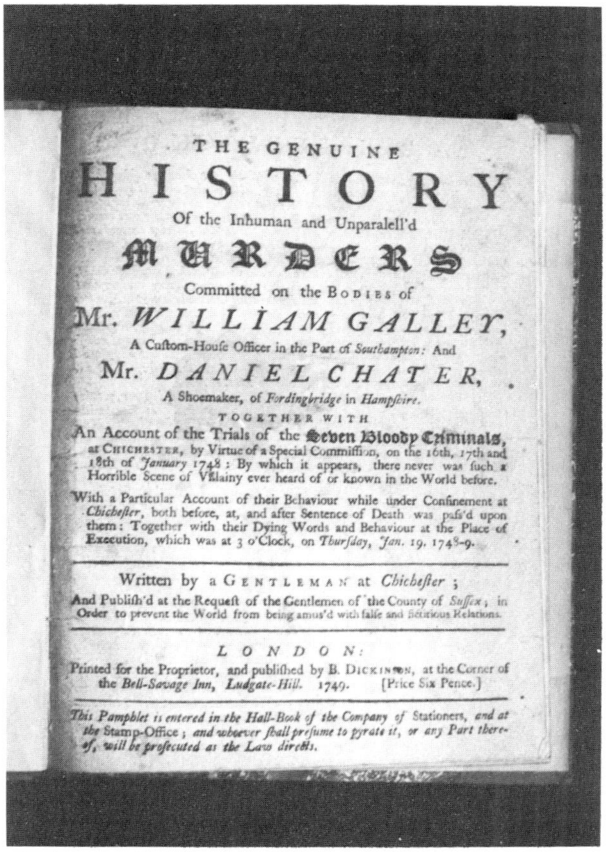

THE GENUINE
HISTORY
Of the Inhuman and Unparalell'd
MURDERS
Committed on the BODIES of
Mr. WILLIAM GALLEY,
A Custom-House Officer in the Port of *Southampton*: And
Mr. DANIEL CHATER,
A Shoemaker, of *Fordingbridge* in *Hampshire*.
TOGETHER WITH
An Account of the Trials of the Seven Bloody Criminals,
at CHICHESTER, by Virtue of a Special Commission, on the 16th, 17th and 18th of *January* 1748: By which it appears, there never was such a Horrible Scene of Villainy ever heard of or known in the World before.

With a Particular Account of their Behaviour while under Confinement at *Chichester*, both before, at, and after Sentence of Death was pass'd upon them: Together with their Dying Words and Behaviour at the Place of Execution, which was at 3 o'Clock, on *Thursday*, *Jan.* 19. 1748-9.

Written by a GENTLEMAN at *Chichester*;
And Publish'd at the Request of the Gentlemen of the County of *Sussex*; in Order to prevent the World from being amus'd with false and fictitious Relations.

LONDON:
Printed for the Proprietor, and published by B. DICKINSON, at the Corner of the *Bell-Savage Inn*, *Ludgate-Hill*. 1749. [Price Six Pence.]

This Pamphlet is entered in the Hall-Book of the Company of Stationers, *and at the* Stamp-Office; *and whoever shall presume to pyrate it, or any Part thereof, will be prosecuted as the Law directs.*

A Representation of ye Smuggler's breaking open ye KING'S. Custom House at Poole.

Mr Galley and Mr Chater put by ye Smugglers on one Horse near Rowland Castle.
A. Steele who was Admitted a Kings Evidence. B. Little Harry. C. Iackson D Carter. E. Downer. F. Richards 1 Mr Galley. 2. Mr Chater.

Galley & Chater *falling off their Horse* at Woodash, *draggs thier Heads on the Ground, while t Horse kicks them as he goes; the Smugglers still continuing thier brutish Usage.*

Chater, Chained in ye Turff House at Old Mills's.
Cobby, kicking him & Tapner, cutting him Cross ye
Eyes & Nose, while he is saying the Lords Prayer.
Several of ye other Smugglers standing by.

The unfortunate William Galley put by the Smugglers
into the Ground &c as is generally believed before
he was quite DEAD.

Chater hanging at the Well in LADY HOLT Park. the Bloody Villains Standing by

The Bloody Smugglers flinging down Stones after they had flung his Dead Body into the Well.

CHAPTER II

Strange doings by night (prosperous times) 1720–1835

Harriet Martineau, writing in the early 1800's, summed up, in one paragraph, most aspects of smuggling in this country:

> There were strange doings by night in the creeks and hollow ways and caves of the southern coast, and a remarkable order of passengers by day in the packets from France. Every now and then a fisherman's great boots were found to be stuffed with French lace, gloves and jewellery, or a lady's petticoats to be quilted all through with silk stockings and lace. Here and there a nice-looking loaf of bread was found to have a curious kernel of lace and gloves; and a roll of sail cloth turned out to be a package of gay lute-string. In the dead of night a large body of men would work for hours, noiselessly, in the soft sands, rolling tubs of spirits, and carrying bales of goods in the shadows of the rock, and through tunnels and up chasms, under the very feet of the preventive patrol, and within sound of the talk of the sentries. While this was going forward on the English coast, the smugglers on the opposite shore were engaged with much more labour, risk, and expense, in introducing English woollens, by a vast system of fraud and lying into the towns, past a series of customs-houses. In both countries there was an utter dissoluteness of morals connected with these transactions. Cheating and lying were essential to the whole system; drunkeness accompanied it; contempt for all law grew up under it; honest industry perished beneath it: and it was crowned with murder.

The success and prosperity of the smuggling trade was due in no small measure to the involvement of the inhabitants at large of Kent and Sussex. The population gave their aid to the smugglers wherever possible and were, in turn, rewarded with gifts of tea, tobacco and the like. A Maidstone man named George Bishop published a pamphlet in 1783 entitled 'Observations, Remarks and Means to Prevent Smuggling' which included the following passage:

> The smugglers are a very powerful body and can raise considerable sums of money on any occasion that offers to promote their interest; they boast of having disposed of large sums in order to prevent any hurt being done to their trade; at one time £3,000 was disposed of. So little care is taken to prevent smuggling that there is not one excise officer at Sheerness where, and in the River Medway, the revenue loses £50,000 per annum, and has done for many years back, which trade has so far increased, as nearly all the spirits, wine, tea, tobacco, raisins, etc. consumed in that neighbourhood are smuggled....

Whilst much of what Bishop wrote in his pamphlet was doubtless exaggerated the overall picture would seem to be fairly accurate and it is certainly significant that it should ever have been felt necessary to produce such a document. The establishment was seriously concerned with the problem and the writings of people like Defoe and Bishop give clear indication of this concern.

On the one hand stood the smugglers; those who carried the goods across the Channel, landed it on the beaches with an accompanying look-out, transported it inland with a guard. In order to ensure speed of unloading and dispersal, great numbers of men were employed as porters and guards. A large number of fishermen, agricultural labourers and village craftsmen were occupied in these part-time pursuits. The great majority of the local population either actively aided them with information and loan of horses and hiding places, or was tolerant of them, or passively wished 'not to know'. On the other hand were the preventive forces, consisting of a small force of riding officers with a small detachment of soldiers quartered in the area on whom they could call for assistance in emergencies. As we shall see these forces were hopelessly inadequate and at this period the smugglers had a fairly easy time of it, and so long as they avoided detection in the Channel, they had a very good chance of landing and clearing their goods successfully.

Religious leaders also lent their voices to the efforts to bring smuggling to a stop. Notably John Wesley the great Methodist leader preached sermons all around Kent and Sussex and wrote on one occasion 'I found abundance of people willing to hear the good word, at Rye in particular. But they will not part with the accursed thing smuggling.' Wesley also published a pamphlet entitled 'A Word to a Smuggler' but, as ever, the populace were unimpressed. A cup of tea or a smoke were felt more beneficial than lofty principles. It is perhaps something of an irony that the Church should campaign against the trade when so many crypts and vestries were used to store contraband and 'Brandy for the Parson' was frequently the price of silence.

One entry in the records of the customs service reads thus: 'As most of the inhabitants of Folkestone, Sandgate and Hythe are in the confidence of the smugglers, no information can be expected of them'.

Even where possible informants felt no sympathy for the smugglers it was rare for incriminating evidence to be given to the preventive men. In Lympne Castle there is an ancient four-poster bed in connection with which there exists an amusing story illustrative of the problems faced by the authorities.

In the nineteenth century the bed was owned by a Mr. and Mrs. Robinson who resided at 'The Warren', Folkestone. One night this couple (decent and law abiding people it would seem) had retired for the night to the said four-poster when a gang of ruffians forced their way into the house. Having woken the Robinsons and summarily tossed them out of bed they proceeded to conceal a number of packages under the mattress. The gang then departed bidding the terrified householders to speak 'no word on pain of death'. Shortly after this the house was invaded again; this time by excisemen who searched the premises but failed to examine the bed and left empty handed. The smugglers duly returned and retrieved their packages which turned out to contain gold. The Robinsons, having kept their silence and their magnificent bed having been broken into the bargain, were offered a handsome reward — smugglers being generally noted for their generosity towards helpers. The disgruntled couple however pointedly refused this and demanded nothing more than to be left in peace. The smugglers took their leave congratulating themselves on a successful ruse and the Robinsons returned to bed. The trade may not have made any new friends that night but neither did it suffer betrayal.

Notwithstanding such somewhat rough and ready treatment, the traders had numerous allies, business frequently being organised and financed by wealthy and respectable citizens living well away from the coastal areas. Farm labourers were often employed to undertake the arduous task of humping goods ashore. It was common practice for them to work for farmers in the summer months and the free traders in the winter. The pay from smugglers was of course much better and in 1735 farmers were forced to raise wages just to get the harvest in! Such was the support for the trade that the small village of Hawkhurst is supposed to have been able to muster a force of up to five hundred men at short notice to undertake smuggling activity. Despite being situated well inland this picturesque township is particularly notorious and the Oak and Ivy Inn which still stands was a headquarters for the most infamous gang of smugglers, not only in Kent and Sussex but anywhere in the country. But more of them later.

A debate on the Smuggling Act 1736 provides another illustration of the extent to which the general population took part in the smuggling trade. Evidence was brought that ... 'in some parts of the maritime counties the whole population was so generally engaged in smuggling that it is impossible to find a jury that will upon trial do justice to an officer of the revenue in any case whatsoever'.

To combat such massive participation the forces of law and order were pitiful. George Bishop's pamphlet referred to the lack of an excise officer at Sheerness, an absence which was conspicuous at a great many other seaboard towns around the county. Customs houses were however located at the major ports such as Deal, Dover and Folkestone and from these a number of riding officers patrolled on horseback in search of illicit cargoes being run. These officers usually operated alone and their effectiveness was greatly diminished as a result. It was an arduous and highly dangerous occupation, the smugglers being quite prepared to use violence to protect their cargoes. Successes were achieved despite all this. A notable feature of the Magistrates records for the Wingham Petty Sessional Division (which covers much of the Thanet area) is the considerable number of smuggling cases. The reports are, on the face of it, fairly mundane — reference to the seizure of goods from persons unknown. Reading between the lines however, one can visualise wild, windy nights with a lonely riding officer coming across a gang of smugglers and galloping in upon them brandishing pistols or sword and forcing them to flee leaving their cargo behind. Great courage must have been needed to attempt this and it says much for the efforts of these men that of twenty-six cases which came before the Wingham Magistrates on February 6th, 1739 twenty-one involved smuggling offences. Bribery and corruption amongst the officers was widespread, certainly, but it is unfortunate that they are frequently dismissed altogether as merely corrupt and totally ineffective. We are reminded of Barham's poem of Smuggler Bill, and of his description of the tenacious and conveniently rhyming Exciseman Gill. Bill having escaped an excisemen's ambush at Reculver (in reality a favoured landing place) is pursued by Gill who, being left behind, sells his soul to the Devil to be provided with a horse capable of catching the smuggler's superior steed:

Smuggler Bill, he looks behind,
And he sees a Dun horse come swift as the wind,
. . . And sparks round his ears, snap, crackle and play,
And his tail cocks up in a very odd way,
Every hair on his main seems a porcupine's quill,
And there on his back sits Exciseman Gill,
Crying 'yield thee, now yield thee, thou Smuggler Bill'.

If we are prepared to accept Barham's description of the dashing Smuggler Bill as being applicable to at least some of his real life counterparts, may we not also accord Anthony Gill the same credibility?

The work of the riding officers was arduous, ill paid and extremely dangerous. Such was the hostility shown to them in Whitstable that it was necessary for the authorities to construct what amounted to a citadel for them where they could be quartered and could store seized contraband in reasonable safety. The violence of opposition in the county is illustrated by a noteworthy incident which occurred at Bromley in 1742. On the August 28th of that year Thomas Quayfe, a customs official was enjoying watching a cricket match when a group of notorious smugglers rode up and attacked him, forcing him to take shelter in Bromley College, and then stole his horse. No reason is apparent for the attack but the most likely explanation is clearly that the unfortunate Quayfe was too conscientious in the performance of his duty. One of the attackers was a man named Jacob Pring who was to play an important role in the smuggling story a few years later.

An attempt at a seizure could be an extremely hazardous affair. In March 1771 three riding officers are reported as having been so seriously beaten by smugglers that 'they scarcely escaped with their lives'. It was not always the smugglers, however, who had the last laugh.

Not far from Dymchurch stand the ruins of the church of Hope All Saints. It was in its present ruinous condition even back in the old smuggling days and became a favoured spot for clandestine rendezvous where plans for running cargoes could be made. They came unstuck however when a Preventative Officer, hiding one stormy night by lying along the top of the dilapidated walls, was able to eavesdrop on such a meeting and thus obtain all the information needed to make a successful arrest and seizure of the smuggler's cargo.

Contraband seized as a result of the efforts of riding officers was, in due course, auctioned off to more honest traders. Newspapers of the period contain frequent advertisements for such auctions. Just one example is the *Kentish Gazette* of June 8th, 1768:

To be sold publicly to the highest bidder at Customs House, Deal on the 17th inst:

600 gallons of geneva	4 gallons of rum
120 gallons of brandy	50 lbs of tea

In addition to attempting to apprehend smugglers in the act of running cargoes the riding officers also had powers to arrest anyone found loitering within five miles of the coast. The records again provide examples of such arrests and details of the punishment inflicted. On December 5th, 1738 for example two men named John Lilly and John Castle were sent to a house of correction for a term of fourteen days and 'there ordered to be whipped'. These unfortunates having been found 'lurking' near the coast were convicted of intending to assist in running uncustomed goods and quite probably that is precisely what they had in mind. The nature of the offence, however, was such that the punishment would have been the same no matter what their intentions.

The waterborne Revenue forces also had occasional successes in their efforts. On June 13th, 1768 the *Macklenburgh* (a revenue cutter) was reported as having taken a sloop of 25 tons with a smuggled cargo from Ostend and Dunkirk and escorted it into Dover. Shortly after this the Winchelsea cutter 'arrived at Sheerness with a smugglers boat laden with brandy'. Such captures were not, however, always without incident.

In June 1771 the Rye cutter gave chase to a sloop from Dunkirk eventually coming up with her some four miles from the French coast. On attempting to board the vessel, however, the Customs men were met, first with strong arguments that they were out of their district and had no right to interfere with the sloop's business and, when they persisted in attempting to do their duty, with stout, violent opposition. The first two officers to attempt a boarding were severely manhandled and a third dragged on to the sloop where he appeared to be in such danger that another of his colleagues felt compelled to open fire on the smugglers with his musket, mortally wounding one of the assailants. In spite of all this, however, it appears that no seizure of any contraband was made. The Revenue forces had not, however, left empty handed a few weeks earlier. On the occasion in point a cutter from Dover overhauled a smuggling vessel and attempted to board her. One of the officers was knocked into the water, however, and the captain of the cutter decided to abandon the case. Very shortly afterwards another Dover cutter appeared and the two boats resumed the pursuit, finally catching up just as the smugglers were attempting to land near Folkestone. As usual opposition to the Customs man was violent and determined, with a crowd on the beach joining in and pelting the officials with stones. Finally one officer fired upon the smugglers with a blunderbuss, killing one and wounding another. The remaining smugglers made off and the officials seized some one hundred and fifty tubs of brandy.

Notwithstanding such intermittent success on the part of the authorities the conclusion has to be drawn, however, that the smugglers were permitted, albeit grudgingly, to practise their nefarious craft comparatively unhindered. The numerous cases brought before the courts were only the top of a very large iceberg. Besides the references in George Bishop's pamphlet to losses to the revenue of £50,000 per annum at Sheerness alone he stated that in 1777 there were smuggled from Dunkirk 2,500,000 gallons of geneva. In 1746 a Royal Commission had looked into the problem and a Captain Cockburn gave evidence to the effect that a minimum of six tons of tea and two thousand half ankers of brandy were smuggled into Kent from the one port of Boulogne. One Robert Hanning claimed to sell contraband to the value of £40,000 a year. During this period the smugglers prospered. The Honourable John Byng (later Viscount Torrington) records in a diary towards the end of the eighteenth century watching smugglers lead horses past the Anchor Inn at Aylesford — apparently unbothered by any Revenue forces and noted that their horses were better than he could afford himself.

The major goods smuggled were spirits, tea, tobacco, silks and laces. Other luxury goods were brought in in smaller quantities; wines, watches, jewellery, music boxes and similar items. Their transport across the Channel, often in the dark and in wintry conditions when detection was less likely, was highly organised, and the skill and seamanship of the smugglers was very high. The financial aspects of buying the goods, and their ultimate placement, was also carefully planned by men with good business acumen. But the part of the transaction which we shall first examine in detail will be the occasion which most of us think of as smuggling — the landing on the coast and the movement inland.

The coastline of Kent and Sussex is very varied and there are many places well suited to smuggling. There are flat areas like Romney Marsh, Caffe Saltings and the Pevensey Levels, or the large flat beaches at Worthing and Goring; the cliffs at Hastings and Folkestone are intersected with wooded gaps that run nearly down to the sea: the Eastbourne cliffs are intersected with gaps such as Crowlink, Birling, and the Hope gap and those nearer Brighton with the Portobello Gap and the Rottingdean gap. The Cuckmere River and the wider area of the Ouse at Newhaven are hospitable to the smuggler, and the desolate expanses of Selsey Bill would seem to be ideal for his needs.

Reference has already been made to the stationing of dragoons along the coast where they could be called upon to render assistance as required. Like all previous measures this met with little real success. Not least of the problems were the difficulties which arose when a solitary riding officer encountered a gang of smugglers and had to summon assistance there being no twentieth century aids to communication to rely upon. Furthermore, the dragoons had little stomach for the work. Their pay was poor enough anyway and fighting smugglers — their own countrymen — involved them in particularly dangerous and unpleasant conditions. In the final novel in Russell Thorndike's Doctor Syn series (entitled simply *Doctor Syn*) one chapter recreates vividly what must have been the thoughts of many of those unwilling antagonists. In it a group of sailors are lying — up to their knees in freezing dyke water — waiting the approach of a gang from Dymchurch. One old salt addresses the boatswain thus:

> Why don't we clear out of this and be done with the folly? We looks to you Job Mallett — I say we looks to you as bos'n — and a very good bos'n you be — we looks to you to save us being' made fools of. We wants to fight the Frenchies and not our own fellows. The Parleyment's a makin' a great mistake puttin' down the smugglers . . . who be hard working fellows and very good fighters too, as we'll soon be called upon to see. . . . I give you my word that I don't like being shot down like a rabbit, and I'm sorry as how its you as is in command, 'cos if it was anyone else I declares I'd get up now and walk home to bed.

In the story the gang avoid a fight by the exercise of wit and cunning and this in truth was the approach most favoured by the smugglers if circumstances allowed. A tub of spirits left for those preventive men known to be less than zealous in the exercise of their duty or for underpaid dragoons could save them a deal of trouble.

Violent encounters could not always be avoided however. In August 1770 two Revenue officers and one dragoon set off in pursuit of some smugglers who were expected in the area of Sturry. A scout had been sent on ahead of the group concerned and he, observing the small force, was able to ride back to his companions and give the alarm. The smugglers proceeded to conceal their goods in a nearby wood (apparently to avoid its confiscation if things went badly for them) and then continued on their way. On coming up with the dragoon they attacked and beat him before continuing after the two Excisemen whom they threatened with death should they attempt to take their goods. It is an indication of the courage and persistence of some officers that the two took no heed of the threats and proceeded to comb the area, finally being rewarded with the discovery of eighteen tubs of gin and brandy and two hundred and fifty pounds of tea.

A much more serious affray occurred near Whitstable in February 1780. On the 26th of that month Joseph Nicholson, the Supervisor of Excise was undertaking the movement of 183 tubs of Geneva from Whitstable to Canterbury. This important seizure had been made when the vessel carrying the contraband had been driven ashore in a storm. Fearing attempts at rescue of the cargo Nicholson enlisted the help of a corporal and eight troopers of the 4th Dragoons. The cavalcade set out at dusk but had only got as far as Borstal Hill when the worst fears were realised an attack was mounted by a group of some fifty smugglers. Fierce fighting ensued during which two dragoons were shot dead and several others wounded before Nicholson and his remaining men were forced to abandon the contraband and flee for their lives.

Shortly after this an advertisement was issued offering £5 reward for information leading to the apprehension of any of those involved. No information was forthcoming and eventually a reward of £100 was put up together with a pardon and a further £50 offered personally of Lieutenant Colonel Hugossin the commander of the 4th Dragoons. This proved too tempting for one Edward Edenden who passed the name of an eighteen-year-old lad named John Knight to the authorities. Knight was arrested and brought to justice. His involvement in the affair was, he claimed, a fairly small one but notwithstanding his pleas to this effect he paid the ultimate penalty at Penenden Heath, just one month after the battle. The *Kentish Gazette* carried the following account of the grisly episode:

> His behaviour at the place of execution, was such as became his unhappy situation, and just before he was turned off, he begged of the spectators to take warning how they assist smugglers. He said he was at that time ignorant of the nature of the crime he had committed, and was drawn in by the persuasions of those who knew better, and were more interested. — He died very penitent, and the people seemed to be greatly affected at seeing so young a man cut off in the flower of his youth. He was not 18 years old.
>
> Monday, his body was brought to Borstal-hill, guarded by a body of dragoons, and hung in chains near the place where the murder was committed.

Ours was a somewhat isolated area until the great era of road building from the 1790's and the coming of the railway in the 1840's. The Weald was still thickly wooded over much of the area, and the roads were deplorable. Enormous rut holes, nearly two feet deep, filled with water in the winter, and in summer the movement of transport caused clouds of dust to rise from the dirt roads. Dr. Burton thought Sussex women had such long legs through years of pulling their feet out of the mire, and Defoe describes the coach of a 'lady of quality' which had to be pulled by oxen as horses could not manage it.

General Hardy in 1746, wrote a letter asking to delay putting his troops into East Sussex 'till the roads were more passable'.

Horace Walpole describes his visit to Sussex in terms which equal his description of his travels through the mountain passes of Italy:

> The roads grow bad beyond all badness, the night dark beyond all darkness, our guide frightened beyond all frightfulness. However, without being at all killed, we got up, or down, I forget which, a famous precipice called Silverhill, and about ten at night arrived at a wretched village called Robertsbridge. We had still six miles, hither to Battel, but determined to stop, as it would be a pity to break our necks before we had seen all we intended. But alas! there was only one bed to be had; all the rest were inhabited by smugglers, whom the people of the house called mountebanks, and with one of whom the lady of the den told Mr. Chute he might

lie. We did not at all take to this society, but, armed with links and lanthorns, set out again on this impracticable journey. At two o'clock in the morning we got hither to a still worse inn, and that crammed with excise officers, one of whom had just shot a smuggler. However, as we were neutral powers, we have passed safely through both armies hitherto, and can give you a little farther history of our wandering through these mountains, where the young gentleman are forced to drive their curricles with a pair of oxen.

It is clear that in physical conditions like these the smugglers would have a very good chance of evading detection altogether. When they were detected, many accounts make it clear that they often dropped or quickly hid their booty and scattered in all directions, jumping over hedges and escaping with relative ease as they had such immense knowledge of their terrain. If they greatly outnumbered the customs men, as was often the case, they usually stood their ground and used violence.

Even these hardy men did not always survive in such harsh conditions, however, and four or five smugglers were drowned while trying to evade pursuit by swimming the Military Canal at Pett levels: the younger men in the party went back for their older commrades, but were not wholly successful. A great many of the operations involved swimming with lines, or hiding in water-filled ditches in the marshes, or hiding under sluice gates; as a great deal of smuggling took place in winter, one would think that the toll in rheumatic diseases and pneumonia must have been high among the less sturdy. An old smuggler described to Lord Teignmouth the physical discomforts of the sea smuggler at work, and told him on many nights the wind was 'fit to blow your hair off'. In addition to these physical discomforts of course were the dangers of the fights with the preventive men. In these cases it was the smuggler's boast that they never deserted a wounded comrade. In February 1827 for example, after a disastrous encounter with the Blockade men when three smugglers were killed, others who were wounded were carried off by their comrades and one smuggler carried a wounded man on his back six miles from Fairlight to Udimore.

When a cargo was being run, the organiser would appoint two or even three possible places of landing, so that if one were endangered by the presence of the preventive force, another could be used. A foreman or gang leader was employed to engage a suitable number of men, who would gather at the appointed time and place. Large numbers of men were often employed, to ensure speed. Roughly half the men would be porters, and half guards. The tubs were usually roped together in pairs so that immediately they could be slung over a man's shoulders, got ashore and on to the waiting horses. They were sold roped together by the French suppliers. The tubs were usually half-ankers, which held four gallons. The tea was supplied by the French similarly prepared for the journey in oil skin bags which would easily sling over a horse's back. The guards were armed, primarily with 'bats' — stout ash poles eight foot long, with which they could inflict terrible injuries and even death, but also carried heavy whips, the but ends of which were lead weighted.

The boat which was attempting to land its cargo would know, by the signal sent by some of the lookout men, whether to land or proceed to the next place. In early times a small quantity of gunpowder was burned in a flashpan, similar to a flint lock pistol. Sometimes the signal was given by an ordinary flint and steel: the sparks could be seen at sea for long distances but did not show up so well on land. Later, in the interests of secrecy, many smugglers adapted the bull's eye lantern by fixing a tapering tube about a foot long on its light face. This was turned in the direction of the boat, and could only be seen at sea and not on land.

A witness at the trial of the Hawkhurst Gang described the method:

> the captain of the cutter fixes a time and place where he designs to land, and seldom or never fails, being pretty punctual as to the time, if the weather permits, as the master smugglers cannot fetch all the goods themselves, so they hire men whom they call 'riders', and they allow each man half a guinea a journey, and bear all the expenses of eating and drinking, and horse, and allowance of a dollop of tea, which is forty pounds weight, being half of a bag, the profit of which dollop, even the most ordinary sort, is worth more than a guinea, and some twenty five shillings, and some more; and they always make one journey, sometimes two and sometimes three in a week, which is indeed such a temptation that very few people in the country can withstand, and which has been the cause of so many turning.

The profits were high; until 1736 the punishment was not great; the master smuggler had mainly to bear the loss of his smuggled goods and the impounding of his ships. In 1736 the Smugglers Act imposed the death penalty for wounding a Revenue Officer. The punishment for unarmed resistance was flogging, hard labour, transportation to America or serving in the Navy. This did not do a great deal to prevent smuggling: it merely made the smuggler more violent and determined to resist capture. In a harsh and brutal age, when men were flogged and transported for quite insignificant thefts, such as a half sack of wheat or a piece of cloth, the punishment for smuggling with the greater rewards was not unduly severe.

ArthurYoung in his *General View of the Agricultive of the County of Sussex*, 1813, puts the payment to smugglers in its economic perspective. A taskworker, he says, will earn 1s. 6d. or 2s. per day (i.e. 7½p or 10p). These men would be skilled workers like carpenters or sheepshearers who undertook specific jobs. The labourers got 6d. or 8d. a day (i.e. approx. 6½p or 7½p). He goes on to say:

> In the neighbourhood of the sea are seen many old labourers, as the young and active find smuggling a more lucrative employ, which is very successfully pursued in Sussex. At Rye and Hastings, Bourne, etc it is highly flourishing, whilst the health of the inhabitants is injured, the revenue defrauded and labour extremely high. It has been computed that the revenue in this line of country is cheated to the amount of 80,000 l per annum: between 3 and 400,000 gallons of gin, rum and other spirits, are annually smuggled in this district. The principals engaged in the business have about 10/6d each night: the common men a guinea a week: and in the

conveyance from the vessel to the shore from 2 shillings to 7 shillings per night: 12,000 gallons of spirit have been landed in a week at Dungeness, in Kent. Light goods from Flanders, into Sussex and Kent, 105,000 l a year, upon which the profit has been so high as 30,000 l.

This great consumption of spirit is very pernicious to the labourers, and equally injurious to the farmers: but the cheapness of gin recommends the sale of it, and unlicensed gin shops are without number.

In the days of riding officers, the smugglers had fairly good expectations of trouble-free runs. The ports had Customs House staff, who could on occasions ride out to meet smugglers, in addition to attending to the boats in port. They depended to some extent for their information on the riding officers, each of whom was responsible for four miles of coast, and whose duty it was to patrol that coast at night. They were armed with a cutlass and two pistols. In an emergency, they could call on a detachment of the military who were stationed in the area for this purpose. These were usually dragoons, but were sometimes hussars or lancers. This arrangement had obvious disadvantages, as there was always a lapse of time before the military arrived. In addition, this duty was very unpopular with the soldier, as it was both unpleasant and dangerous. Even if it did not involve actual fighting with armed and desperate smugglers, it involved hours of hanging about in the cold and dark, and some riding officers more keen than others sometimes required exercises like hiding buried up to the neck in shingle in order to surprise the smugglers. While the riding officers received a reward for any seizures of contraband which they made, the dragoon's reward was shared with the whole regiment, *pro rata* according to rank so clearly a dragoon who had endured hours of waiting in the cold and dark was not terribly happy to know that a sergeant sitting in the warm mess would get a greater share than himself. There are several cases in which the dragoons were slow to arrive when sent for, or in which their leader demurred, on one excuse or another, from taking part in an affray.

The preventive service as a whole at this period appears to have been fairly easy going, (although, as we have seen, not as entirely ineffectual as is sometimes suggested) and there are many tales of bargains struck between riding officers and smugglers. It seems sometimes to have happened, that when discovered, a bargain would be struck, the smugglers would depart rapidly, leaving a percentage of their tubs on the beach, then when they were well clear the riding officer would fire his pistol to summon assistance, announcing that he had 'seized' so many tubs.

It was also commonly accepted at the time, and often stated in the literature of the day, that there was a fair amount of outright bribery of riding officers. As they were nearly always so greatly outnumbered by the smugglers, one must admire the fact that they did attack them at all, for they were barbarously treated. After a particularly bad affair in Kent, when great numbers of smugglers were collected together, and sentries were posted who drove ordinary travellers away from the affected area, in effect creating a 'no go area' in today's jargon, a writer of a letter in the Collier correspondence said, 'the time will come when few will accept of places in ye Customs where their duty requires riding'.

When the men at sea received the light signal to land, the goods were off loaded into tub boats, special open boats, and silently rowed ashore. Sometimes the 'dry goods' went into the tub boats; while the tubs, attached to a line — strung out like clothes on a washing line, but still in their pairs — were towed behind. In this case, the porters had to be very smart in picking them up when they landed, for the men cutting the tubs free from the towing line worked very quickly and it was not unknown for a porter to get cut hands. Great care was taken to clear away all traces of the tow rope afterwards — pieces of rope being a sure give-away of their activities. On some beaches sometimes the boat could come really close to the shore and the tow rope be dragged ashore by a man swimming. Tobacco, lace and silks were supplied in oilskin packages done up with yarn. All these pre-packed goods were supplied at large warehouses on the French coast at Dunkirk, Calais, Boulogne, Fecamp, and after 1760, Roscoff, which grew rapidly from a tiny village to a thriving trading post entirely on the proceeds of English smuggling.

The usual groups of men numbered about twenty to fifty, but quite often really large runs involved two or three hundred men, besides a hundred or more horses and carts. During the early 1760's we read, either in the local newspapers or in official letters, of innumerable engagements between smugglers and preventive men, or of the unopposed landings of contraband material, and the number of men involved ranged from about twenty to two or three hundred. If a large cargo was being landed, dozens of men would be employed as speed was essential: the master smuggler's aim was to get the stuff off the beach and into its temporary hiding place as soon as possible. Some items, especially tea, appear often to be sent up to London straight away. A great many inns depended for their supplies on the smugglers, and possibly some nearby inns took 'immediate delivery'.

Two hundred men assembled on a flat beach at Goring in July 1720 armed with guns, pistols, clubs, swords and blunderbusses. A quantity of wool was shipped out and a large quantity of brandy came in, which was quickly loaded, on to horses carrying two, three or four half-anker tubs. One does sometimes read of horses laden with three half anker tubs, so perhaps they were sometimes supplied in threes, although two was the usual number. It is interesting to note that the writer particularly mentioned the wool going out, and one would suspect that this happened more often than was reported: the particular interest seems to have been focussed on the incoming tubs in most cases. The coastal area behind Goring was famous for its huge flocks of fine sheep. As late as 1769 a newspaper was reporting attempts on the part of the smugglers to load a flock of live sheep in a French boat near Rye: the preventive men were watching, and in a somewhat comic performance the smugglers made repeated attempts to drive the sheep on board at different places, but were always stopped by the preventive men. On this occasion at Goring, a customs officer who challenged the smugglers was first sworn at and then assaulted, and injured.

In July 1720 a small group of smugglers at Cuckmere Fell were armed with 'pistols, Cutlesses, and Clubbs' as they guarded twenty or thirty horses loaded with about one hundred half ankers of brandy. At Ferring on June 21st, 1720 the Custom House Officers clashed with sixty armed smugglers, and one of them had his horse shot under him. This was only seven days before the Goring event. The three events, taking place within a month, give some idea of the scale of operations, most of which went unrecorded.

In April 1733 three Rye Officers saw 'thirty men arm'd, about fifty horses laden with oyl skin baggs'. They sent for two dragoons and a foot soldier from Rye, then the six men pursued the thirty smugglers and caught up with them. The smugglers, however, 'swore at the officers, damned them what were come to rob them and came up with their pistols cocked close to their heads'.

They were tied up, led to Lamberhurst in Kent, a journey which took four hours, and then released and threatened that they were not to follow the smugglers.

Sometimes, however, the preventive officers did have a success. In September 1721, together with a small group of Grenadiers, they surprised a party of smugglers at Burwash, among them Jervis and 'Gib Tompkin' two well-known smugglers. There was first an armed skirmish in a wood, then a long pursuit lasting a day and night and finally at Nutley the officers captured four smugglers, five horses, 'and all their Ropes and Running tackle'.

A letter of August 1739 describes a group of fifteen men riding near Malling in Kent, who may have been a mixed band of Hawkhurst and Sussex men, with twenty-one horses heavily laden, he noted their arrogance and the fact that one man had 'a great brass blunderbuss slung over his shoulder', and concluded that these men could only be taken by a 'strong military force'.

Sometimes, the smugglers temporarily imprisoned the officers. In June 1733 when the Newhaven officers tried to take ten horses laden with tea which had been smuggled in at Cuckmere, thirty men with blunderbusses and pistols fired on them, and then took them prisoners until the smuggled goods were taken clear. In August, at Greenhay, twenty smugglers with horses laden with tea knocked a customs officer off his horse and confined him for an hour until the contraband had been removed. In July 1735, officers at Arundel watched a suspected smuggling vessel, waiting for the goods to be brought ashore, but twenty smugglers armed with pistols and blunderbusses took them and kept them prisoner until several boat loads of goods had been brought ashore and unloaded. At Eastbourne in June 1744 the Eastbourne Customs officers with five dragoons challenged a group of smugglers on the beach near Pevensey. One hundred mounted smugglers appeared, fired repeatedly at them, slashed at them with their swords, while the goods were loaded on horses and sent off towards London.

The difficulties of fighting a large number of desperate men, when outnumbered, and in the dark, can be seen in an engagement at Hollington in October 1734. The Customs officers at Hastings had reason to believe that there was to be a landing inland from the coast. There were three Customs officers led by Mr. Carswell, and the local detachment of military — five men of Brigadier General Cope's Regiment of Foot, led by Sergeant Angell: ten men in all: clearly an insufficient number to deal with a large gang, but lack of government funds to supply a sufficiently large preventive force was one of the causes of the growth of smuggling, although the authorities seemed unwilling to accept the fact.

They found a suitable wooded hiding place by the road, and disposed the men in two parties, one nearer the sea than the other, in order to trap the smugglers between the two. Then, crouching behind trees and bushes, they waited tensely. It was bright moonlight. About midnight, a solitary rider came, riding at ease from the direction of the sea. Guessing that this man was the scout for the smugglers, they let him go by in silence. About a quarter of an hour later, the main body arrived, 'about thirty horses all laden with Goods in Canvas baggs and a great many men'.

Mr. Carswell, with considerable courage, leapt into the road in front of the column, and asked the first rider what goods he had. The man reigned sharply, and 'answered with a great Oath none for him'. At this Mr. Carswell tried to grasp the horse's bridle, but the man turned his horse sharply and 'called out to the Gang to turn', where upon they all 'fell a whipping their horses in great confusion'. The rear guard of the Customs party nearer the sea now came out of hiding, in an effort to prevent their escape, but the smugglers attacked them

> several of them struck at the officers with the great ends of their whips and the clubs they had in their hands, and being so assaulted and not so able to stop the Gang or seize any of their 'horses or Goods, Hide (one of the customs officers) called out to the soldiers to fire.

However, the smugglers made good their escape, 'all getting off with the Goods', and the two parties of officers and soldiers joined forces again, and coming along the road, some distance from their hiding place, 'they saw something lye in the road and Robert Jones the soldier went up and said it was a dead man upon which the officers carried him into a neighbouring alehouse'.

The Coroner passed a verdict of manslaughter by the soldiers without naming any particular man and the three Customs officers and Sgt. Angell were bound over to give evidence at the next Assizes. The dead man was a carpenter called Peen who lived at Hawkhurst. In their evidence to the Coroner Mr. Carswell and Sgt. Angell thought that Peen had been killed in the retreat by the horses hooves, and each of the men emphasised the distance at which the body was found from the actual struggle. They were clearly apprehensive of a murder charge. The attorney's brief contained strict instructions that he was to plead first manslaughter, and second, that Peen was employed by the smugglers. The difficulties under which the Customs officers laboured are obvious — the darkness: the confusion of large numbers of mounted men trying to gallop off: the rearing of the frightened baggage horses, who were led, riderless; the violent stream of blows from the heavy, lead weighted whip handles and murderous clubs: the fact that they were heavily outnumbered: the reluctance to use firearms as this might lead to a murder charge.

This incident is remarkable in that it had an independent witness, Thomas Pettit, who was in woods nearby (poaching?) observed the smugglers 'in great confusion' as they broke into neighbouring grounds 'and were much depressed'. He eavesdropped on two as they planned to 'carry their goods to Hollington to be concealed in Turners Hole' and watched them as they stowed away as much as 'the private place would hold', and then, their secret hiding place full, rode off with the surplus. Amazingly, he agreed, to be a witness, and showed Mr. Carswell the secret cache so that the contraband could be recovered. The letters he wrote, and his reason for testifying, will be looked at later in the section on legal aspects. He seems to have survived, and not to have received any terrible punishments usually meted out to those who dared testify against the smugglers. Mr. Carswell was murdered in 1744 in another engagement.

It is hard to sympathise with a regime as harsh as that which governed Britain in the eighteenth century but the sheer ineptitude of some of the measures taken to stamp out smuggling and the ease with which they were countered somehow draws out a feeling of pity for the inadequacy of it all. At one point a ban was imposed on the building of the type of boats favoured by smugglers. The traders, however, simply had them built at Calais. Another idea was to grant licences to privateers to arm vessels and work in conjunction with the revenue forces and so increase the number of ships able to patrol the coast. There was no shortage of volunteers as the smugglers themselves all enlisted their services. They were thus provided with an ideal cover under which to ply their trade and made full use of this 'government sent' opportunity. The smuggler relied heavily upon popular sympathy and the generous use of bribes. He was, however (as some of the preceding accounts show), well prepared to resort to violence and the 'forced run' was a primary tactic during the eighteenth and early nineteenth centuries. Gangs were highly organised for this purpose, being divided into those employed to carry tubs and those whose job was to fight off the unwarranted attentions of the authorities. Pitched battles were not uncommon.

It is between the two factions of the gangs that an important distinction must be drawn. The fighting men were, on the whole, those most deeply involved in the trade and to them the term 'criminal' might be more readily applied than to the tub-carriers, the latter being usually nothing more than local labourers earning a little extra money to supplement their all too meagre income.

Naturally, gangs operating in this way required a high degree of discipline and by necessity they exercised considerable influence in the communities involved with their activities. A time was to come when the violent measures adopted and their terrorist approach was to alienate some of these gangs from the public support which had always been such a great advantage.

Most infamous of all was the Hawkhurst Gang.

CHAPTER III

The Hawkhurst Gang — a tale of contempt for all law

During the 1740's smuggling reached huge proportions and was heavily tainted with violence. The Sussex Assize records tell of the running of three tons of tea at a time, and there are frequent accounts of killings and pitched battles. A letter to the Commissioners of Customs, from an informer calling himself Goring, comments on a killing at Bulverhythe in 1737 and provides a fascinating account of lawlessness and corruption in Kent and Sussex

> May it please your Honours, — It is not unknown to your Lordships of the late battle between the Smuglers and Officers at Bulverhide; and in relation to that Business, if your Honours but please to advise in the New Papers, that this is expected off [sic], I will send a List of the names of Persons that were at that Business, and the places' names where they are usually and mostly resident. Cat (Morten's man) fired first, Morten was the second that fired; the soldiers fired and killed Collinson, wounded Pigon, who is since dead, William Weston was wounded, but like to recover. Young Mr. Bowra was not there, but his men and horses were; From your Honours.
>
> Dutifull and Most faithfull servant,
> GORING
>
> There was no foreign persons at this Business, but all were Sussex men, and may easily be spoke with.
>
> This is the seventh time Morten's people have workt this winter, and have not lost anything but one half-hundred of tea they gave to a Dragoon and one officer they met with the first of this winter; and the Hoo company have lost no goods, although they constantly work, and at home too, since they lost the seventy hundred-weight. When once the Smuglers are drove from home they will soonall be taken. Note, that some

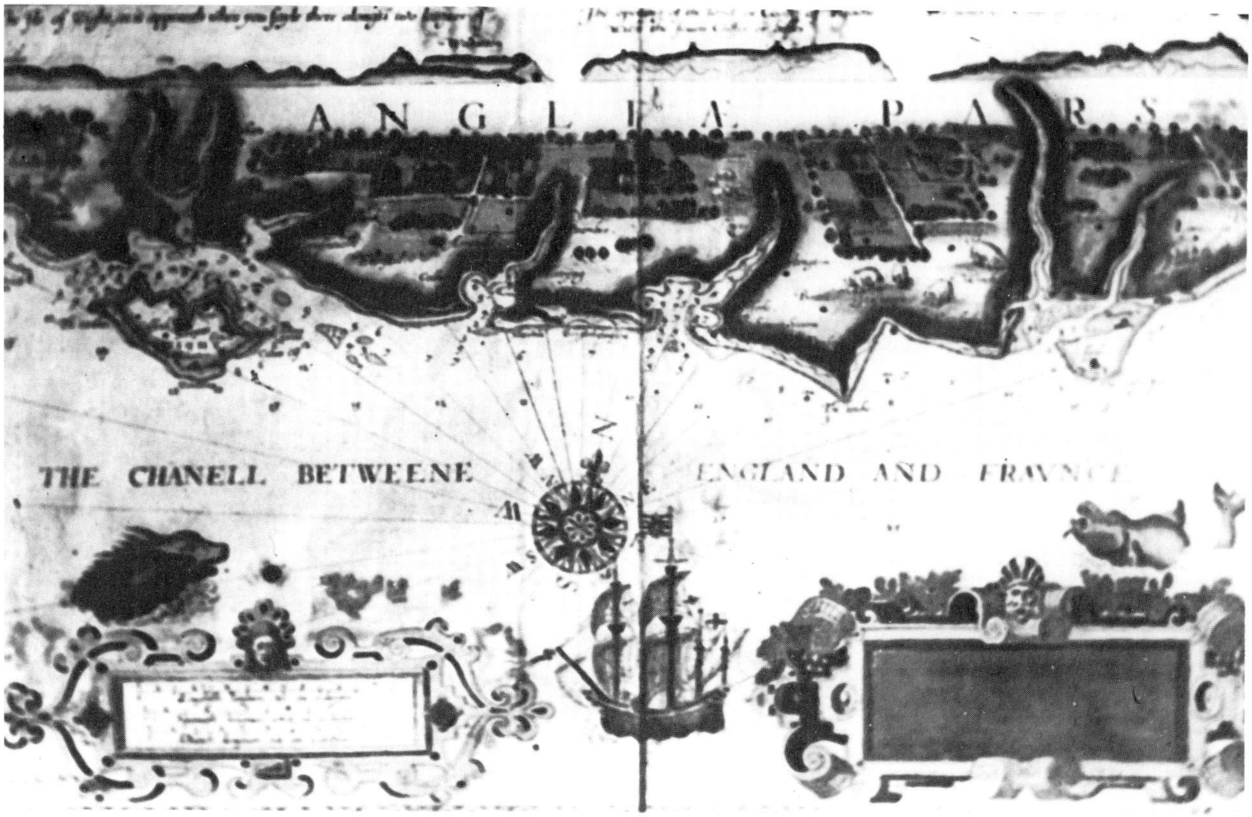

The oldest known map of the Marsh coast. Ashley's Mariners Harbour, 1588.

W. Stocks, Rye

VIEW OF HASTINGS FROM THE WHITE ROCK.

Published by Geo Wooll Printseller High St. Hastings Dec. 1825

Near Beachy Head

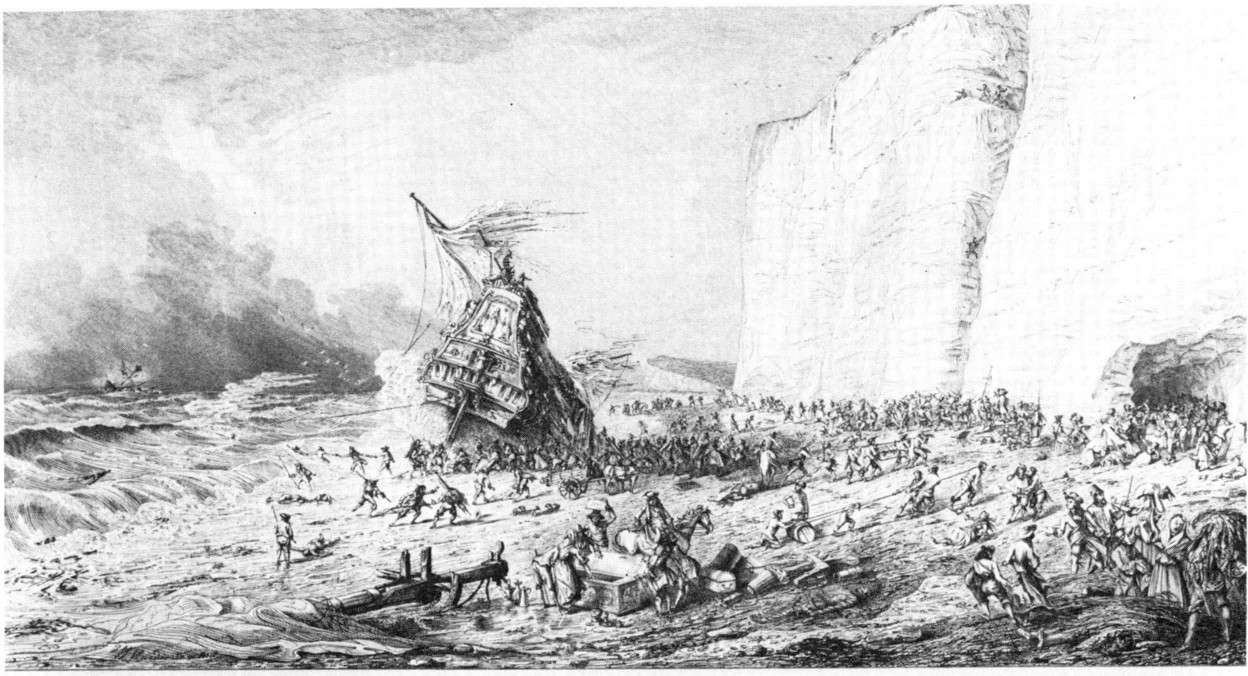

The Wreck of the Nympha Americana, a Spanish Corsair, near Beachy Head.

Published by the Artist, Newick, near Uckfield, Sussex. November 29 1747 Vide Pamphlet

'Smugglers running spirits', 1807.

By courtesy of H.M. Customs and Excise.

The old derrick crane, near Rottingdean, Sussex, 1812.

The Coast Guard House—Eastbourne.

say it was Gurr that fired first. You must well secure Cat, or else your Honours will soon lose the man; the best way will be to send for him up to London, for he knows the whole Company, and hath been Morten's servant two years. There were several young Chaps with the Smuglers, who, when taken, will soon discover [i.e. reveal] the whole Company. The number was twenty-six men. Mack's horses, Morten's and Hoak's, were killed, and they lost not half their goods. They have sent for more goods, and twenty-nine horses set out from Groombridge this day, about four in the afternoon, and all the men well armed with long guns.

And if I hear this is received, I will send your Honours the Places' names where your Honours will intercept the Smuglers as they go to Market with their Goods, but it must be done by Soldiers, for they go stronger now than ever. And as for Mr. Gabriel Tompkin, Supervisor of Dartford, there can be good reason given that Jacob Walter brought him Goods for three years last past, and it is likewise no dispute of that matter amongst allmost all the Smuglers. The Bruces and Jacob fought about that matter and parted Company's, and Mr. Tompkin was allway, as most people know, a villian when a Smugler and likewise Officer. He never was concern'd with any Body but Jacob, and now Jacob has certainly done with Smugling. I shall not trouble your Honours with any more Letters if I do not hear from this, and I do assure your Honours what I now write is truth.

There are some Smuglers with a good sum of money, and they may pay for taking; as Thomas Darby, Edward King, John Mackdanie, and others that are rich.

The Hoo Company might have been all ruined when they lost their goods; the Officers and Soldiers know them all, but they were not prosecuted, as [they] was not at Groombridge, when some time since a Custom House Officer took some Tea and Arms too in Bowra's house at Groombridge.

The first of this Winter, the Groombridge Smuglers were forced to carry their goods allmost all up to Rushmore Hill [just north of Hindhead, in Surrey] and Cester Mark, which some they do now, but Tea sells quick in London now, and Chaps from London come down to Groombridge almost everyday, as they used to last Winter. When once they [i.e. the smugglers] come to be drove from home, they will be put to great inconveniences, when they are from their friends and will lose more Goods than they do now, and be at more Charges. Do but take up some of the Servants, they will soon rout the Masters, for the Servants are all poor.

Young Bowra's House cost £500 building, and he will pay for looking up.

Morten and Bowra sold, last Winter, some-ways, about 3,000 lb. weight a week.

This letter describes a gang of well-organised and fearless men, with good sources of supply and regular business deals, who were equally ready to use either bribery or violence. The comparison with the gangs of prohibition America is inescapable. The reference to the possibility of the Hoo Company being ruined is especially interesting. Far from being broken this group was to continue to dominate North Kent for another 80 years!

One of the trends of this period is the inclination of the smugglers to defy authority even when their goods had been seized and there are several instances in the records of gangs re-taking their seized property. At Christmas time in 1740, Thomas Carswell, the brave officer who had been involved in the Hollington ambush, was shot in the head and killed instantly, in broad daylight. He and five other officers were attacked by twenty smugglers 'on the King's Highway from Silver Hill to Hurst Green' as the gang battled to retake the seized contraband which the officers were escorting. Most of the smuggling party were labourers from Salehurst, and a contemporary note in the court record said that George Kingsmere (possibly Kingsmill? see post) fired the shot. Nevertheless, nine years later in July 1749 the same records list Richard Double, known as 'The Ensign' as condemned to hang for the murder, and yet a year later Thomas Carey, alias the 'Lame Jockey' was condemned to hang for the murder, as he fired the shot. The records were not particularly well kept over these years, and in any case, Richard Double, whose sentence had been changed to transportation, was pardoned in 1750, and a letter exists:

To Mr. Dubel at the Crown Inn in East Grinstead
Sussex, by bagg.
Sir,
I have sent you the true copy of Holman,
Dubel, Geren, and Trower,
I am your umble servant
Thomas Cooper

The smugglers went heavily armed at this time, as in a run at West Wittering in 1743, when 2,000 lbs of tea was run by a large group of labourers from Aldingbourne. In a big run at Bexhill in 1745 three tons of tea, as well as brandy, was moved by a company of mounted smugglers, most of them labourers from Bexhill. They were heavily armed, and one who was killed was carrying 'a brass loaded carbine and a large whip with a lead loaded end'. As well as cutlasses and firearms they nearly always carried heavy whips, sticks and cudgels and sometimes scythes welded to long sticks — a murderous weapon. In this run, on their way to the meeting place the smugglers raided the house and attacked the family of one officer and assaulted another. As a result a detachment of thirty soldiers of Harrison's Regiment were hastily fetched, but the smugglers stood up to them and attacked them with 'whip and club' as well as with firearms.

While the violence of import smuggling caused it to be the subject of contemporary comment, owling still went on to some extent. William Dunk and other labourers of Winchelsea were caught in 1748 stealing 600 lbs of wool in order to ship it to France.

The events described above show that the smugglers had grown into large, highly organised and heavily armed groups, based either in convenient landing places on the coast, like Rye, Hastings, Pevensey and Bexhill, or strategically placed villages on the roads to London and the interior, like Brede and Bramber. These gangs travelled widely: one reads of Rye cutters fetching goods from Guernsey to run on the Sussex coast: of a Folkestone man sailing to Flushing for goods to run in Pevensey, and so on.

The most feared gang of all, though, was the Hawkhurst Gang, which roamed widely over the South of England. It is clear from contemporary records that at times there was a complete breakdown of public order as Customs officers, the soldiery and the courts were all unable to deal with these large bands of armed men riding through the isolated villages and towns. The Hawkhurst Gang took its name from the village of Hawkhurst in Kent, and had great influence there and in East Sussex, but they roved as far as Hampshire. Their worst action, that plumbed the depths of human degradation and cruelty, and that was the cause of their downfall, took place in Sussex. The greatest blot upon the annals of smuggling is without doubt the murders of William Galley and Daniel Chater, two elderly and inoffensive, if somewhat foolish men. This action finally changed the public tolerance of the smuggler (who, after all, if a bit of a rogue and a rebel, had a kind of Robin Hood reputation in that he robbed the Exchequer in order to sell more cheaply to honest citizens), into one of horror and revulsion at the cruelty shown by organised gangs who had grown above the law. Most details of smuggling activities are sparse, and have to be gleaned from Court records or official archives, but a full contemporary account of this exists, by 'A gentleman of Chichester' who prudently remained anonymous. It was taken down in writing from the mouths of witnesses, and the writer 'frequently conversed with the prisoners both before and after condemnation'. The reader is recommended to the book which is called

> Smuggling and smugglers in Sussex — The genuine history of the inhuman and unparalleled murders of Mr. William Galley, a Custom-House officer, and Mr. Daniel Chater, a shoemaker, by fourteen notorious smugglers, with the trials and executions of seven of the criminals at Chichester 1748–9. Illustrated with seven plates, descriptive of the barbarous cruelties.

The village of Hawkhurst lies in the Weald of Kent, well away from the coast and would seem to be an unlikely location for the home of the most notorious gang in the history of English smuggling. But then again it is a popular misconception that all smugglers were seafaring types; woollen hats, peg legs and all that sort of thing. In fact whilst seamen were employed in transporting contraband across the Channel the other participants in the trade, and these made up the majority, frequently had no connection with the sea. Thomas Kingsmill, the leader of the Hawkhurst Gang during the height of its notoriety, had formerly been a farm worker and in that respect, if not in others, he was typical. Hawkhurst is situated fairly close to a number of waterways, the River Rother, the Kent Ditch and the Hexden Channel, all of which were navigable from the coast for a considerable distance inland during the heyday of smuggling. The village was also an important staging post (the Oak and Ivy Inn in particular) for illegal goods being transported overland from the sea — frequently by means of an efficient system of small carts drawn by teams of dogs — and could claim to be as deeply embroiled in the trade as many other more obvious locations.

Just when the Hawkhurst Gang came into being is uncertain but it came to prominence in the early eighteenth century under the leadership of one Arthur Gray, a master-smuggler and highwayman of some repute. He was successful enough to be able to build the mansion later known as 'Gray's Folley' at Seacox Heath, a short distance from Hawkhurst, and arrogant enough to include some large and not particularly well-hidden smugglers' stores in its construction. It was not Gray, however, but Thomas Kingsmill, otherwise known as Staymaker, who brought the gang to everlasting infamy.

When later Kingsmill was in Newgate, he was described by the Ordinary of the prison as

> for some years past employed by the chiefs of the smugglers, the moneyed men or merchants, as they are usually amongst themselves called, in any dangerous exploits. As his character in general among his countrymen was that of a bold, resolute man, undaunted, and fit for the wicked purposes of smuggling, and never intimated, in case of any suspicion of betraying their secrets, ready to oppose King's officers in their duty, and being concerned in rescues of any sort or kind, so he wanted not business . . .

By the year 1746 Kingsmill had risen from the lowly rank of tub-carrier to undisputed captain and the gang had embarked upon a course of murder and terrorism which was shortly to lead to its downfall but at the same time was to set a trend for future companies of smugglers. The maintenance of internal law and order was virtually non-existent by modern standards to the extent that a petty thief might be hanged whilst desperate characters like Kingsmill and his cronies were able to operate almost without let or hindrance. The local historian William Holloway makes reference to the Hawkhurst Gang frequenting the Mermaid Inn at Rye — which may still be seen looking much the same now as it must have done then — where they would sit, in full view of Revenue men, with their pistols on the table and openly discussing their plans or boasting of successful exploits past.

When one Customs officer was ill advised enough to seize an illegal cargo at Shoreham, he and his three assistants were overpowered, bound and sent to Hawkhurst. Two of these unfortunates were, it seems, former smugglers who had changed sides. Upon discovering this fact they were tied to trees and flogged almost to death before being transported to France and abandoned there. Despite a reward being offered and it being no secret among local people as to who was responsible no one was ever brought to justice.

It took the sleepy little village at Goudhurst to end Kingsmill's reign of terror. The East Barming register of burials records the funeral in 1801 of a man named William Turley who had died in the Poor House aged 83. Not a grand old gentleman this; poor but honest. He is described as 'blasphenous and in every way worthless', and having escaped from an affray at Goudhurst in 1747 with a broken foot had ridden to Wrotham, had the foot cut off and made good his escape on a fresh horse. The affray in question had been the defeat of the Hawkhurst Gang and had happened as follows:

It was the usual practice of organised smuggling gangs to commandeer horses to use as pack animals and store goods in barns if circumstance required whether or not the owners objected.

One is reminded of Rudyard Kipling's 'Smugglers Song':

> Running round the woodlump if you chance to find
> Little barrels, roped and tarred, all full of brandy wine;
> Don't you shout to come and look, nor take 'em for your play;
> Put the brishwood back again — and they'll be gone next day.

Invariably a person who had his property used in this way received a present of tea or tobacco or the like by way of payment. The Hawkhurst company operated in this way but soon found the payments an unnecessary requirement and began simply taking what they wanted when they wanted and returning it if and when it pleased them. Their activities were duly extended to taking provisions and ultimately to straight-forward burglary and highway robbery. Goudhurst suffered particularly from these unwanted attentions. The gang often frequented the Star and Eagle Inn which at that time was connected to the church by a subterranean tunnel and this establishment together with 'Spyways' their sentry house overlooking the main street may still be seen today. By the time of our story the terrified villagers would hardly dare to venture out, even in the broad light of day. Kingsmill and his men made a practice of riding into town to plunder any houses where they thought the pickings might be good. Anyone resisting was either murdered or put to torture. Travellers between towns and villages in the area undertook their journeys at great personal risk and only when absolutely necessary.

Deliverance was at hand, however, in the person of a young man named William Sturt who, returning to his native Goudhurst, having secured an honourable discharge from the army, was appalled by what he saw and proposed the formation of an armed force to protect the town with himself as leader. The Goudhurst Band of Militia was formed on April 17th, 1747. Its existence was intended to remain a secret from the smugglers but by whatever means it very quickly came to the attention of these thugs who waylaid a member and tortured him into divulging full details of the plan. Such was the contempt with which Kingsmill heard of the Militia that the prisoner was released and sent back to Goudhurst with the message that one hundred of the smugglers proposed to attack the town, lay seige to it, plunder every house, murder all the inhabitants and burn it to the ground. In his confidence Kingsmill stated the exact date and time of this dreadful appointment.

With what horror was this message received by the simple farm workers who thus found themselves suddenly in the unenviable position of champions of law and order? How many must have regretted their bold course and wished Sturt had never returned? We can only guess. Sturt however was not to be underestimated. He mustered his men and having made to them a stirring speech set them to gathering all the weapons they could find. Musket balls were cast and some two hundredweight of gun powder procured. A spot at the upper end of the town was chosen for the battle, barricades erected and the church tower fortified and manned.

Thomas Kingsmill and his ruffianly crew kept their appointment almost to the minute. Appearing outside the town on April 28th, stripped to the waist and heavily armed with pistols, cutlasses and bats (the clubs used by the fighting gangs) they must have presented a terrifying sight. Before battle commenced Kingsmill bellowed out that he would be damned if he did not broil four of the towns people's hearts and have them that night for his supper. Fighting thereupon broke out, musketry volleys being received and returned by both sides. The Militia had the best of it and soon killed two of the smugglers, one of them George Kingsmill, brother of the leader, and wounded a number of others. Unaccustomed to such treatment the gang showed little stomach for further violence and before long were in full flight. The heroic villagers set off in hot pursuit turning the battle into a rout. Several more smugglers were cut down and a great many captured and ultimately brought to justice. Sturt received the undying gratitude of his townsmen and lived out the remainder of his life in a fairly uneventful fashion, being appointed eventually to the position of master of the Goudhurst Workhouse.

What of Kingsmill? Accounts of his fate vary. According to one version he was shot dead in the churchyard, although in fact it was his brother George who died in this way (by local tradition a headstone in the churchyard exhibiting a skull and crossbones marks the resting place of George Kingsmill but this is probably not so). Another source states that he was lynched by the villagers at nearby Horsmonden. Much as he may have deserved such treatment the truth of the matter is that he escaped from the field of battle and lived to do further mischief before coming to his just deserts almost two years later:

On September 22nd, 1747 a gang of smugglers from Dorset suffered the loss of a boat carrying two tons of tea and thirty-nine casks of spirit from Guernsey. These confiscated goods were sent to the Customs House at Poole. The smugglers, however, like so many of their contempories, were desperate men and not prepared to take this set-back to their business quietly. Thomas Kingsmill had been lying low in the months following the Goudhurst affair but his reputation was such that it was to him and those of his associates who remained at liberty that the Dorset men looked for assistance in the recovery of the contraband. It says much about the nature of the man that Kingsmill commanded such widespread notoriety being at this time still only twenty-six years of age.

A band of between thirty and sixty men assembled near Rowland's Castle in Hampshire early in October. Of these only a comparatively small number were from Kent and Sussex but they were without doubt the most violently disposed and Kingsmill together with his second in command from Hawkhurst, one William Fairall, assumed immediate leadership of this lawless company. Two other members of the group were an arthritic ex-carpenter called Perrin, reputedly one of the purchasers of the tea, and a man called Edmund Richards, a violent man described as 'that notorious wicked fellow'.

The men with Kingsmill and Fairall at the head rode round Southampton Water to Lyndhurst, where they rested themselves and their horses. They were all heavily armed and among the horses was a little grey horse loaded with extra guns. Then, when they were refreshed, this large body of men, entered the outskirts of Poole at about 11 o'clock at night. There is no need to comment on the fact that a large group of men, openly riding with long guns slung over their shoulders, could pass through a large area of southern England with not a single person in authority to stand against them. Kingsmill sent two scouts into the town to see if the Customs House was guarded or if there was any trap, while the main party proceeded more slowly. Soon Willis, one of the scouts, returned, with bad news. A Navy sloop was moored at the quay, exactly opposite the Customs House, so that her guns could be trained at the door. There was, however, no sign of life on her. There was now a long argument, as the Chichester men wanted to give up and go home, but Kingsmill said that if they went home the Kent men would go ahead themselves. This decided the Sussex men to go ahead after all, for they knew very well that if the others rescued the tea alone they would keep it. At this point the second scout came up to say that the tide had gone out and as the water had dropped so had the ship, and her guns were now below the level of the quay. Perrin and another of the gang therefore stayed to take care of the horses, while the rest went towards the Customs House, taking with them a boy they met on the road, in order to prevent him from raising the alarm. He was released unharmed at the end of the break-in. Then, with hatchets and iron bars, they broke down the doors of the Customs House. Rapidly, the two tons of tea was carried out and stacked outside. They then carried the tea to a suitable open space, fetched the horses and loaded them up. They then set out on the road to Fordingbridge During this whole time, no Customs officer, no dragoons, nor person in authority appeared, no one challenged them, no one reported them, no one sent for help. At Fordingbridge they rested their horses and took refreshments themselves. When they were rested, they set out on their journey again, in broad daylight along the main street. They had almost certainly been drinking heavily and were very merry, and large numbers of ordinary people gathered to watch them go by. One of the smugglers riding by was a John Diamond, or Dymer, alias 'The Shepherd', and he was hailed by one of the men in the crowd, who had once worked with him at harvest time at Selsey. This man was Daniel Chater, a shoemaker, Dymer laughed and joked with the old man for a few minutes, then as he rode off he threw Daniel a bag of tea. This simple little happening was to lead to the poor man's death, and to lead inexorably to the shocking events that at last forced the authorities to take firm action against these smugglers. From this single act, a train of events proceeded like a Greek tragedy, inevitably progressing to the death of the two humble victims. Dymer was taken into custody at a later date at Chichester; a witness was needed against him, to prove that he had been connected with the raid at Poole. It was here that cases almost always fell down, for lack of a witness to stand up and testify in the courts, for witnesses were invariably bribed or terrorised by the smugglers.

Daniel Chater had probably talked about the encounter with Dymer for knowledge of it reached the ears of the Collector of Customs for the Port of Southampton, a Mr. Shearer, who sent for the shoemaker and took his story from him, under oath. Dymer was held on suspicion, and Chater was required to travel to the Surveyor-General of Customs, Major Battine, who lived at East Marden, just north of Chichester, for further questioning. His feelings are not recorded, but we may imagine that he looked to the event with apprehension, knowing the hatred of the smugglers for informers, and possibly with embarrassment, as Dymer was an acquaintance of his. However, he had no choice — apart from the legal requirement to bear witness, it was known that he had accepted tea from the smugglers, and pressure could be brought to bear upon him, and, as so often happens, the forces of the law can more easily act on the innocent than on the guilty. Chater may have been promised a reward, and this may have encouraged him. At any rate, he did not simply disappear, as so many would have done, for there was a price of £500 on every man who had broken into the Customs House, and it was obvious that the smugglers would make every effort to avoid effective action being taken against them, as, if they were caught and convicted, it was certain hanging for them.

In these circumstances, as Chater would have to ride from Southampton to Chichester, through country heavily infested with smugglers, who were known to act violently to informers and witnesses, and who had a most efficient intelligence service, the intelligent reader would take it for granted that Chater would be sent off to Major Battine in a well planned operation, carefully timed and routed, and with an escort of a dozen or twenty soldiers. After all, as the only witness — and witnesses were hard to come by — Chater was a very valuable property, quite apart from the humanitarian grounds of his safety. The intelligent reader, however, would be wrong. He was sent with a single escort, a man as elderly as himself, a minor customs official, a tide waiter called William Galley. Neither of the men seems to have been sure of the way, and they set out on Sunday February 14th, at the very worst time of the year for travelling on the shocking Sussex roads, on hired horses, dressed in their Sunday best — Chater in a light coat with red breeches — carrying a letter addressed to Major Battine explaining the circumstances of their visit — a letter that was to be their death warrant.

If those in authority were culpable in ignoring the attack on the Customs House when it was actually taking place — and sixty men clattering on horseback through a town, and smashing down an immensely strong oak door must have caused a considerable disturbance, as must the ride back through Hampshire in triumph — they were criminally negligent in sending two elderly men unescorted through known smuggler country on a mission that was vital to the survival of so many of the leading smugglers.

Shortly after setting out, the two men called on a friend of Chater's who lived in Havant, to ask the way. He directed them to continue by Stanstead, near Rowlands Castle, but they lost their way, so they called at the inn at

Leigh, had a drink and asked the way. Here two brothers, George and Thomas Austin and a Mr. Jenks, who were going to Rowlands Castle, offered to show them the way. They took them to the White Hart at Rowlands Castle, run by Elizabeth Payne, a widow. The two men were now in the net, for Mrs. Payne's two sons were smugglers, and they were in smuggler country, where Dymer was well known and liked.

Mrs. Payne told George Austin that she was worried, for Galley was a customs official. He replied, not to worry, for they were merely taking a letter to Major Battine. This reply probably sealed their death warrant, for she knew Major Battine to be a high official in the Customs service. She therefore sent one of her sons for William Jackson and William Carter, two important smugglers in the neighbourhood. When Galley and Chater wished to leave, she told them that the ostler had gone off with the stable keys in his pocket, and they would have to wait for his return. The two men accepted this, and continued drinking. From this time onward they had no hope of reprieve. George Austin was now advised by the landlady to leave and he did so, but his brother and Mr. Jenks were by this time drunk and they remained, still drinking, and clearly no threat to the smugglers. Drink played a not unimportant part in this affair. Some of the smugglers said later that they were drunk the whole time, and this probably led to some extent to their cruelty. Chater and Galley might not have been so compliant in the beginning had they not been fuddled with drink, and in fact, as one of the smugglers admitted at the trial, their aim was to get them drunk.

Mrs. Payne's other son arrived, with four more smugglers. The smuggler called Jackson took Daniel Chater outside and got him to talk. Chater foolishly told him about Dymer — yet another inexorable step in the tragedy had been taken. Galley, suspecting some indiscretion, came to get Chater away from him, but Jackson swore horribly at him and slashed him across the face, knocking him down. He protested he was a King's officer, and Jackson shouted, 'You a King's officer! I'll make a King's officer of you: for a quartern of gin I'd serve you so again!'

Then they apologised, and amazingly they all sat down and started drinking again. After a little while, the two men were so fuddled with drink that they fell asleep on a bed in a small side room. Their pockets were searched and the letter was taken and read. The smugglers John Race and Richard Kelly slipped silently in. There was a very threatening atmosphere as man after man quietly entered the inn until a crowd of them had gathered in the small room.

A long discussion raged as to what to do with the two men who were still asleep in the side room. There were some quite extraordinary suggestions — one being that a loaded musket should be propped against the head of each, with string tied to the trigger and that they should all pull simultaneously, so that none should be innocent and none should be in a position to bear witness against another.

Another was that each should contribute 3d. a week for food to keep the two prisoners alive until the verdict was given on Dymer, and that then the same punishment should be meted out to the pair, whether it was hanging, imprisonment or freedom. The matter was apparently decided by the wives, who shouted out, 'Hang the dogs, for they came here to hang us!'

So the proceedings were set in motion by Jackson, who went into the little room where the men were sleeping, jumped on the bed, slashed them across the face with the sharp steel spurs on his riding boots, pushed them to the floor and kicked them as hard as he could. The two elderly men were then whipped through the kitchen and out into the freezing February night, confused, injured, terrified and shaking with cold and fear.

They bound the two men together on one horse, their legs tied together, and set out in the dark towards Rake, with Jackson shouting continuously, 'Whip them, cut them, slash them, damn them!'

The roads were very bad in the winter weather conditions, and they could only travel slowly. This terrible progression, with the shouts and oaths of the smugglers, the cracking of the whips and the groans and screams of the prisoners continued through the dark night, while the Sussex people cowered behind their cottage walls and none dared come to their aid. At Wood's Ashes, half a mile away, the two men's bonds loosened slightly and they slipped upside down on the horse, their wigs fell off and with every step the horses hooves hit their heads. They were pulled upright and whipping continued, but the same thing happened at Goodthorpe Dean, so each man was put up separately behind a smuggler, and the whipping continued all the way to Lady Holt Park. Galley was now almost unconscious, so he was slung across a horse 'as a butcher does a calf' and Jackson now inflicted on him some unspeakable indignities. After a mile further on poor Galley fell off the horse and appeared to be dead. They therefore went to the Red Lion at Rake, taking his body with them. Here they went to a nearby cottage, belonging to the smuggler Mills, and in an outhouse, on a bitter winter night, they flung the wounded Chater down and left him, chained by the leg to a post. They returned to the Red Lion and drank a great deal, then borrowed a candle, lantern and spade and went out to bury William Galley. They enlarged an old foxhole and put him in it, but it is thought by some people that he was not quite dead as when he was found his hand was protectively over his mouth in the light soil.

They told the landlord of the inn that they had been in a battle with the King's officers and this accounted for the body and the injured man. They now stayed all day Monday drinking at the inn, on Tuesday they went home, returning to the inn on Wednesday night. All this while Daniel Chater remained chained in the outhouse. On Wednesday night fourteen of them assembled to deal with the poor old man. It is too unbearable to quote the contemporary account of the terrible beating and knife slashing to which he was now subjected, almost gouging out his eyes, or to tell of the terrible journey to Harris's Well near Lady Holt Park where he was forced to climb over the fence although there was a gap he could have walked through. He was hanged by the neck over the well, but as he had not died in a quarter of an hour, he was thrown down the well. As he could still be heard groaning, the smugglers borrowed a ladder from a nearby cottage in order to go down after him. As they could not fit the ladder into the well, they searched around for some large rocks and a tree trunk, which they threw on top of him.

At last the poor man's sufferings were over and there was silence. This terrible story, and these hideous atrocities help to explain why large areas of the South of England were under the sway of the smugglers, and why people were afraid to stand up to them. Not only had the smugglers a good intelligence service, great strength and numbers, and on occasions, great cruelty, any civilian who crossed them and got into their clutches was on his own: there was no help from the authorities.

These events were described in the most horrifying detail at the trial of the smugglers, and the mixture of sadism, bestiality and brutality provoked such a storm of indignation and revulsion that never again would the smugglers be able to terrify the South of England and intimidate witnesses to the same degree as they had done for the last few years.

This time the smugglers had gone too far and when their hideous crimes were discovered a concerted effort was made to bring those responsible to justice. A man named Jacob Pring, himself one of the Hawkhurst Gang though not involved in the Poole affair, changed sides and became a thief taker. Largely as a result of his endeavours a number of those involved in the murders were arrested. Later an informer implicated one William Steel and when he turned King's evidence the remaining members were soon rounded up.

The murderers were tried at a special Assizes at Chichester on January 18th, 1749 and three judges presided, and a sermon was preached by the Dean (afterwards the Bishop) of Chichester. Some of the prisoners had been in Horsham Gaol, and a letter exists which describes how they were taken to Horsham Church each Sunday, and stood in their chains in the aisle, looking very dejected throughout the service.

Benjamin Tapner, a bricklayer, of Aldington, John Hammond; a labourer of South Bersted, John Cobby, William Jackson and William Carter of Hampshire, Richard Mills the elder, a horse dealer of Trotton, and Richard Mills the younger of Stedham, were sentenced to be hanged, and all of them except the two Mills were also sentenced to be hanged in chains. This was often done at this time, to such criminals as highwaymen and pirates as a terrible warning to others. Even in an age so brutalised, this struck terror into criminal hearts, although one feels that the judical punishments were only a few degrees removed from the original crimes. After the body was removed from the gallows it was soaked in tar to preserve it, and then enclosed in a network of metal strips to keep it together. It was then hung on a gibbet on a high place, so that it could be seen for a good distance.

A macabre touch was that the smith who was to make the irons needed measurements, as reported in the contemporary account:

> The afternoon preceding their execution a person came to take the measure of Jackson, Cobby, Hammond, Carter and Tapner in order to make their irons in which they were to be hung in chains, which threw the prisoners into very great confusion, and they seemed under a greater concern than ever they had showed before.

Jackson was so upset or terrified that he died about two hours later, he had been in bad health for some time.

Thus ended one of the most violent episodes in the history of smuggling: it only remained to act out the grim ceremony of execution. The smugglers had become so strong and so arrogant that they were corrupted by their own power. They overstepped the mark, and forfeited public tolerance. They had become terrorists and dictators instead of helpful Robin Hoods. At this trial, for the first time, witnesses were found who would testify freely, revolted by the horror of the events. Mill's servant testified against him, and he was visibly shaken by her testimony. Several smugglers testified against their erstwhile comrades.

The execution party was escorted by a company of foot guards and a detachment of dragoons, as there were still fears that a rescue might be attempted. The six smugglers were marched through the town and up the Midhurst Road to The Broyle, where the gallows had been erected. Executions were held in public as a means of conveying an awful warning to possible criminals. They were attended by huge crowds and there was often a holiday atmosphere, with piemen and fruit sellers and hawkers of broadsheets, which often contained the 'last confessions' of the condemned roughly printed out with a wood-cut portrait that usually bore no visible likeness to the unfortunate subject. The accused were allowed to make a speech before sentence was carried out, and they often warned the crowd to mend their ways in case they too should end on the gallows. As a large range of crimes (e.g. horse stealing and house breaking) carried the death penalty this warning struck an answering chord in many of the spectators. There was a curious attitude to the awful spectacle of death: the crowd liked to see a man die well, to make a speech of repentance and resignation and then step calmly on the scaffold. Many criminals played up to the occasion until the last few minutes, joking and calling out to the crowd. There are many newspaper accounts of hangings at this period, written for decent middle-class families, and they usually give a precise account of the prisoner's last moments, and details of the duration and movements of his struggles as he died.

The six smugglers hanged at Chichester therefore went through the horrible ceremony of the time: a long cart was drawn up underneath the gallows — a crossbar on two supports, and each in turn was tied to the beam by the executioner. The rope for the elder Mills was rather short and he was obliged to stand on tiptoe, shouting out so that the bystanders could hear, 'Don't hang me by inches!'

When the noose had been tied around the necks of all six men, the cart was driven away and they were left to dance the 'hempen jig'. Carter's body was hung at Rake near the Portsmouth road, Tapner's at Rook's Hill, near Chichester, Cobby's and Hammond's on the coast near Selsey Bill. These men had inflicted terror and violence on Sussex in the last few years, and they now looked out over the Sussex countryside through which they had roamed, in awful warning to those who should think of following in their footsteps.

Among those who had been arrested were Thomas Kingsmill and William Fairall. These two, however, were considered to be criminals of such importance that they were sent for trial at the Old Bailey together with Richard

Perrin. Throughout their trial Kingsmill and Fairall exhibited the utmost contempt for all concerned with their prosecutions and leered defiantly at the judge when sentence of death was passed on them. In the days leading up to their execution these two took to attending chapel showing repentence but certainly never any fear. Their bodies had been ordered to be hung in chains and when Perrin, also under sentence of death, commiserated with them on this Fairall laughed and said, 'We shall be hanging in the sweet air when you are rotting in your grave . . .' They were executed at Tyburn on April 26th, 1749 almost two years to the day after the battle of Goudhurst. Fairall's body was hung in chains in his home village of Horsmonden in the road still known as Gibbet Lane and Kingsmill's body exhibited at Goudhurst Gore, not far from the scene of the battle.

Between the Poole attack and their arrest the Hawkhurst Gang practised housebreaking and highway robbery. Four of the gang were hanged for highway robbery and at their trial admitted to smuggling and robbery but denied ever having murdered anyone. Two of them, brothers by the name of Kemp (who had been captured by Jacob Pring*) are reported as being of good birth. Thomas Kemp and another of the gang named William Gray had once been confined in Newgate prison for a Crown debt. Three other Hawkhurst smugglers secured their release by ringing the prison bell at a pre-arranged time and knocking out the turnkey when he came to the door. Two more of the gang were tried at Rochester Quarter Sessions for housebreaking and executed at Penenden Heath, Maidstone.

With the execution of Kingsmill and Fairall the Hawkhurst Gang was finally broken up. A similar but rather less infamous group was operating simultaneously in north Kent and they continued to force runs and show violence to those who dared to interfere for many years.

CHAPTER IV

The reigning commerce of the coast

In the eighteenth and nineteenth centuries the greater part of the population in southern England was implicated in smuggling, either by helping the smugglers in their work or by buying their products. When the Act putting Pitt's window tax into operation was passed at roughly the same time as yet another Act aimed against the smugglers. the *Sussex Weekly Advertiser*, printed the following comment:

> June 28 1784
> Though the minister's new smuggling bill may, in great measure, operate to the suppression of that illicit and pernicious traffic, it is nevertheless hugely objectionable as it will be most severely felt by the middling classes of people. Many persons in this town [i.e. Lewes] whose consumption of tea is 8 to 12 pounds a year (principally souchong, smuggled in the retail way at six shillings a pound and purchased off the fair trader at seven shillings) have from 20 to 30 windows, so that, for a saving from 16s. to 24s. per annum on the article of tea, according to the proposed plan, they will be burthened with the enormous additional tax on their windows, of from £2 = 15s to £4 = 10s the year. The remedy therefore prescribed in this new bill, will, to the most useful part of the community, be far more grevious than the disease.

So many people were planning to block up their windows to avoid the tax that the newspaper's item continued:

> The glaziers, it is thought, will petition the House of Commons against the new window tax as odious and impolitic; in which case it is said the grocers and tea dealers will throw in a counter petition.

Everyone drank tea, the poor as well as the rich, and despite the mystique that today surrounds antique Georgian tea caddies, with their locked compartments, tea could be found in thousands of humble homes in the eighteenth century and a high proportion of it was smuggled. The tea drunk then was Chinese tea, imported by the East India Company under monopoly conditions, stored in special warehouses and sold by the Company. England did not become a heavy user of Indian tea until much later, when Queen Victoria was on the throne. The smugglers in the main imported the cheaper sorts of tea, a very black tea called Bohea, and green tea. This was partly because their methods of transit would have caused the more delicate sorts to deteriorate, but also because they wished to sell as cheaply as possible. The large warehouses which catered for the smugglers on the French and neighbouring coasts supplied the tea ready packed for the journey in oilskin bags, so shaped that they could be flung over a horse's back.

Smugglers sometimes used agents, sometimes they went abroad to buy the tea themselves. The Hawkhurst Gang sent to Guernsey, where great stocks of tea were held. In July 1734 the *Prince George* sloop from Hastings took Thomas Darby to Flushing in the Netherlands for the same purpose. The duty payable was 4s. a pound, but the smuggler could go to France or the Netherlands and buy tea for only 2s. a pound. Even with all his expenses of transport and guarding, and the possibility of losing some cargoes to the customs men, he could still make a good profit. Quite astonishing amounts of tea were smuggled into the country, and in the 1730's and 1740's tea was the

* See page 50 post.

predominant article run. Sometimes the revenue cutters took huge hauls of smuggled tea in the Channel, in 1776 the *Stag* cutter of Rye had over two tons of tea. In 1745 a 'committee to inquire into the most infamous Practice of Smuggling* produced some fascinating details about the economics and techniques of tea smuggling:

> The present price of such Bohea as is imported by our Company is about 2s 10d a pound: That the Expenses are, for Freight £1. 1s per Hundredweight, for their Bags, containing 27 pounds-weight each, 2s per bag, to their Porters 4s per Hundred-weight; for Warehouse room 5s; and 20s per Hundred-weight is allowed to their agent, whos disposes of it to the Hawkers; their whole Expense amounts to betwixt 1s and 1s 3d per pound; and this Tea the Smugglers sell for about £20 per Hundred Dutch Weight, which is about 100 Pounds English: That he has been informed by Smugglers, that they do not now get clear above 20s per Hundredweight: and he himself believes that their profit cannot amount to 3d per pound.
> As to the Loss which Smugglers sustain by Seizures, he said, it is a mere Trifle: That he formerly dealt with a considerable Trader in run Tea for Six of Seven years, who never had any goods seized in all that time, and that although the Danger of Seizures is greater at Sea than on land, yet the Smugglers more commonly escape the Custom-house Sloops, by means of Intelligence sent from the Inhabitants on the Coast when those Sloops sail out of Port, and that the generality of the people on the Coasts are better Friends to the Smugglers than to the Custom-house Officers.

The smugglers' gain, and the cheaper price of smuggled tea for the consumer, naturally involved the government in a heavy loss of taxation to which it was due. The loss of revenue was not merely a local phenomenon affecting the coastal area, but a national problem with serious economic consequences, commented upon by many writers of the time. One of the most voluble on the subject was George Bishop.† He said that great quantities of tea were imported by France and Holland, most of which was smuggled into Britain. The European nations imported 17,400,000 pounds of tea a year, and that 5,400,000 was drunk by the European nations and 12 million pounds by the English.

However, there was a monopoly importer in England — the East India Company, and that body officially imported 6 million pounds of tea. Therefore, Bishop argued an equal amount — another 6 million pounds — was brought in by the smugglers. These figures were for 1766. By 1778, he calculated 13,190,993 pounds of tea was imported, whether legally of illegally, while 24,000,000 pounds was actually drunk. The difference was made up by the adulteration of tea by the addition of ash or sloe leaves dyed to look like tea. His figures for smuggling are in rough agreement with the official estimates of a parliamentary committee in 1783.‡ 'The Quantity of Tea supposed to be brought Annually into Great Britain by the various Methods of illicit Importation, amounts, according to the Estimate of the Commissioners of Excise, to near Seven Millions of Pounds.' The Commissioners computed fake tea production as slightly less than Bishop had thought. 'The Quantity of factitious Tea which is Annually manufactured from Sloe Liquorice and Ash Leaves . . . to be mixed with Genuine Tea is computed at more than Four Millions of pounds.'

Neither Bishop nor the report makes it clear whether the smugglers adulterated their tea as well as the 'fair trading' grocers. One of the reasons fair traders adulterated their tea — and there are many contemporary complaints of this practice, was of course that they were trying to compete with the lower prices of the smugglers. As the population of England and Wales at the first Census in 1801, was 8·9 million people only, it is clear that tea drinking was a widespread habit.

The 1783 report enumerates the national consequences, all due to smuggling, such as loss to the Revenue of 'not less than One Million Sterling' (which was a huge sum in those days) and an 'unfavourable balance' caused by paying for this huge illicit import of tea. In fact, this report has numerous echoes of many of the financial statements of today, with smugglers cast as the sole cause of all difficulties. The report continued by blaming them for using shipping that should be used for the good of the nation as a whole, preventing men from serving as sailors for the good of the country, damaging the entire 'China Trade' and being the entire ruination of a great many fair dealers in tea and generally damaging the grocery trade. Although one does not at first connect a band of busy men, on a quiet beach after dark, busily unloading bags of tea and kegs of brandy, with national financial crises and employment trends, it is obvious on reflection that the figures in the report had a fair basis, and that as the greater part of smuggling was done on the South and East Coasts, the Kent and Sussex smugglers had a very large share of responsibility for the situation.

The authorities were so alarmed at the escalation of smuggling on the Southern coast that the marine surveillance was increased, and the following cutters were on duty:

1777–1780				
Newhaven	*The Dispatch*	138 tons	26 men	12 carriage guns
Shoreham	*Enterprise*	90 tons	18 men	8 carriage guns
Chichester	*Falcon*	92 tons	18 men	8 carriage guns
1780–1783				
Newhaven	*The Surprise*	135 tons	28 men	14 carriage guns
Shoreham	*Enterprise*	90 tons	18 men	8 carriage guns
Chichester	*Roebuck*	97 tons	21 men	8 carriage guns

* House of Commons Journal 19 Geo II. † *Observations, Remarks and Means to Prevent Smuggling*, 1783.
‡ First Report from the Committee appointed to inquire into the illicit practices used in defrauding the revenue. Dec 1783.

The Smuggler's Retreat
Hythe
G.A.H.

The Three Daws, Gravesend. Three secret tunnels led from behind the chimney breast (now removed). The Pilots House (foreground of picture) has seven staircases to confuse Revenue men and press gangs.

Shades House, Hoo Peninsula — smugglers' haunt.

An old smugglers' tunnel runs under the Hogarth Inn, Isle of Grain.

Said to be the home of Dr Syn, Dymchurch.

Dymchurch beach — a famous landing place.

New Hall, Dymchurch — used as a courthouse in the time of Dr Syn.

Martello Tower, Dymchurch.

There are many reports in the local newspapers of sea battles between revenue cutters and smugglers' vessels, which were also armed, but as this is a study of land smugglers we shall do no more than point out that there were often quite violent marine engagements, in which men fought and died as in naval war. Usually the ships' guns were used, the smugglers' principal aim being to smash the rigging of the revenue cutters, so that they could escape without pursuit, and there are interesting accounts of their guns being loaded with old horseshoes, nails and scrap metal, and then fired at the rigging, as these missiles did the required amount of cutting and slashing damage. Men too, were horribly wounded, and one could imagine that a flying horseshoe could do a great deal of damage. Newspaper reports tell of people in Rye hearing the screams of the wounded at sea. One of the saddest of the casualties was a young man of eighteen, Capt. Haddock, of Rye, who was killed by a canon ball although he was crouching behind the bulwark of the revenue ship he was commanding, a young man of great courage and spirit. Sometimes the revenue officers boarded the smugglers' boats and hand-to-hand fighting with pistols and cutlasses ensued. More often, however, the smugglers' boats, which were built for speed, outsailed the revenue cutters and simply changed their place of landing. Even here the smugglers had an influence far wider than the simple landing of goods, for various Acts were passed controlling the method of shipbuilding of all non-government boats in order to prohibit the smugglers from building fast ships. The fact of clinker building, the length of the bowsprit, the number of oars, the shape of the hull to size, all were controlled, and there were many complaints from honest shipbuilders that they could not design the best possible ships because these regulations prevented them from doing so. The smugglers, of course, simply carried on building clinker-built boats, and if they wanted more oars than the legal limit, well, they just had movable or hidden thwarts to contain them, and threw the oars overboard if they were searched.

However, despite the increasing alarm, the running of tea continued throughout the eighteenth century, although most experts think the 1730's and 1740's to be the greatest peak. Most of the runs were undetected: a typical one was this at Eastbourne in May 1733.

> Thomas Hurst, one of the riding officers, seeing the tracks of a great many Men and Horses on the Sea Beach, summoned some other Officers and two Dragoons, and went in Pursuit of them, imagining they had been running some Goods: and tracking them six or seven miles into a place called Wilmington Wood, searched about and found their Cargo, which they seized, amounting to one Thousand seven Hundred and fifty Pounds of Tea, and one Hundred and ten Pounds of Coffee.

In 1745 the duty on tea was reduced to 1s. a pound, in order to inhibit smuggling, and this certainly did have an effect. As the smugglers now had to reduce their prices in order to compete with the lower price of legal tea, their profit margins were cut, and they could no longer afford to lose many cargoes. It had been their boast that they could lose one cargo in five without suffering a loss, but this was not so with the smaller profit. Consequently, they became more vicious as they had to stand and fight rather than lose a cargo. There were many operators in a big way among them, and it was believed that they had even sent agents to attend the East India Company's legal tea auctions to send the price up by giving feint bids, and withdrawing at the last moment. Another witness to the Commission referred to the smugglers' difficulty since tax was lowered:

> Since the late Act, there has been a sale at East-India Company's Warehouse at which Sale, the lowest Black Bohea Tea (the Species chiefly run) was sold by the Candle at 3s 4d per pound; to which Price must be added, the Excise of 1s per pound, and 25 per cent ad valorem; and from thence there is to be deducted 6½ per Cent on the prime cost for prompt Payment, also an Allowance for Tret and Super-tare, which brings the price of this tea to the Trader to about 4s 8d the Pound; and the Witness, and Others, sell it for 5s per Pound, in order (if possible) to prevent Smuggling; That in Holland the same Sort of Tea is sold for about 24 Stivers per Pound, which is about 2s English; and the Buyer has rather larger Allowance than what our East-India Company makes: That in Sweden Tea is rather cheaper than in Holland.
>
> The Expense which the Smugglers are at in running Tea, in this Time of War, he said, he believed might be 14d per Pound; and Supposing them to sustain a Seizure of One Cargo in Five, it adds to that Expence 4d per Pound more; and they sell Tea, as he is informed, for about 4s per Pound; but that now they have great difficulty in disposing of it, since the present Act was made; and though they could formerly afford to lose One Cargo in Five, he apprehends they cannot at this time.

Another witness said that tea run into the 'South Part of England' is brought by 'Vessels employed in Smuggling from Holland, France, Jersey, Guernsey'. The tea duty was increased again in 1759, as England was again at war and needing increased revenue, and tea continued to be smuggled.

We complain today of government interference, of planners, of taxes like VAT, and imagine that previous ages lived in freedom from interference in business matters. This was not so; a large range of materials and manufacturers in eighteenth-century England were taxed heavily, or even forbidden altogether (although they were smuggled) or their manufacture hedged with a list of tiresome regulations, like the innocent — one would have thought — craft of candlemaking. These difficulties simply meant that the smugglers moved into that line of business. Bishop tells us, 'the inhabitants of the sea coast have their tea, spirits, wine, currants, raisins, starch, soap, china, glass and tobacco mostly smuggled'. Many of the accounts in the *Sussex Weekly Advertiser* refer to packs of 'light goods' as well as tobacco, spirits, tea. Articles mentioned in customs reports included pepper and cinnamon.

This enormous traffic involved a great deal of transport, and Bishop, forgetting that many horses were borrowed from farmers, and returned to do their ordinary farm work, calculated, 'one fifth or one sixth of all the horses kept, are for smuggling, which horses consume more corn than is used in distillery', and he makes the somewhat ludicrous calculation that were it not for the smugglers' horses England would not have to pay to import oats. On firmer ground, he makes the same point as the Commissioners of the damage to the national exchequer, 'the smugglers pay for the articles which they buy either in cash or by the illicit exportation of English wool (no other article of any consequence being carried abroad by them), and like Arthur Young he bemoans the misuse of manpower: 'there are employed in smuggling 60,000 of the younger men and best able to labour . . . one twenty fifth part of the whole of the labourers in the Kingdom: and one thousand women and children in retailing and hawking about the country spirits and tea'.

The volume of spirits smuggled into the country was equally as astonishing as the volume of tea: the loss to the revenue must have been immense. A smuggler called Hannay, when reprieved of murder, told Sir Robert Walpole that before 1736 the annual cost of goods smuggled in England was, he estimated, one million or one million one hundred thousand pounds, of which eight hundred thousand pounds was for tea. This was an immense amount when the relative value of money in those days is considered. This estimate was agreed by a witness to the 1745 Commission, who thought, 'that there is carried out of this Kingdom at least one Million Pounds per Annum, in Specie [i.e. in gold] to purchase the various goods run here'.

There are innumerable contemporary references to the heavy drinking of the people at large, as well as to the drinking of the smugglers. The well known cry 'Drunk for a penny, dead drunk for tuppence' fell on the unreceptive ears of those dealing with the problem of heavy drinking as they affected the nation — the problem of drunkenness, the murderous affrays, the spin-off crimes, the sexual licence, the ill-treatment of children, all often engendered by too much drinking. Smuggling thus played a not insignificant part in the moral as well as the financial problems of the nation.

In fairness to the smugglers, it must be pointed out that not all cheap spirits came from them. Many distilleries used their basic products three or four times, and bribed the revenue officer to enter in the record only one distillation, 'by which means they made very bad spirits but as they pay but little duty can afford to undersell the London distillery'. In addition London and Bristol had many illegal distilleries which paid no duties and according to the all-knowledgeable Bishop, about ten thousand secret stills in Scotland sent their produce to London (although I suspect this to be an exaggeration). In this positive deluge of spiritous liquor, whether half-excise paid, nil-excise paid or smuggled, one wonders how the revenue officers managed to continue as a viable corps at all.

According to Bishop in 1777 two and a half million gallons of Geneva (gin) were smuggled from Dunkirk alone. He estimated four million gallons of gin as being smuggled into England each year, as well as great quantities of brandy, rum, other spirits and claret. Special distilleries were founded at Calais, Dunkirk, Ostend, Newport and Gottenberg to supply the smuggling trade. Twelve ships of 200 tons regularly brought rum from the West Indies to Guernsey for smuggling to England: much of this went to the West Country but it is thought that some came to Sussex. In January 1743 nine smuggling cutters sailed from Rye to Guernsey 'to take in large Quantities of Goods, to be run on the Coast'.*

The disposal of this huge volume of spirits was contrived by various means, including the species of deception that Harriet Martineau tells us was involved in selling smuggled English wool in France. Cases were reported in Sussex newspapers of visits by excisemen to liquor stores in the country, under a 'mistaken' impression that some of the spirits were smuggled. Just one example is that of Mr. Liffen, of Hove, a 'reputable' dealer in spirits, whose cellar was visited by Customs men, but cleared. Perhaps Mr. Liffen was a wronged citizen: perhaps he 'got away with it'. We are not in possession of sufficient facts to decide after this lapse of time.

According to Bishop:

> smugglers are taking every method to improve their trading and convey immense quantities of spirits into London with permits they get with spirits bought at the Custom-House sales, or permits bought in London for that purpose. They have warehouses at proper distances on the roads, the more easily to convey it forwards, as is best suitable to their purpose.

Arthur Gray had such a storehouse in Kent, an unofficial smugglers' bonded warehouse as large as many official ones of His Majesty's Government. Another gang of smugglers in Southern England had a seafront warehouse complete with quayside crane. This magnificent effrontery really compels our admiration. The spirits sold by the smugglers were very often better than the official kind, and Bishop tells of 'stronger and better' spirits sold on false permits that were purchased with 'low' spirits. Smuggled brandy was often sold inland as 'genuine Crowlink' as a mark of great approval: Crowlink, of course, was the famous gap in the cliffs near Alfriston, much favoured as a landing place for contraband.

There was good profit in the importation of spirits, which were supplied by the French warehouses in casks slung together by ropes in pairs: half-ankers holding four gallons each, to go across a man's shoulders, and often carried longish distances on foot, and ankers, double that amount, for slinging across a horse. A four gallon tub of gin or brandy cost £1, and could be sold in Sussex or London for £4 (and which of us today would not like to buy four gallons of brandy for £4?). A witness at the 1745 Commission stated that he bought, 'hundreds of dozens of Claret, with the bottles for sixteen shillings the Dozen, and French brandy at three shillings and sixpence per gallon'. Wine was often shipped in bottles, then packed in straw in saddle-sacks, to avoid legislation affecting hogsheads of wine.

When one considers that this contraband spirit was usually 40 per cent and sometimes 100 per cent above proof, the quantity of alcohol flushing down English throats was truly remarkable. One old smuggler told Lord

* Witness to the 1745 Committee.

Teignmouth that he did not think the process of bringing the spirit down to proof was worthwhile, as there was the problem of finding containers. John Banks tells of such a 'bottle party' at Hastings, where large earthenware bowls were filled with the spirits and mixed with water until floating marked glass baubles reached the height that indicated the correct rates of alcohol to water. As Banks himself in his youth lived in a Hastings house infested with rats, mice and bugs, and as the water was almost certainly from a well, and may therefore have been contaminated with typhoid germs, one suspects that cautious buyers would prefer to haggle with the smugglers for a whole, unopened keg, and most middle-class people — Adam Smith the economist among them — seem to have purchased in this way. One of the witnesses at the trial of the murderers of Galley and Chater confessed to having a 'very wicked liver' ever since he took up smuggling, and this could be believed. Many of the acts of violence done by the smugglers were probably done under the influence of drink and no doubt some of the violence and indolence generally in the slums of Southern England was due to smuggled spirits. However, there was another side to the picture, and a little drink must sometimes have made bearable a life almost insupportable in its misery and squalor. The working men from towns like Brighton and Hastings who helped the smugglers as lookout men and porters lived in conditions of unbelievable squalor. As early as 1847 the Board of Health sent Edward Cressy to report on conditions in Brighton and several new coastal towns, and he described the small tenements of the back streets, many of which had been built soon after the turn of the century. Many of these houses, crowded round small courts and narrow alleys, were completely airless. In Brighton, it was common to have more than a dozen people crowded into a small house of two bedrooms. These people used an overflowing and unemptied cess pit in the tiny backyard. On some occasions the cess pit's contents even seeped through the walls of the houses. The wells were badly sited, and the water frequently, contaminated with typhoid and cholera germs: it was safer to drink beer than to drink water. Small-pox, tuberculosis, and a killer strain of measles, were prevalent. A survey written in 1860, which says the conditions had been retrospective for many years, stated:

> Men, women and children must not be suffered to herd together like brute beasts, in pestilential dens, where every instinct of propriety and decency was effectually smothered. Parents, brothers, sisters, cousins, male and female, must not be huddled together in the same apartment, often only a few feet square, where birth and death are going on at the same time; where the new born child, the dying and the dead, all lie scattered on the floor.*

The relief offered by drinking smuggled spirits, and the higher rates of pay offered for a nights smuggling, was an understandably attractive relief from a life of poverty, drudgery, ill-health and squalid conditions.

The living conditions in Hastings were only marginally better: in both towns open drains ran down the centre of many of the narrow alleys, filled in addition to rainwater, with rubbish of the foulest nature. Numerous small local slaughter houses threw all their offal out in to the streets and corners to rot. Village dwellers had slightly less disgusting living conditions and better food, but theirs too was a hard life of grinding drudgery and unrelenting poverty. It is small wonder that the farmers complained in the *Gentleman's Magazine* that they could not get labourers when the smugglers wanted men. For a week of unrelenting toil on the farm, they were getting little more than 12s. plus their cottage; a craftsman in a town did not earn a great deal more, and a labourer less than a craftsman. A half-guinea for a night's work, however cold and dangerous, plus the 'perks' must have seemed a great blessing to them, by working for the smugglers. Then too, the smugglers looked after their men: they boasted that they never left a wounded comrade behind, and there are many reports in the local papers of men who had been taken by Customs officers, being released, or attempts made to release them by their fellow smugglers.† It is true that this esprit-de-corps went hand-in-hand with the application of the most vicious punishments to anyone who 'squealed', but that was a different matter. While in ordinary life there were many good and fair employers by the standards of the time, there were also many harrowing stories of men being used, worked out, and thrown aside.

There were, however, other benefits for Kent and Sussex smugglers in addition to the money earned, and the luxuries of spirits for themselves, and tea or silks for wife or girlfriend. The gathering at the appointed place, the anxious waiting for the boats, the frenzied work of unloading, the intense satisfaction of clearing an assignment at speed from the beach and seeing it safely on the road had a nerve-stretching satisfaction rarely felt in fishing, ploughing or thrashing (the usual winter occupation of farm labourers). When the well-known Hastings smuggler Roper was asked if he would not like to give up smuggling, he is supposed to have replied, 'What, would you have me sit bobbing an eel all day, to catch six penn'orth of whitebait'. Then too, although he was outside the law, the smuggler had a certain status the farm labourer did not. Anyone who doubts this — and there is little contemporary evidence for this — can ask any housewife who lived through the last war if she can remember the deferential treatment displayed by customers to food suppliers. When the Hawkhurst Gang rode through the Dorset and Sussex countryside after raiding the Customs House at Poole, crowds of people turned out to watch and many of them cheered. There was also the comradeship, and the boozy relaxation at the inn after a successful run, echoed in many contemporary descriptions. The Hastings smugglers were accustomed to smoke and drink on the clifftop on fine evenings, relaxing, and on one such occasion Roper was shot in the leg by a Customs officer, because they refused to 'move on'.

Finally, in the age when revolution was always rumbling beneath the surface — in the 1790's, the 1830's and 1840's the fabric of English life was badly shaken, taking part in smuggling, was a gesture against officialdom. It is

* 'Brighton as it is', by a graduate.

† A smuggler who was in prison apparently could rest assured that his family were being looked after by the other smugglers.

significant that an official inquiry, taken in 1833 into the disturbed state of Sussex linked smuggling with the Swing Riots. These agricultural riots were particularly bad in Sussex and Kent: groups of farm labourers, their faces blacked, and after dark very often, went from farm to farm and to the houses of landowners to persuade them to promise to pay higher wages. The report suggested that the prevalent habit of labourers to gather together in large groups for the purpose of smuggling encouraged them to gather in groups for the Riots.

In conclusion of this survey of the amounts of spirits run into the country by giving the inventories of two seizures: one listed by John Banks for 1803:

477 casks of brandy containing 1,650 gallons
109 casks of rum containing 375 gallons
421 casks of gin containing 1,460 gallons
8 packages of tea containing 188 pounds
173 packages of tobacco containing 6,432 pounds

The other seizure was noted in the Sayer manuscripts:*

Nov 28 1825
1 cask of 3 gallons and 2/8 gallon foreign Brandy
1 cask of 3 gallons and 4/8 gallon foreign Geneva
1 cask of 3 gallons and 4/8 gallon foreign Brandy
3 cannisters containing 4 pounds and 2/8 pound weight of Black tea, foreign
1 cannister containing 1 pound weight of a mixed tea, foreign
1 cannister containing 1 pound and 1/8 pound of Green tea, foreign
1 Paper parcel containing 4/8 of a pound weight of tobacco, foreign
1 Foreign silk shirt
1 cask containing 3 gall and 2/8 gallon foreign Brandy
1 cask containing 3 gall and 2/8 gallon foreign Geneva
2 casks containing 6 gallons foreign Geneva
1 cask containing 3 gallons and 2/8 gallon of foreign Geneva
1 cask containing 3 gallons of foreign Brandy
13 casks containing 3 gallons and 2/8 gallon of foreign Brandy
1 cask containing 3 gallons and 2/8 gallon of foreign Brandy.

It is amazing to learn that the estimated value of this haul was £93 7s. 10¼d.

Many middle class shops and trades depended heavily on smuggled goods. It is highly probable that a great many inns would have gone out of business had they not had smuggled spirits. Many other shopkeepers were dependent on supplies from the smugglers. A well-known tradesman in Hastings, after hearing that soldiers were being sent to the town as a result of the activities of the Ruxley Gang, disappeared, hiding in fear of what would be discovered.

Another interesting case concerned a Brighton trader, a draper called Powell. A boat taken at Newhaven turned out to have hidden store places, and not only a great quantity of contraband was found, but an incriminating letter and even an invoice. Mr. Powell was truly caught! The invoice reads as follows:

Dieppe 6.11.1822
Send de Inwois of de Gods you bought. mont of de Plain Silk f 7223.99 Gros de Naples, twill'd Tipre and Glowes mont F10 300.9 I tanck you to credit me for de amount, haf credit you for de two Bills a 3 an 4 months for de Plain Silk, de remainder you mai depend by de nachts term by Mr Castell. I saw teim send you de Patterns directed to John Rode London.
Remained your Humble Serveter
D'L WITT
Mons P. Powell, No. 16 North Street, Brighton.

The goods taken from the hiding places show an astonishing range of imports: 950 yard silk, 3½ yards ribbed silk, 48 pairs long kid leather gloves, 174 pairs short leather gloves, 10 yards silk lawn, 6 pairs silk garters, 4 silk purses, 292 yards silk net lace, 10 pairs ruffles, 4 pairs lawn ruffles, 6 musical boxes, 12 musical works for boxes, 14 opera glasses, 1 pair of gold bracelets, 6 gold watches, 11 brushes, 1 watchchain, 2 pairs earrings, 2 brooches, 3 bead purses, 46 hair necklaces, 14 pairs hair bracelets and hair girdles, 134 toys.

A letter announcing the despatch of 3,000 yards of silk and 86 pairs of gloves was also found together with the invoice. It is quite clear that a draper's shop doing business on this scale was heavily involved in smuggling. Mr. Powell's establishment was one of several flourishing drapers in Brighton, and his shop was situated in a busy and popular part of North Street. As the date was 1822 this was at the height of Brighton's popularity as a Regency watering place. Many of the demure middle-class and upper-class ladies attending balls at the Castle or the Old Ship Assembly Rooms or even being presented to the King at the Royal Pavilion, would therefore be clothed in smuggled goods.

A few years earlier in 1818, Robert Hardy, the Vicar of Walberton, in Sussex wrote:

smuggling has not been confined to the lower orders of people: but from what I have heard, I apprehend that it has very generally been encouraged by their superiors, for whom no manner of excuse, that I know of, can

* Add MS 1879.

be offered. I was once asked by an inhabitant of a village near the sea whether I thought there was any harm in smuggling. Upon my reply that I not only thought there was a great deal of harm in it, but a great deal of sin, he exclaimed 'Then the Lord have mercy upon the county of Sussex, for who is there that has not had a tub'.*

However, one suspects that Robert Hardy was not particularly representative of Sussex parsons, and that Kipling's 'brandy for the parson' had more of truth in it. Although the smoking of pipes became less common as the eighteenth century progressed, snuff becoming very popular, country squires and parsons were old fashioned and kept to their pipes, and it was generally accepted at the time that a great deal of the tobacco they smoked was smuggled. Similarly country vicarages were well known for the good quality of their brandy and claret, and we have Parson Woodforde's own word for it that he paid a smuggler for some 'hyson tea'. (Parson Woodforde, of couse, being a Norfolk parson.)

Parsons generally were often associated in popular tradition with smuggling, probably because they were in control of the parsonage cellars, the church and the graveyard, all good hiding places for contraband. The involvement may sometimes have gone further: a story is told of the lady who on hearing that a revenue cutter had made a big capture of contraband at sea, exclaimed 'I hope that it is not the parson's boat'. This association may have provided some inspiration to Russell Thorndike in his creation of Doctor Syn or Daphine Du Maurier with the evil Francis Davey.

It was not unknown for public figures to express toleration for the smugglers. Adam Smith wrote that the smuggler, while 'no doubt highly blameable for violating the laws of his country, is equally incapable of violating those of natural justice, and would have been, in every respect, an excellent citizen had not the laws of his country made that a crime which nature never meant to be so'. A Chancery case in 1874, in which a Hastings slum area called 'America' was made over to the Crown, produced an interesting comment from a witness: 'You were not thought respectable if you were not a smuggler . . . they were all smugglers, parsons and all . . . oh yes, they used to take a Keg for Christmas sometimes'. Even the great Duke of Newcastle, so powerful in his political influence that he was called 'King of Sussex', was supposed to tolerate smugglers, and to have used his influence to secure the release of a smuggler from Horsham jail.

But perhaps the final word on the extent of smuggling could be left to Defoe, who before he became a journalist had been a tradesman and a haberdasher: his enemies called him a 'sock-seller', and so understood business methods: 'I do not find they have any foreign commerce, except it be what we call smuggling, and roguing, which, I may say, is the reigning commerce of all this part of the English coast, from the mouth of the Thames to Lands End.'

* Serious cautions and advice to all concerned in smuggling.

CHAPTER V

Such a gang of profligates

There was a general belief in the eighteenth century that collusion with the smugglers was widespread and that illegal trade was often allowed to proceed unhindered by preventive men, dragoons, magistrates and officials as a result of bribery and coercion. There are innumerable stories of smugglers leaving a barrel or two behind in barns and other buildings as payment for overnight storage — bribery of a sort, but there is no doubt that corruption on a Mafia-like scale existed. Threats and bribery, often used together, were the causes of this.

The annals of smuggling in both Hastings and Rye contain many instances of quite inexplicable discharge by magistrates of obviously guilty men. In October 1734 the Commissioner of Customs in London wrote to John Parnell, Mayor of Winchelsea, rebuking him for acquitting Thomas Darby, a known smuggler. In February 1735, Gabriel Tomkins, a bailiff of the Sheriff of Sussex, arrested Thomas Moore of Rye for smuggling, but he was bailed by the magistrate. The bailiff Tomkins stayed overnight at the Mermaid Inn, and Moore returned with several other men, and with the help of Thomas Bean the landlord, broke down the door of Tomkin's room, dragged him downstairs and frogmarched him through the streets, forcing him on board a boat, where he was locked up, to be taken overseas. Fortunately, Catain Pigram, commander of the Rye revenue sloop, *Amelia*, sent his men to search all the ships in the harbour, and Tomkins was found, not surprisingly in a state of great anxiety, and set free. There are several instances of men being taken by smugglers in this fashion and set on the coast of France and left to fend for themselves. As we were often at war, their predicament must have been very perilous. In March 1748, Mr. Springer, a Sussex customs man, was put on board a ship near Brighton to be sent to France against his will, and there are several other examples. Not only smugglers adopted this method of getting rid of people inconvenient to them — the writer Smollet describes such an event, and Stevenson's *Kidnapped* is based on it.

All the indications are that very large bribes could be offered, Bishop says, 'The smugglers are a very powerful body and can raise considerable sums of money on any occasion that offers to promote their interest: they boast of having disposed of large sums in order to prevent any hurt being done to their trade; at one time three thousand pounds was disposed of.'

Often acquittals were made in the face of overwhelming evidence; when the Collector of Customs at Rye took 49 lbs of tea from a William Lingfield's house, the magistrates, one of whom was the mayor, acquitted him. In many cases charges were not brought, obviously because the local revenue officer had accepted bribes, or was so terrorised by the smugglers that he preferred to turn a blind eye to their activities, despite the fact that efforts were made to prevent this by not employing local men. In November 1822 two of the Newhaven waterguards were reprimanded because, 'however guiltless they may be of collusion with the smugglers they have betrayed a want of energy almost amounting to cowardice . . .'. Just before Christmas in 1822 a report on John West and James Woolgar of Eastdean, complained about their activities, or lack of activities, in the Eastbourne area in similar terms. There are many other reports like this at this period. The Collier letters seventy years earlier speak of a man in Kent who 'squealed' and gave details of bribes to customs officials, and there are recorded instances of bribes in Hampshire — the custom was widespread.

The reports of the men on the Sussex coast to the Comptroller of Customs at Newhaven have several interesting accounts. One reads:

> On the fourth of September 1825 I was posted as sentinal on duty at the point near the mouth of Cuckmere Haven when two men came up to me. One of them, who has since called himself John Clare, laid money on the beach, desiring me to pick it up. I told him I did not want it. The two men then sat down for some time underneath the cliff when John Clare put on a lump of chalk £20 and pointing to it said ther should be twenty pounds for me and a cart in readiness to carry me to what part of the country I pleased admitting them to work tubs, asking me at the same time which was the most convenient place for that purpose.*

Equally important in gaining the support of ordinary people was the fear of reprisal if they informed against the smuggler or refused a favour asked. A farmer getting a request for horses on a certain night would leave his stable door unfastened: refusal would almost certainly lead to a mysterious fire in his barn. Similarly, one of the Collier letters describes the treatment meted out to informers: 'Some time ago a person these villiams suspected to have been an informer was, at or near Tarring in this county, barberously beat and abused by them.'

A Hastings man called Harrison who gave information on Hastings smugglers which led to arrests, was so hated in Hastings that it was stated that 'nine parts of ten' of the Hastings people 'would as freely murder Harrison as they would eat or drink'. The unfortunate Harrison was in fact pursued almost to death. As he left the town protected by dragoons he was followed by a 'posse full of Revenge and Malice' who very nearly caught him as he sat in a drunken daze in an alehouse near Fairlight Church. Fortunately he was on his journey again towards Rye just two or three minutes before the avengers arrived.

There is no doubt that magistrates were threatened and terrorised: the power and influence of the smugglers remind one very much of the workings of the Mafia. We shall quote two examples only, here, of ways in which individual representatives of the law were treated. In 1748, William Fairall, a known smuggler of the Hawkhurst Gang was captured and taken to magistrate James Butler, near Lewes. Mr. Butler sent him to London for trial, under guard. The guard got him as far as Borough, near London Bridge, where they put up for the night in an inn. Part of the weakness of the judicial system was lack of police stations, with staff and cells, and consequently prison parties put up at inns and escapes were frequent, especially when men started drinking. Fairall escaped, dashed into the street, leapt on to a horse, and galloped away in full view of the startled Londoners, and went straight back to Sussex. No effort was made to recapture him, but he was not satisfied with this, and made plans to be revenged on Mr. Butler. First he plotted to destroy all the deer in his park, then the plan escalated to burning the mansion, with Mr. Butler in it, but some of the gang objected to this. Finally Fairall and several of his comrades armed themselves with a brace of pistols apiece and lay in wait one dark night for Mr. Butler, who was due to ride home from Horsham. By tremendous good fortune for Butler, he was delayed and did not go home that night, or he would have been a dead man. Moreover the affair was discovered by some means and he was told of the plan, so he collected a bodyguard. As the smugglers were now outnumbered, they dropped the plan.

Mr. Butler was a brave man who did his duty. Many others did not. The behaviour of a magistrate called Partington, a century later was curious, though from what combination of fear or persuasion it is impossible to say. Mr. Mathias, a preventive officer at Newhaven, detained a French boat with more than four oars (this was illegal as it enabled smugglers to outrow revenue men), and took the three crew before Mr. Partington at Lewes. However, he was not in. Acting on the advice of his household, the unfortunate Mathias went to several places in Sussex, including Brighton, but everywhere just missed Mr. Partington. Returning to Lewes, he found that the magistrate was at dinner, but refused to see him. On enquiring whether Mr. Partington would make a definite appointment to see the men the next day, the reply came that the matter needed two magistrates and could not be

* B. F. Richards, 'Smuggling in Sussex 100 years ago'. *Sussex County Magazine.*

dealt with until the following Tuesday. He went back despondently to the inn at Lewes where the prisoners were in charge of his men, only to find that two had escaped, which is hardly surprising as his men were exhausted.

The interesting sequel is that in the official record the unfortunate Mr. Mathias was sharply reprimanded: no one seems to have inquired into Mr. Partington's actions. The remaining prisoner, Louis Preara, was finally seen by Admiral Rainer, as no magistrate was available. He was fined £100, and as he could not pay spent six months in the House of Correction at Lewes. This building, now demolished, had a treadmill, which ground corn for the town, on which prisoners walked at roughly sixty steps a minute, timed by a watch, for several hours a day, so Preara probably heartily wished he had escaped with his comrades.

If the case went before a jury there was no better chance of success, as most juries were either composed of smugglers paid by smugglers, or terrorised by them. *The London Gazette* June 1747, noted, 'The audacious behaviour of the smugglers in the courts, of their menaces to the Justices of the Peace, the Officers of the Revenue, and all others who shall dare to obstruct their proceedings.'

John Collier, the Surveyor-General of the Customs of Kent and Sussex writing about the murderers of Mr. Carswell, the Hasting Customs officer, said, 'the smugglers either bought off the chief evidence, or else murdered him, so that there is not sufficient for conviction. . . . These persons as I am informed, pretend to have intelligence if anything is taken out against them, and keep a person in perpetual pay for that purpose.' John Collier then asked for his name not to be mentioned!

A government report in 1733 described the 'doctoring' of witnesses, and tells how they learnt their story by heart:

> Before any Tryal came on, they were used to summon together so many of their Posse as they thought they should stand in need of, and acquaint them, as far as they could, with sort of Opposition they expected to meet with: and then give everyone his cue, taking Care that each had his Part according to his Capacity: if it happened to be long, or in any way difficult, they commonly gave it to him in Writing, that they might con it over, so as to be perfect on the Tryal, as indeed they most commonly were.

In a Hampshire case a dragoon was persuaded to testify for the smugglers instead of his own colleagues. His reward was a suit of clothes for the trial and '55 Hogsheads — a Hogshead of French white wine, and about 5 guineas in money, besides maintaining him in London and on the road'. The same Hampshire smuggler (Boyce) paid over £200 to witnesses in another case 'besides giving the Jury an elegant Entertainment, and (as he himself declared) two guineas each man'.

When Arthur Gray of the Hawkhurst Gang was taken before the Kent magistrates with ample evidence against him, the Colliers letters tell us he was discharged and 'has become more insolent than ever, as he has been one of the most notorious Fellows, and concerned in running many thousands of pounds'. In short, the smugglers who operated in Sussex, Kent and Hampshire (and the large gangs roamed widely) knew they could control the local juries.

For an important matter, the smugglers were sent for trial to London, but matters were no better there. A crooked lawyer supplied witnesses who would swear whatever was needed. They learned their lines as an actor learns his parts.

> Ye person who is Solicitor for the Smugglers when in Newgate is one Kelly, an Irish Roman Catholic. He has his assurance from his country and his principles from his religion, or from Hell itself, to make a gentleman so accomplished completely a man of business he has 40 or 50 fellows of his own country and religion at his command who are ever ready to swear whatever he cares to dictate.

The Mafia-like ramifications of the smuggling network were impressive. From the most minor to the largest affairs they had an intelligence service for their support. This extended from the simple Sussex shepherd tilting his crook one particular way to indicate danger, through the tip-off from the local dragoons to a 'mole' in the courts.

> They likewise employ an Agent (one Norton) to defend against prosecutions: and he searches to see when Capia's are taken out in the Exchequer against any of his Clients, and accordingly apprises them to get out of the way: that this Norton was formerly clerk — to the Solicitor of the Customs: and [he sees] all the Informations that were given in at the Customs House against persons running goods — the smugglers have such Intelligence, and use such artful Management and are withall so resolute and desparate — that not One Pound in Twenty of rum Tea is seized.

It was difficult to get the smugglers to prison to await trial in the first place. In 1721, a Lieutenant Burnett of General Grove's Regiment captured Jacob Walters, a well-known smuggler and took him to London with a guard of twenty men. He wrote, that being apprehensive of a rescue attempt, he had, at his own expense, had all the men 'quartered in one room every night from Battle to London'. He was wise, because there were many occasions in which smugglers, taken by the military, were released a few hours later by other smugglers. It was not unknown for them to be released while held in prison. Some of the Hawkhurst Gang were actually 'sprung' from the Fleet Prison in London, while in Sussex, Tapner and Carter, two of the murderers of Chater and Galley, confessed to Simon Hughes, the Vicar of Donnington, that they planned to rescue Dymer from Chichester prison, but the plan fell through.

When a smuggling cutter was taken off Hove and two of the men were landed as prisoners at the foot of Hove Street, a large party of smugglers appeared, knocked the officers over, attacked them with sticks and stones cut off their belts, and rescued their comrades. There are accounts of rescues in Rye and other parts of Sussex. One daring escape was made from the top of the famous Bo Peep tower. A smuggler imprisoned there was visited by his mother, who gave him a rope; he was allowed to exercise on the top of the tower each day. So on his next exercise he hitched the rope to a chimney at the top of the tower, slid down to the ground and calmly walked to a nearby inn, where a horse and cart was waiting for him.

A letter from Thomas Petitt, who was to have given evidence against the smugglers involved in the Hollington ambush, exists in the Sayer files. He is fully aware of the danger to witnesses 'for i don't know But what it may cost my life, for them Holkhourse genge ear blourthoursty fellows'. and he asks for 'som mony for to by me clouse fitten to a peare for a witness'. and he admits that he is motivated by the desire for 'prophit'. According to K. M. Clark he later promised not to testify as he was roughed up by the gang, and was lucky to stay alive.

On the other side, the smugglers had no difficulty in getting witnesses. A Collier letter complains about a Sussex case coming up, as 'the smugglers and their well wishers throng the courts to be ready to serve on the Jury'. The waywardness of juries went beyond the freeing of guilty smugglers — it placed vengeance on the King's servants who administered the law against them. A lawyer's brief in the Sayer file gives most particular instructions that a manslaughter charge is to be sought on behalf of the Customs official who killed a smuggler in the course of duty. The fear implicit in this document was very real, as murder charges were sometimes brought against officials who had killed in the course of duty, and they could not be certain of an automatic acquittal.

A murder charge was brought against a preventive man, George England, who killed Joseph Swain, a smuggler, at Hastings in 1821. This case excited tremendous interest throughout Sussex. It was customary for the officers at this time to search the fishing boats on their return to the beaches at Hastings, to see if they had any tubs hidden under the pile of nets in the boat. This was necessary, as tubs were sunk beneath the surface of the water at prearranged spots and taken up discreetly by fishing boats in broad daylight and thus brought to land. As there were over seventy fishing boats going in and out, it was not possible to search each boat by hand, and a large fork like prick was used to probe the piles of nets. The fishermen did have a legitimate grievance in that these pricks damaged the nets.

As Swain's boat was being beached, England got into it to use his fork. Swain, who was not in the boat but alongside, leapt into the boat, threw England out, snatched his cutlass from his hand and hit him. England got his pistol out as the two men struggled. England staggered back, his pistol went off and Swain was killed instantly. A murder charge was brought against England, who was justifiably worried as there was very strong feeling indeed against him in Hastings. There were irregularities in the trial and matters were obviously biased against the unfortunate England. The prosecution alleged that he deliberately stepped back, aimed and shot in cold blood. The defence maintained that he staggered back in the struggle and that his pistol went off as he lost his balance. The judge in his summing up clearly directed for an acquittal. Nevertheless the jury brought in a guilty of murder verdict.

Even after this passage of time, the predicament of the unhappy England is painful to the mind. The judge commented that the sentence was not what he had expected, but that he must pass the sentence of the law. The prisoner was greatly agitated on hearing the verdict and burst into violent grief, exclaiming 'My Lord, have mercy on me'. The judge, however, as he must, continued inexorably to pronounce sentence, with frantic interruptions from England

> That you be taken from hence — Consider I was in execution of my duty — to the place whence you came — Gentlemen of the Jury, pray consider your verdict again — and from thence to the place of execution, on Friday next, where you are to be hanged by the neck until you are dead, and may the Lord have mercy upon your soul. — Oh Gentlemen of the Jury, pray consider your verdict again!

England was taken out, but he did not have to suffer much longer as a very speedy pardon was granted. Before this shock, he had also to endure immense worry, as the people of Hastings, at the time of the killing, caused quite serious riots, and violent threats against his life. The riots were put down only by calling in customs men from other stations nearby, and parties of dragoons from Hastings and Bexhill. There was a breakdown of order in the town which only a military force could put down. The resentment did not die down for some time, and it is highly probable that England would have been 'executed' if he had returned to the town. A stone with a lyrical eulogy was erected over Swain's grave, depicting him as a martyr, and England was given an immediate discharge from the service and smuggled away.

In this case, through a biased jury and the established legal system, the smugglers attempted to administer their own punishment. Sometimes, however, they executed a kind of rough justice of their own, inflicted with brutality to strike terror in to the hearts of serving officers. Thus, on the beach at Seaford, they pegged out two customs men, below high water mark, and then rode off and left them to drown, inch by agonising inch as the tide came in. Sometimes officers were pushed from the clifftops to crash to the beach below; so many mangled bodies of officers were found at the foot of the cliffs that it could not possibly always have been accident. On one occasion a 'punishment' taking advantage of this fact was inflicted. An officer was blindfolded, then led to the clifftop and pushed over. However, as his enemies walked away he managed to hold on, and held on in agony and terror for what appeared to be hours. At last he managed to tear the blindfold from his eyes, and peered down fearfully into the abyss. The earth was a few feet beneath him: he had been pushed down a small declivity in the rocks. The terrified and humiliated man let go, and dropped safely to earth.

The smugglers not only perverted the course of official justice, and offered a rough 'Jeddart justice' i.e. hang first and try after, they also sometimes administered an alternative justice. In September 1783,* a small group of

* S.W.A. September 1783.

The Ship Inn at Herne Bay — Sydenham Snow was killed outside.

The grave of Sydenham Snow in Herne Churchyard.

The Crown Inn, Sarre — contains a hidden staircase which can only be entered from a cupboard in a bedroom, often used as a hide.

Smugglers' cottages, Pegwell.

Coastguard Cottage, Pegwell.

The Bull Inn at Sissinghurst was used as a local courtroom (but housed a smugglers' hide in the attic and a tunnel led from the cellars to the local church).

The Customs House, Sandwich.

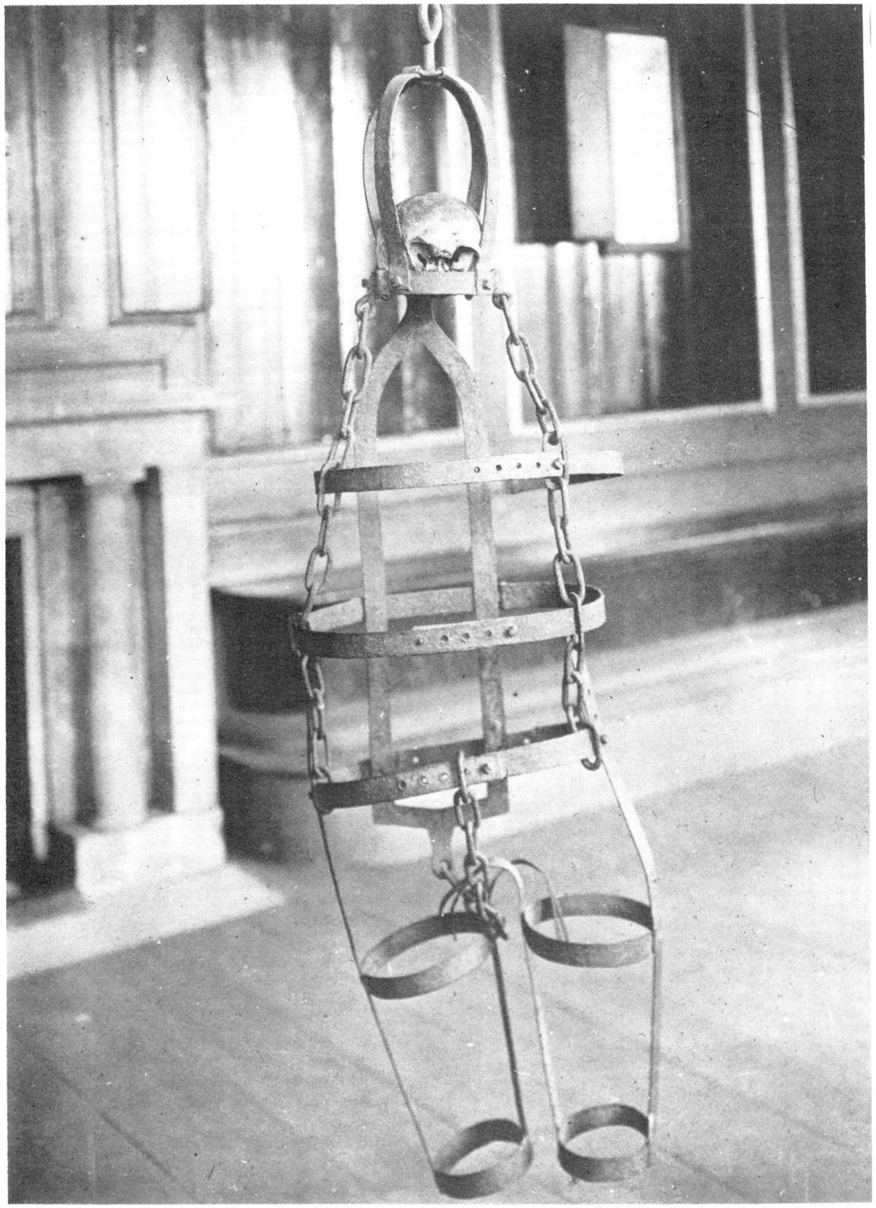

Gibbet irons — the skull is alleged to be that of a smuggler.

Mermaid Street, Rye.

smugglers captured a Mr. Matson, a Newhaven Customs officer who had recently shot a smuggler. He was taken as a prisoner to a quiet part of the coast, where, on the 'sea-side', he was presented to a company of two hundred smugglers, who tried him for murder. They questioned him, and argued freely about the rights and wrongs of the case for a considerable time. After much discussion, argument and counter-argument, a vote was taken. By a majority of ten, he was found innocent. The smugglers released him instantly.

CHAPTER VI

A curious kernel of lace

Tea was not always stored, but often taken straight to London, or to an agent at Groombridge for distribution. Another ingenious method was described at the 1745 Commission

> As for Seizures on Land, he said, they very seldom happen: for when Tea is landed, it is carried by ten or twelve armed Persons in a Body, on Horseback, into the Inland Counties where there is no Danger of having it seized, and it is disposed of, at certain Markets, to People who take 1000 Pounds weight at a time: That there are likewise a Number of men called Duffers, who go on Foot, and have Coats in which they can quilt a Quarter of a Hundred-wieght of Tea, and bring it to London in that manner, undiscovered: and that these Duffers supply the Hawkers, who carry it about the Town, and sell it to the Consumer.

Walking sixty miles to London in a coat containing twenty pounds of tea must have been hot work indeed. Thigh pieces and caps were also quilted. However, in the annals of smuggling in Kent and Sussex, one can find no parallel to the action of the quick-witted Suffolk woman, when surprised with tea by a Customs officer searching her cottage. She whipped the bag under her apron and started groaning with labour pains. The officer, however, speedily delivered her of a fine healthy seven pound bag of tea.

The tea sellers did not always escape detection. In May 1733 the watchmen of St. Paul's, Covent Garden and St. Martin's-in-the-Fields took a large consignment of tea, which was being carried by nine men to their London customers. Six men escaped, but two men and a boy were captured. The men were 'prosperous farmers from Rye'. The Lambeth area of London was well known as a centre for illicit tea dealing. The most surprising hiding place of all was a temporary illicit tea store in the Fleet prison.

Houses and shops often had ingenious hiding places. The houses were often panelled, and stairs winding, with many nooks and crannies. Kitchens and outhouses had stores, boilers, coppers, stoves, ovens, storage tubs. Sometimes kitchen ranges had unused ovens leading to hiding places. Mr. Weston of Brighton ran a profitable draper's shop at 18 and 19 North Street. He came of an old Seddlescombe family, a village noted for smuggling, and was watched and visited by Customs men for some time. On one visit, after being shown round politely, as always, and offered refreshment, the officer, as an afterthought, went back into the kitchen. This large room had a range against one wall. He found the range had hidden wheels, and by operating a pulley it swung open to reveal a veritable Alladin's cave, stuffed with silks and laces. These had been shipped to Weston on the smuggling cutter *Master Wren*. He was fined £10,000 which he apparently paid without difficulty. A great many drapers along the coast appear to have relied heavily on the smugglers for their goods. In those days, when almost no clothes were ready made, women bought the materials of their choice and had them made up by dressmakers. The drapery trade was therefore far wider in extent than it is today. Many smuggled items were actually forbidden to be imported at all, and without the smuggler would have been unobtainable. For example, a Member of Parliament named Huskisson, speaking in the House of Commons, attacked the folly of high duties and actual prohibitions, saying 'members were well aware that Bandana handkerchiefs were prohibited by law, and yet I have no doubt there is hardly a gentleman in the House who has not got a Bandana Handkerchief'. As he spoke, to the roars of laughter of the whole House, he drew a Bandana handkerchief from his pocket.

When in the country, the smugglers on occasions used sunken roads in which they were fairly free from observation while the goods were actually in transit. Such a road near Mayfield was marked on one map as 'Smugglers lane', and in Brighton a road, now lost, between Patcham Church and Standean was popularly connected with the smugglers. Many of the paths they were supposed to have favoured were of great antiquity.

When the goods were in temporary hiding places they were usually well hidden, but even in fairly open situations fear usually assured their safety. Tradition has it that near Ewhurst in Surrey casks were often hidden in light scrub, and in the piles of tubs would be two or three with marks on them. This was a signal to the local people that these tubs were for them, the price of their silence.

When a smuggler's cache was raided, retribution was likely to follow, as the terrible story of Richard Hawkins so chillingly illustrates. Tea had been hidden near a barn at Slindon in which Hawkins was working. It was owned by four smugglers — Jeremiah Curtis (a dangerous man) of Hawkhurst in Kent, John Mills, Richard

Rowland, nicknamed 'Little Fat Back', and Thomas Winter, called 'The Coachman'. Two bags of tea were found to be missing from the store, and three people were suspected — John Cockrel, an innkeeper of Walberton, his son John, an innkeeper of Yapton, and his son-in-law, Richard Hawkins, a farm labourer. The smugglers were exceedingly angry, as always when they lost their property. Curtis, drinking in the Yapton inn, expressed their reaction by shouting loudly 'damn him — he would find it out — for damn him he had whipt many a rogue and washed his hands in their blood'.

On January 28th 1748, Hawkins was working in the barn at Slindon, when Curtis and John Mills rode up and curtly ordered him to go with them. Hesitantly he did so, and climbed on to the horse behind Mills and all rode off. The similarity of this technique to that of the modern gangster, taking his victim for a ride, is obvious. They first went to his father-in-law's inn at Yapton, where he was cross-examined over drinks, but no violence was offered. There was a cold build-up of intimidation that was very frightening. They then left for the Dog and Partridge at Slindon. Hawkins protested, but after some argument he got up behind Mills and they set off. The landlord at the Dog and Partridge was a James Reynolds, who appears to have been on good terms with the smugglers. Thomas Winter and Richard Rowland were already in the inn when Curtis and Mills arrived with Hawkins, so he was outnumbered by five to one. Curtis dismounted and bustled into the inn shouting, 'We have a prisoner here', so there could be little doubt about their intentions. They asked the landlord for the use of a room, then, standing menacingly over Hawkins, started interrogating him. The innkeeper tried to persuade him to confess, saying, 'it will be better for you, Dick' but when Hawkins continued to protest his innocence, he left the room so as not to be a witness to what he knew must follow.

First Hawkins was punched. Then his outer clothes were removed so that the violence which was to be inflicted upon him should be felt more severely. Then Winter and Curtis stepped aside to allow Rowland and Mills sufficient room to swing their whips. The deliberation with which the smugglers acted, and which is described very fully in the contemporary account makes chilling reading. Struck viciously across the face and shoulders, Hawkins fell to the floor, crying out that he was innocent and begging them for God's sake and for Christ's sake, to spare his life for the sake of his wife and child. Ignoring his pleas, his captors continued the sadistic whipping. This was followed by a heavy kicking all over the body. At last Hawkins, who had been incredibly brave, broke, and cried out 'my brother and my Father' i.e. his in-laws. Whether they had in fact stolen the tea or whether he said this in pain and desperation is unknown. At this Mills and Curtis put on their coats and set off to fetch the two Cockrels. The others flung Hawkins in a chair and started drinking. After a time, they looked at him and saw that he was dead. They immediately locked the parlour, taking the key with them, and set out for Walburton to tell Mills and Curtis.

These two had gone to the inn at Yapton and asked Cockrel to stable their horses while they had a drink. Curtis followed Cockrel into the stable and demanded his tea. When Cockrel denied that he had it, he beat him viciously with an oak club. He then forced him on one of the horses and they all set off for Walberton, where they dragged out the elder Cockrel and put him on the back of the other horse. All four then set out for Slindon where they meant to continue the interrogation in the Dog and Partridge. However they were met on the road by the other two smugglers, who were travelling post haste to tell them of Hawkins' death. These two called out urgently that they wanted a word in private. Mills and Curtis therefore shouted at their prisoners to dismount and stand a little way off. Although it was dark both men did as they were told and waited tamely, without trying to escape from their tormentors. This is a measure of the extent to which the Hawkhurst Gang had terrorised Kent and Sussex. The four smugglers now had a long argument. The brutal Curtis wished to go through with the beatings, but the others dissuaded him. So they told their two prisoners to go for the time being, threatening them that they would come for them when they wanted them. The Cockrels made good their escape, and were so terrified of the whole affair that they never reported Hawkins as missing. History does not record the feeling of the unhappy sister and daughter, Hawkin's wife, nor the fate of his young child.

The first thought of the murderers was to fling Hawkins down a nearby well, but Reynolds the landlord objected as he thought this would incriminate him in the matter. They therefore put the body over a horse and travelled twelve miles to Parham Park and threw it into a large pond there, weighted with stones. It was found some months later, and a proclamation of January 1749 offered a free pardon to anyone who would give information leading to the arrest of the murderers. Jacob Pring, the former Hawkhurst Gang member, bargained with a high official that he should be pardoned if he could bring 'Smoker Mills' in. This he did by finding him in an inn in Bristol, drinking with the two notorious Kemp brothers. As they were all outlawed as smugglers by the recent Act, and had instead taken to robbery, he did not have much difficulty in persuading them to go with him to his comfortable home in Beckenham, Kent, where they thought they would be safe and secure. There, on an excuse of going for good horses for them, he galloped to Horsham, returning with Mr. Rackster, an exciseman, and eight armed men, and burst in on the unsuspecting smugglers just as they were sitting down to a meal. After a struggle all three were overpowered. Mills was tried at East Grinstead. The smuggler called Coachman saved himself by testifying against Mills, and Reynolds the innkeeper got off. Curtis escaped to Graveslines in France and joined the Irish regiment there.

The gibbet was built on Slindon Common near the Dog and Partridge, and Mills hung there in chains for a long, long time as a warning to all evil doers. There was a rumour that when the tea was finally moved the two bags were found and that the whole sad tale had all been for nothing.

As the preventive forces became more efficient attempts were made to run cargoes by means of tricks, some more ingenious than others. A family called Ashcroft earned a living by shipping pebbles to the Staffordshire potteries, and loads of chalk up river from Newhaven to Lewes. Sometimes more than chalk was shipped and after much watching the Customs men finally made a catch. They watched Ashcroft's boat as it entered the harbour, and as he ran the boat in to the bank to tow her, one cried 'I can see a tub'. Ashcroft dropped his tow rope and ran threequarters of a mile before going to earth in a cottage where his Mother lived. One officer watched while another fetched a constable and he was finally arrested in the house of a carrier called Pratt. He was sentenced to five years naval service, this being the usual punishment for small-time smugglers with marine experience. There were many cases of small, unimaginative runs like this.

Often, however, things were better planned. Holidays and Sundays were often used. The Coronation of George IV was much celebrated in Brighton as might be expected, as the town housed one of the King's homes. The charity schoolchildren were given a feast and a medal, while the reknowned Phoebe Hessel, by then over a hundred years old, watched the festivities from Mr. Wagner's (the Vicar) carriage. The Customs men appear to have been taken up in the general rejoicing, and the smugglers took advantage of this to shift a load of tubs from the stables of the Old Ship hotel.

In 1855 a travelling wild beast show and circus visited Shoreham. Such shows were very popular in early Victorian England. While almost the entire town watched the circus, a group of smugglers moved fourteen tons of tobacco inland. It was hidden under ninety tons of stone in a barge which they took up to Beeding chalk pits. It was there unloaded into four carts. One went through Horsham, a second through Cuckfield and the other two effectively disappeared as they left Beeding. None of them was found and all the tobacco was cleared, the affair only being discovered by a accomplice getting drunk and talking. The barge had been calmly taken off to Brighton, the crew saying they had a buyer for the stone. As a result of this all the Customs officials at Shoreham were replaced.*

John Banks tells of an amusing incident at Hastings Pier Rocks. A lugger laden with French goods was due. Two young men swam out to the ship, which had come as close to the shore is it could. They took the line, on which were slung the tubs in pairs, and two of the crew, rowed with muffled oars towards land, towing the line of tubs behind them. At a certain point, one of the boys, Jack, slipped quietly over the side of the boat and swam to the Pier Rocks, towing the line of tubs. The boat rowed on to the other side of Hastings, acting as a decoy should the Customs men be watching. From here we should let John Banks tell the story in his own words,

> Jack, quietly swimming in, sees the dark outline of the Pier Rocks against the somewhat lighter sky, and after a minute or two, fancies the rocks are in motion. It is the company, who have managed to get there and are waiting for him. 'Is that you, Jack,' says one, in a quiet voice "Yes' says Jack, 'It's me.' 'You can touch there, I think. Give us your line.' The goods are soon hauled silently in and as silently distributed, the company making their way along some sand which had purposely been sprinkled across the beach: and as it happened on that particular night, the Coastguardman on duty at the Western end of the Parade was held in conversation by one (a tradesman) in the secret of the company and the goods were soon away. They went into West Street, through Russell Court, along George Street, up the Light Steps and along Hill Street. On this street they saw a light: old so and so was not gone to bed. It being Saturday he was having a hand of cards with a friend. No sooner thought of than done. One goes in and borrows the key of the shop of which he had the charge. (Jack and Sam and Jem too worked in the same shop): the goods were stowed away in the shop until the next night, and then, all being quiet, they were taken to their destination, nobody the wiser — the transactors excepted.

If there was an air of humorous ingenuity about some of the ideas for hiding places, many of the smugglers themselves seem to have had a streak of rough humour in their characters. George Roper of Hastings was well known as a relaxed and humorous man who at the end of his life became the Master of a pleasure steamer, and died, universally respected in 1850. John Banks quotes an article in *The Battle and the Breeze* giving what he calls an 'overdrawn portrait'.

> One of the principal free traders at Hastings ... was a fat, good natured fellow, named Roper, who, commanded a remarkably lucky, fast sailing lugger, called the 'Little Ann'. So far from assailing the 'warriors' with taunts and abuse like the rest of his comrades, Roper conducted himself with undeviating civility, so that had it been possible for fire and water to unite, he would have been esteemed even by his opponents. He usually wore a long white frock of gabardine over his flushings, and it was his custom when not engaged in illicit adventure, to sit smoking his pipe swinging his legs upon a crab or capstan, fixed in the beach in front of the Cutter 'public house'.

Similarly, Jack Jig, of the inn at Jevington, seems to have had a sense of humour. He had many brushes with the law, and on one occasion when the inn was surrounded by Customs men, he is supposed to have rushed out, dressed in bonnet, cloak and petticoat, with his riding boots showing underneath, crying like an hysterical woman. A little later one of his fellow smugglers, Creampot Tom, was arrested in London, and Jig himself was taken in his inn. The Customs officers had searched the house fruitlessly and were leaving when they heard a noise and found him concealed in a narrow hiding place in the roof. At Battle he bribed his keeper with 50 guineas, cut his chains and escaped. He was recaptured and taken to Horsham prison. From here he was moved to East Grinstead, and for some reason, released. Creampot Tom was less lucky and ended on the gallows in Oxford for horse stealing. Jig continued free, but was now considered an informer, and was chased and nearly lynched on Lewes racecourse. He returned to his inn but was soon in trouble again, for horse stealing. He was acquitted, and by December 1792 he was working with the Customs officers, helping to take fifteen horses and a large amount of tobacco at Newhaven, as 'the noted Jig and other ten shilling men in service of Mr. Walter of Horsham'.†

* Cheal, *The Story of Shoreham.*

† *Sussex Weekly Advertiser*, December 24th, 1792.

He seemed unable to keep out of trouble and was soon in the news again, for assaulting a Mr. Vine of Wilmington with a bludgeon. Vine was wearing a stiff and high crowned hat which saved him from serious injury. In 1793 he was charged with stealing two hams of bacon from a Mr. Smith of Jevington and sentenced to be transported for seven years, but this appears not to have been carried out, for in 1796 we find him charged with stealing hay. The jury had difficulty in coming to a verdict and tradition has it that the judge caused them to be locked in a room without candles or fire on a bitter winter night as an aid to a speedy decision. He was found not guilty. After other adventures he was charged with horse stealing at Salisbury and sentenced to death. This was transmuted to transportation for fourteen years to Botany Bay.*

These stories which have come down to us about Jevington Jig illustrate a point that emerges with respect to several of the smugglers of this period — a tendency to indulge in minor crime and horse stealing when times were bad. We have not researched the truth of all these stories about Jevington Jig, but the general picture is a believable one. His connection with Mr. Walter was reported in the local paper, and is interesting. Mr. Walter's exploits were often reported in the *Sussex Weekly Advertiser* as he was very successful in seizing contraband. One month's haul was 203 bags of fine teas. On one day alone he took 18 bags of tea, 36 tubs of gin and 11 horses at Ditchling, and on the same evening 15 bags of tea. The newspaper estimated that in rewards 'he has £4000 or £5000 in some years'. He fitted his men out at his own expense in a smart blue and silver uniform, with a hat decorated with silver lace. He appears to have been an unusually successful Customs officer. Jevington Jig does not seem to have been in a very big way of business, but always to have been on the outskirts of small-time smuggling and petty crime. His neighbour, Stanton Collins and the Alfriston men are credited in the stories handed down with a rather larger sphere of influence. He is supposed to have emptied a Dutch ship which had been wrecked, in two nights, despite mountainous seas, and carried the goods as far as Alfriston. He was apparently so taken with the figurehead of the ship that he took that too, a large gargoyle-like carving, that was for some time at his own house — the Market Cross, and then at a later date it was moved to the Star Inn. Stories have been handed down of several cutters unloading after dark, and the goods being cleared by upwards of 300 men. Jeffrey Farnol's *Sir John Dering* relates to the doings in Alfriston and district. In another story about Stanton Collins he is supposed, in order to get rid of some Customs men who were searching his house, to have placed a piglet in a shawl in bed with his wife and explained with great concern that she and the child were unwell. The piglet tradition is a delightful touch and appears in several smuggler stories. Sometimes it is placed alone in a cradle stragetically placed over the entrance trapdoor of a hiding place. When pinched, it would squeal, and in smugglers' stories the officers could not tell the difference between the squeal of a piglet and the cry of a new-born baby, and always retired in gentlemanly confusion. The idea of using a piglet or a lamb to impersonate a baby is a very old one and goes back at least to the medieval mystery plays.

There are several tales about Stanton Collins, who appears to have been a colourful figure and respected at least by his immediate circle, althouth he too is supposed to have been involved in petty thieving on occasions, snatching purses from cart drivers. On one occasion he was reputedly approached by members of the congregation of a local non-conformist church. One of the congregation, aggrieved because the minister refused to marry him to his deceased wife's sister, ousted the Minister and installed a friend in his place. Stanton Collins bodily removed the interloper and re-instated the rightful minister — an occupation not normally associated with smugglers.†

Sometimes, instead of relying on women friends and piglets to avoid trouble, smugglers tried to avoid arrest by feigning sickness themselves. The Hastings Customs officers, acting on information, searched the room of a sick man 'but upon looking about the Chamber, they found some baked Herrings in a plate, and plenty of other Victuals, which the Officers thought was Odd dyet for a sick person: they asked him what was his Name was, who replied Smith, upon which Mr. Bailey took up his handkerchief which was tyed round his head and face and knew him perfectly to be John French, a Notorious Outlawed Smuggler'.‡

It is difficult to make an assessment of the territorial coverage and detailed working of the gangs. They were based in towns and villages which were strategically placed in good landing places or in good transit centres on the routes inland; i.e. Hastings, Rye and Hawkhurst are foremost examples. There are tantalising references in the newspapers of the eighteenth century to the Bramber, Worthing, Brighton, Bognor men, etc., and sometimes an individual is named as 'the noted smuggler', but the details are usually scrappy and disjointed. The contemporary account of the earlier Hawkhurst Gang and their trials is very full but it is also sometimes rather confused. However, it is clear that the strength and stature of the gangs shifted with the quality of the leadership, the calibre of the opposing officials and external historical considerations, such a wars, alterations in the rates of the various duties and the effects of the never ending stream of legislation against smuggling. Over two thousand Acts were passed from the reign of Edward III to Victorian times — most of them without any noticeable improvement in the situation.

Many of the smugglers — the leaders as well as the batman and tubman — appear to have had a trade of their own. Many were inn keepers — an occupation that had obvious advantages in a link with smuggling, offering meeting places for smugglers, hiding places for contraband, markets for goods and centres for information gathering. Farm labourers are frequently named as smugglers in the records, as are blacksmiths, carpenters and horsedealers or colt breakers. Apart from their duties as tubmen or batmen, blacksmiths and carpenters would be useful in maintaining the running tackle that is sometimes mentioned in the reports of the time. Horse dealers and farm labourers would be as useful in dealing with the horses.

* P. M. H. Smart, *Jevington throught the Ages.* † *The Times*, April 25th, 1758.
‡ J. Manwaring Baines, *Historic Hastings.*

A manuscript of 1814, describing Rottingdean, now in Brighton Reference Library, describes Captain Dunk, the butcher, who was also a smuggler, who paid a £500 fine, while ten of his '. . . worthy friends were lodged in Hawsham Gaol, or in their elegant language were sent off for a few months to colledge to improve their manners'. The youthful writer notes Rottingdean is 'a village famous for bringing things on shore without paying the Revenue duties'.

The smugglers had a wealth of colourful nicknames. This was partly in the interests of security, but also a fashion of the times, when many public figures had nicknames. Also it was part of the freemasonry of smuggling, indicating a part of their life in which they were not citizens, husbands, fathers. 'Nasty Face', 'Spinner', 'The Miller', 'Curse-Mother Jack', 'Coachman', 'Smoker', 'Joseph Nobody' and 'Towzer' are just a few of the names. Places too, also for security reasons, were given nicknames. Banks tells of a Marrow-bone Gap at Fairlight, and Jinn's Stool, a large rock near Galley — hill. But in the last resort the smugglers always relied on force to preserve their secrecy if necessary. The owner of the *Brighton Herald*, walking along the Shoreham Road late one night, some time in the 1840's, suddenly heard the sound of many horses approaching. He stepped aside, and as he did so, the leader rode up to him and put a pistol to his head. The threatened man looked up and recognised a well-known and respected local inhabitant, and indeed, a friend of his, and called out his name in surprise.

> At the same moment, the leader of the smugglers — for it was a large body of these men engaged in 'running' the contraband cargo of a vessel off the coast — recognised him and exclaimed 'If you had not spoken, I should have shot you'. They had taken him at first for a Revenue officer, and if he had been one it would have gone hard with him. As it was, there was a laugh, a shake of the hands, and the party rode off.*

* Fleet, *Our Sussex Ancestors*.

CHAPTER VII

Intrigue: of Jacobites, spies and guinea boats

The eighteenth and early nineteenth centuries were a period of almost continuous war against France and in the early part of the period there was the added threat of a Jacobite uprising in favour of the deposed Stuart kings. Throughout this era the smuggling fraternity of Kent and Sussex occupied such a unique position of neutrality — using their activities to benefit both sides — that it is sometimes hard to believe that those concerned were in fact Englishmen. Whilst one might reasonably suppose that the increased naval activity in the Channel would affect the trade this was not so. The French Government encouraged the English smugglers, causing as they did much harm to the economy of Britain. Part of Dunkerque was actually allotted to them and more than five hundred were from time to time accommodated there. The Oak and Ivy Inn at Hawkhurst was a notorious smugglers' haunt and frequently used as a hiding place for Jacobite spies. Indeed it's name derives from the recognition badge used by the Jacobites.

The English authorities entertained grave misgivings as to the loyalty of the local inhabitants of these seaboard counties. For example for some weeks during 1689–90 a privateer was being fitted out at Shoreham, and the crew, eighty stalwart and boisterous men, frequented, naturally the inns in the area. Some anxiety was felt in official quarters — could they have Jacobite leanings? — and Edward Lawrence, the local Collector of Customs was told to make enquiries. He reported that the men 'drink their Majesties health' and the doubts seem to have been put at rest. A Sayer letter echoed the fear of the Jacobite influence, requesting in 1721 'a company of Dragoons, to take up these villains or in a short time they will rise up in a Rebellion, the number of them is not less than 200, and every man of them for the Pretender'.

This connection between the Jacobites and smuggling is borne out by a letter of the poet Pope in 1717

> I beg you to do me a familiar or rather domestic piece of service. It is, when a hogshead of good French wine falls into your hands — whether out of the skies or whatever element pays no custom — that you would favour me with about twelve dozen of it at the price you gave.

This letter was to John Carryl, a Sussex squire of known Jacobite sympathies.

During the wars with France, the smugglers were known as a means of transport, both of men and letters, and also of information to the French, our enemies. This is no more surprising, really, than the Jacobite connection, for in both cases it depends on the fact that the smugglers had excellent lines of communication with France, the Jacobites, of course, being exiled and mainly based in France.

Cooper quotes many proven examples of the communications of the smugglers with France while the two countries were at war, and here are quoted only a very few examples. This traffic was after all only to be expected, as the smugglers continued trading with the French throughout the wars. 'July 25 1702. Some French letters sent from a privateer, and others found on the beach near Seaford. May 3, 1703. A Frenchman with papers, from Calais, with letters and papers, under Beachy Head in the night.' This traffic was still going on in 1746, when Pelham wrote, 'They tell me there are regular boats going between Hastings and Bullogne not only upon smuggling affairs, but also carrying on a very improper correspondencys.'

However the smugglers apparently also acted as sources of information to our own authorities. A letter in the Sayer file written just before the outbreak of the Seven Years War stated: 'Our intelligence from the French coast is at present over, for all our smuggling rascalls with their vessels are seized at Boulogne, Calais, Dunkirk etc.'

This traffic in intelligence and letters between smugglers and France continued throughout the century, and Cooper states that a Bexhill family of whom he had knowledge, regularly carried correspondence to France during the Napoleonic wars.

Material aid was given to the enemy. Ammunition was occasionally shipped together with wool, as from Rye in November 1747 (possibly the Hawkhurst Gang again) and there are instances of smugglers supplying guns for French ships: 'Smugglers from Rye and Hastings have carried to France 60 or 70 swivvel guns . . . and openly carry over wool' (Sayer, June 1749).

During the Napoleonic wars the intrigue reached a level which was never to be surpassed. French prisoners of war who escaped from English prisons made their way to the coast and would be carried over by the smugglers, who needed only a description of the man, a token of trust from French relatives and money for the passage. At the same time, however, one smuggler from Lydd reported how he and others like him would use part of their time in France to gather information on the French fleet and pass this on to English men-of-war on the return journey. It is unlikely that Napoleon was not aware of such double dealing, but clearly chose to continue with his support of the smugglers of whom he said, 'They have the courage and ability to do anything for money'. He also said:

> They did great mischief to their government. They took from France annually forty or fifty millions (francs) of silks and brandy. During the war they had a part of Dunkirk allotted to them, to which they were restricted, but as they latterly went out of their limits and committed riots, and insulted everybody, I ordered Gravelines to be prepared for their reception, where they had a little camp for their reception.

One of the most notorious smugglers of this period was Thomas Johnstone. Johnstone is generally referred to as 'the celebrated Hampshire smuggler'. He did, however, operate in both Kent and Sussex. Having been forced to flee to France (setting sail from Brighton) after a daring escape from prison he was approached personally by Napoleon and asked to pilot the French invasion force across the Channel. To his everlasting credit, Johnstone turned out to be a patriot and refused, being imprisoned in France as a result. He did, however, escape again and later assisted Lord St. Vincent by giving him detailed information concerning the French forces.

Probably the most noteworthy development in the smuggling trade during this period was what was loosely known as 'guinea smuggling'. The French needed gold in large quantities to support their armies in mainland Europe. In order to provide the necessary money large sums were required to be transported across the Channel. Since the Royal Navy was mounting a blockade of the French coast open transportation was clearly impractical and, on occasions, smuggling vessels were found to be ideal for swift and unobtrusive crossings.

The following anecdote in the Sayer file illustrates the exploitation of this situation:

> When the exportation of golden guineas to France was prohibited, a lucrative business was done in running boats over to Boulogne with the guineas. There were four men in particular at Hastings who made this their regular occupation and did very well at it.
>
> They decided to make a great coup by smuggling a thousand guineas over at one time. They had gone some distance when the Captain sighted the Revenue cutter bearing down on them. He deliberately threw the whole bag overboard. The officers came on board, searching everything, and went away unsuccessful.
>
> Very soon afterwards the Captain purchased a nice house and retired from business, while his unfortunate comrades were nearly ruined by their loss.
>
> It afterwards appeared that the whole thing was a piece of collusion between the Captain of the smugglers and the Revenue officials. The bag of gold was safely at home in the Captain's house; what had gone overboard was a bag of stones.

Special galleys (or guinea boats as they were termed) were built for this purpose, originally six-oared but later rowed by anything up to two dozen men. These latter craft were over thirty feet in length and could make the crossing in about six hours in calm weather. One account tells of how a galley leaving Dover and faced with a stiff northerly wind obtained a tow from the Dover steam packet until clear of the shore. After slipping the cable the smugglers pulled away rapidly, arriving in France ten minutes ahead of the steam ship

The crews who undertook this work were selected with care and well paid for their efforts. This would be hard earned money, six or more hours of unrelieved rowing being no small undertaking. It was usual for the guineas, prior to despatch to be spread around the town in comparatively small catchments amongst a number of reliable people. Accounts exist of old clock cases, etc. being seen stuffed with guineas in humble Folkestone homes and of children being locked safely away where wagging little tongues could do no damage.

A story is told of how one night a man responsible for the shipments appeared, heavily muffled, on the doorstep of a cottage just after the occupants had gone to bed. The cottager and his wife hastily admitted their mysterious visitor and were informed that they were to be entrusted with custody of some one hundred thousand guineas. This sum was duly concealed in the mattress of their bed where it stayed until the following night when smugglers came and took it away — every last guinea. No reward at all was left with the couple but shortly after their son was given an opening at a bank — a very good job for the son of a Folkestone fisherman.

As much as £30,000 might be transported at any one crossing, the coins being carried in long leather money belts concealed about the persons of the smugglers. The Boatswain of each galley carried passes from both the English and the French and so could virtually guarantee a trouble-free crossing. As a result the smugglers enjoyed a period of considerable prosperity, being for the most part let well alone by the Revenue men and no doubt taking advantage of the state of affairs to ensure an equally profitable return trip from France carrying more conventional contraband.

The crossings were not entirely without incident and danger however. Not least of the problems for those concerned was the weather. Then as now the Strait of Dover was notoriously unpredictable and a gentle swell could, within minutes, become a raging sea, well capable of capsizing the small-draughted galleys and putting a quick untimely end to the aching of the muscles of those who laboured interminably at the oars. Furthermore, whilst the authorities frequently turned a blind eye to the smugglers some measure of interference was not unknown, it sometimes being necessary to run a gauntlet of blockading naval ships which occasionally chose to fire on them. The danger was such that one story tells of how a young guinea smuggler named Will Baker had his trousers and underpants hidden by his wife in an attempt to dissuade him from undertaking an excursion across the Channel.

The degree of vigilance varied greatly from one Revenue cutter to another. In one episode a galley carrying guineas was intercepted shortly after leaving Folkestone and the crew had to abandon their precious cargo overboard. Naturally the spot was suitably marked and the smugglers returned shortly afterwards and retrieved it, the incident being remarkable in that the whole thing occurred within sight of the Folkestone Custom House.

On another occasion a galley was run ashore near the east pier and the loading of the guineas begun. The bows of the vessel rested upon a shingle bank whilst the stern remained float. The weight of the gold eventually broke the galley's unsupported back and another craft had to be brought and the cargo transferred before the crossing could be undertaken. Where were the Customs officers whilst all this was going on? In the words of one concerned — 'Oh, they was squared; it warn't worth their while to interfere'.

As this guinea smuggling is a matter of some importance it is worth quoting again Napoleon's own words:

> I got bills upon Vera Cruz, which certain agents sent by circuitous routes, by Amsterdam, Hamburg and other places to London ... the bills were discounted by merchants in London, to whom ten per cent and sometimes a premium, was paid as their reward. Bills were then given by them upon different bankers in Europe for the greatest part of the amount, and the remainder in gold, which last was brought over to France by the smugglers.

He also refers to the more direct part taken by smugglers in the war:

> They brought over newspapers and dispatches from the spies that we had in London. They took over spies from France, landed and kept them in their houses for some days, then dispersed them over the country, and brought them back when wanted. They came over in boats no broader than this bath.

A further variation on the more usual smuggling activities during the French wars were the excursions by a number of free traders into the business of privateering, the Cinque ports being particularly involved. It was common between the sixteenth and early nineteenth centuries for private ships to be licensed to raid enemy ships. Not surprisingly many full-blooded pirates — notably Captain Kidd — began their careers as licensed 'privateers'. The practice added to the general air of lawlessness and free-for-all so much a part of the smuggling scene and acts of piracy in the 'narrow seas between England and mainland Europe' became a frequent occurrence. In August, 1758, Nicholas Wingfield and Adam Hyde who were masters of privateer cutters boarded a Danish ship and stole twenty casks of butter. For this they were tried and sentenced to be hanged. Despite this other smugglers continued to board ships coming up the Channel. The most notorious group was that from Hastings which came to be known as Ruxley's Crew. The *Kentish Gazette* reports in 1768 of this band of 'piratical smugglers who have lately been terrorising our district'. In the same year the gang boarded a Dutch ship and killed the Master, Peter Bootes, by breaking his back with an axe (Hastings fishermen were nicknamed 'chopbacks' for many years afterwards as a result!). After this act of such extreme cruelty the government sent a detachment of 200 Inniskilling Dragoons (The Skins) to Hastings to arrest the smugglers while a man-of-war was achored just offshore. This surprisingly energetic action on the part of the authorities, who had hitherto been continuously lethargic in their dealings with the smugglers is some measure of the violence and brutality of the Hastings pirates which clearly shocked even the case hardened public of the day. The Mayor was pestered by the townspeople to explain what was going to happen, and when he refused, was violently assaulted. In due course information was forthcoming and a net closed around the villains. It is interesting to note that they were first betrayed by their own drunken boasting as to how the unfortunate Dutchman wriggled when they split his backbone.

When it became clear that arrests were certain one wealthy shopkeeper absconded hastily. It seems that he had been 'fencing' the proceeds of piracy and smuggling — allegedly to the value of ten thousand pounds — and, not unnaturally was anxious to avoid punishment when his suppliers were brought to justice! The inevitable arrests occurred and a number of smugglers sent to London for trial, it being thought unlikely that they would receive fair treatment in Sussex. Four of the crew, Thomas Sisbury, William Geary, Richard Hyde and William Wenham were ultimately sentenced to death for the murder of Bootes and as pirates were duly turned off at execution dock, Wapping. It can only be said that the doing of Ruxley's Crew were a disgraceful episode — ranking with the worst of the Hawkhurst Gang. Ships were hailed on the pretence of civil business, then boarded, the crew shut in cabins, the cargo looted, and the whole ship scuttled, leaving the crew to drown. It is almost inconceivable that this could have been tolerated for so long in a civilised country only two hundred years ago. Fortunately, when the authorities acted, they acted vigourously and Ruxley's Crew was destroyed.

It was gangs such as this that were eventually to bring smuggling into such a state of disrepute that the determination of the authorities to crush it was greatly increased and the popular support upon which the free traders relied so heavily diminished. When the French wars ended the situation changed drastically.

CHAPTER VIII

The nineteenth century and the blockade

Wellington's victory over Napoleon at Waterloo in 1815 finally brought to an end a series of wars which had lasted in all for over one hundred years and left Britain as the greatest international power of the nineteenth century. The Industrial Revolution had transformed the country into a modern and prosperous industrial nation well in advance of many of its European neighbours. The situation internally was nevertheless far from satisfactory. The very industrialisation which had brought such economic prosperity also resulted in widespread degradation of the working classes. Furthermore, oppressive criminal laws created more than two hundred crimes for which the penalty was death.

Smuggling was such a crime and, what is more, a crime very much on the increase. The wars so recently ended had employed huge numbers of men who were no longer required. The thousands of discharged servicemen found themselves without work and in the early nineteenth century that meant without money. Not surprisingly many of those who found themselves in this unfortunate position turned to the trade as a means of keeping body and soul together. After all a not inconsiderable number had been compulsorily enlisted in the first place as a punishment for smuggling offences. Clearly action, and decisive action at that, was required. Against a background of increasing social unrest the Royal Navy was entrusted with the task of mounting a blockade of the Kent and Sussex coast, a method of warfare which had proved reasonably successful against the French. In 1817 a 44-gun frigate, H.M.S. *Ganymede* was stationed in the Channel. She was replaced sometime later by the 74-gunned H.M.S. *Ramillies* together with H.M.S. *Severn*, a further ship the *Hyperion* (42 guns) being anchored off Newhaven in Sussex.

The Martello Towers which have become so familiar a part of the south coast had been constructed in 1804 as part of the anti-invasion defences. In order to increase the effectiveness of the Navy these now became shore stations for the Blockade officers. Each was manned by a naval lieutenant, a midshipman and a minimum of eight seamen. The towers were soon supplemented by purpose-built barracks and there were eventually 73 stations in Kent alone between the Isle of Sheppey (Harty) and Lydd. Each station was required, weather permitting, to mount a nightly 'rowing guard' along the section of the coast for which it was responsible. In the event of conditions being too severe for this a shore patrol was undertaken. In order to further strengthen these forces the Revenue service was increased in numbers to form the 'preventive water guard' which maintained boat crews at the places where smuggling was most rife and additional riding officers were recruited to police the territory inland from the coast.

Discipline amongst the Blockade forces was severe to the point of savagery. The commander of the *Ganymede*, Captain McCullock, became known to the free traders as 'Flogging Joey' as a result of his brutality towards his men who, none the less, responded to their duties with such vigour that they earned the nickname of 'Flogging Joey's Warriors'. The sailors concerned were comprised in the main of Irishmen and as such would have had little love for their English quarry. A letter to the *Sussex Advertiser* complaining of the treatment meted out to these men read thus: '. . . There was no less than twenty six of these poor creatures tied up yesterday and flogged. . . . Their cries were piercing and reached Rye. . . .'

Service with the Blockade must therefore have been very unpopular as in addition to the harsh discipline the work to be undertaken was both arduous and dangerous. Smuggling activity usually took place on nights when weather conditions were bad and so favoured concealment. Furthermore the smugglers were, of course, quite prepared to use violence in order to avoid capture or the loss of their cargo. Not the least notorious at this time were the North Kent Gang some of whose escapades have already been illustrated. Numerous other incidents took place at this time, the local newspapers carrying frequent notices issued by Customs House and offering rewards for information leading to the arrest of those involved:

On 7th July 1819 Thomas Parker, a seaman from H.M.S. *Severn* came across a group of some twelve armed

Cave entrance leading to tunnels at Pegwell Bay, Kent.

Alleged smugglers' tunnel, Pegwell Bay, Kent.

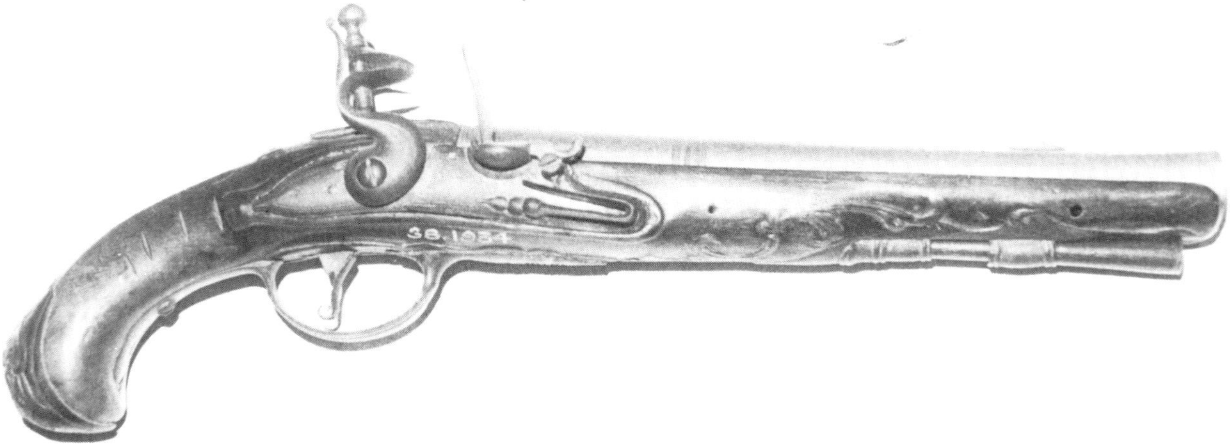

Hawkhurst Gang pistol.

'Spyways', Goudhurst, haunt of the Hawkhurst Gang.

Ypres Tower, Rye, used as a prison — frequently to house smugglers.

Watchbell Street, Rye.

Smugglers' cottages at Herne, showing the lookout window by the chimney used by the North Kent Gang.

The Smugglers Inn, Herne — also used by the North Kent Gang.

Windmills like this one at Herne were used for signalling.

smugglers at Shakespear Cliff, Dover. He was immediately set about and beaten to the ground. His attackers threatened to beat his brains out but finally contented themselves with attempting to tie him up. However Parker managed to wriggle free and escape, kicking one of his assailants in the face as he did so. No further attempt was made to apprehend the smugglers that night.

Not long after this a group of Blockade men were patrolling together near to Martello Tower number 26 at Dymchurch. Observing a vessel coming ashore they moved in quickly and seized an illegal cargo of 105 tubs of spirit as well as the boat itself. The smugglers themselves were forced to retreat but not before striking one of the officers a severe blow in the eye and attempting to shoot another.

On October 25th, 1819 another Blockade seaman, William Press Williams was the victim of a serious and determined attack. The incident began whilst on patrol near Pegwell Bay. He was surprised by a group of five smugglers who beat and then attempted to strangle him. Williams was able to get a hand to his pistol which he fired and the smugglers, presumably fearing that Blockade reinforcements would soon arrive, were forced to flee. They were nevertheless resolved to make a further attempt and later the same night, with two additional accomplices, renewed the attack. This time Williams was better prepared and able to beat off one of the smugglers with his cutlass. Once again, however, he was overpowered and this time an attempt was made to suffocate him by stuffing clay into his mouth and to throw him over the cliff. Fortunately for Williams he managed for the second time that night to fire his pistol and the desperados abandoned their efforts and this time chose not to return.

In 1820 another Blockade man — George English — was on duty near Dymchurch when he saw a boat (the *Rover* from Folkestone) being pulled up on the beach. He fired his pistol to give the alarm and was immediately set upon by 'a large body of armed men who had been lying in wait' on each side of a nearby mudbank. Two of the gang threatened him with their pistols and forced him to remain silent while the landing operations were completed. In due course the smugglers departed leaving English to give the alarm. On this occasion the authorities got the better of the incident the vessel being seized later the same night and English being able to give evidence in due course.

Despite such frequent use of violence the co-operation of the public remained a major factor in the success of the smuggling fraternity. In 1817 an attempt by blockade midshipmen to apprehend some smugglers at Deal resulted in an affray when locals came to assist in resisting the arrest. The blockade men took refuge in a shop but were themselves arrested on the instructions of the Mayor on charges of assaulting the smugglers. Strange to relate there was some justification for this action as Deal, being a member of the Cinque Ports, claimed the ancient right of a two-mile free zone in which no Customs duties were payable. The ancient charters granted to the ports and their various limbs and members specifically provide that 'For the faithful service of the Barons of our Cinque Ports . . . We have granted . . . all their liberties and freedom so that they may be quit of all customs, to wit, of all Lastage, Tollage, Passage. etc . . .' (these being customs duties, particularly Passage, which was a tax on landing). Reason prevailed, however, and a magistrate by the name of Holroyd ordered the midshipmen's release. This event, though bizarre, was not unique as the affair of George England (see Chapter V — 'Such a gang of profligates') illustrates.

On the occasions that smugglers were successfully apprehended it was frequently the case that the real trouble was only just beginning. Such was the feeling of favour of those involved in the trade that once captured determined efforts were often made to secure a speedy, if illegal, release. The attacks on Dover Gaol referred to later were the most spectacular of the rescues which occurred at this time. They were not however unique. On May 8th, 1820 two smugglers, Thomas Harcourt and George Jenkinson, were arrested and incarcerated in Winchester Gaol. The following morning they were found to have been spirited away, the only clue left behind being a length of rope dangling from the window of their cell.

A more violent rescue took place on the night of August 4th in the same year. John Kelty, a Blockade man, encountered a lone smuggler at the West Pier, Folkestone and took him, together with a tub of spirits to the nearby watchhouse pending removal to Dover. Shortly afterwards however an 'immense mob' descended on the watchhouse brandishing bludgeons, throwing large stones and firing pistols. In the mêlée which followed one Blockade officer was wounded and the smuggler made good his escape. Despite a reward of £100 being offered for the smuggler and £200 for any of the attackers no further arrests were made.

In the event of smugglers being brought to trial convictions continued to be extremely difficult to get. In 1823 occurred a famous incident involving men from Folkestone. A vessel called *The Four Brothers* carrying contraband to the value of some £10,000 was intercepted by a revenue cutter just off Dungeness. A fierce battle ensued in which four smugglers were killed, six injured and one preventive man killed. The remaining sixteen smugglers were captured and sent to the Old Bailey for trial. Things looked black. Smuggling was a capital offence and with the death of the preventive man, hanging looked certain. Fortunately for the accused the charge proved not to be smuggling, but firing on a King's ship. The *Four Brothers* however, which had sailed from Flushing, was a Dutch vessel and more than half of the crew, technically at least, were Dutch. Acquittal followed and a heroes' welcome home to Folkestone. At this time it was quite common practice for pregnant women living along the Kent coast to go across to Holland to have their babies as by doing so the children would not ultimately be eligible for service in the Royal Navy and so escape the unwanted attentions of the press gangs.

A full account of this interesting episode is given in Appendix 2.

At the East Kent Quarter Sessions in January 1825 a much less significant but nevertheless interesting case took place when one George Taylor was charged with assaulting Daniel Hardy a Blockade seaman in the execution of his duty at Houghan the previous December 12th. The affray in question appears to have been a fairly serious one with eight smugglers including Taylor being captured. The defence counsel raised the novel defence that Hardy was merely a common seaman serving on H.M.S. *Ramillies* and that in attempting to apprehend smugglers he was not therefore acting in the execution of his duty and that the charge against Taylor was therefore ill founded. This argument met with little sympathy and the trial continued with Thomas Stockwell being called to give evidence for the defence. The cross examination by the prosecution ran thus:

Question — 'How came you to meet together that evening?'
Answer — 'We fell in with one another as we often do!'
Question — 'Did you meet by appointment?'
Answer — 'Yes we did. Taylor an I and three others concluded upon a meeting; I will not say there were ten more persons besides me altogether; there might be twenty!'
Question— 'Did you go to the beach?'
Answer — 'We did!'
Question — 'Did you see a boat?'
Answer — 'There were boats swimming about!'
Question — 'Did not one come near the shore?'
Answer — 'Yes!'
Question — 'Did it ground?'
Answer — 'No!'
Question — 'Could anyone get at it?'
Answer — 'If they were not afraid of getting wet they might!'
Question — 'Did you go up the cliff?'
Answer — 'Yes and then we laid on the grass!'
Question — 'What did you do that for?'
Answer — 'I don't know — to rest I believe!'

The evidence of the next defence witness — Edward Smithson — was equally flimsy and at variance with that of Stockwell. Notwithstanding this, however, and a sound case being presented for the prosecution, the prisoner was found 'not guilty' and discharged.

And so the skirmishes and pitched battles continued through the era of the Blockade. Coroners court papers for Romney Marsh include statements taken from Blockade men at 'The Ship' Dymchurch in 1825 give a wild account of the hardships and dangers of their work. Patrick McImerhany, a 'landsman' from H.M.S. *Ramillies* states that he was on patrol at five o'clock in the morning of the December 30th, 1825 when he surprised a group of smugglers. He challenged them and was pelted with stones. He attempted to fire his musket but this failed to go off and when the smugglers attacked he pulled out his pistol and tried to fire that. It must have been a raw, damp morning, one can picture the lonely marsh, shrouded in mist and landsman facing the angry group of smugglers. His pistol would not fire either. The gang advanced, brandishing sticks, hurling curses and abuse at McImerhany and threatening to kill him. At this, most desperate of moments, his luck changed and Midshipman Richard Morgan, the leader of the patrol came to his assistance. Morgan too had trouble with his firearms, the first pistol failing to discharge. A second attempt, however, was successful and he fired, killing one of the smugglers, the remainder thereupon scattering, leaving the dead man, Charles Keely, and two tubs of spirit.

The grave of Charles Keely, can still be seen in the churchyard at Dymchurch. As for Richard Morgan, his name was to figure again in the story some months later when it was to be he rather than a smuggler who was to lie dead in the grey early morning; a death which (as with Sydenham Snow and the North Kent Gang five years before*) was to provoke the establishment into another all out effort to rid the Kent coast of the most successful and notorious gang of the day.

To leave behind dead or wounded was an unusual occurrence in fights of this kind. The following year a great battle was fought near Camber in which one blockade man died and several more were wounded. Heavy losses are reported as having been inflicted on the smugglers. Precise numbers, however, are not known as the smugglers escaped, taking their casualties with them in addition to their contraband. Such action often involved men carrying wounded or dead comrades over a distance of some miles in the cold and dark and across rough and marshy terrain. We know the traders too well to make the mistake of thinking that they were prompted purely by motives of loyalty and fellowship. Running of illegal cargoes carried the risk of the hangman's rope and it was clearly advisable not to leave behind possible informants for the authorities to work upon.

Large-scale runs continued to be made in the old way, with large numbers of tubs being landed on beaches and then removed on horseback, in carts, and sometimes the transport is even described as 'a coach'. A newspaper account of a landing that went wrong said 'and a coach and four was driven off at speed, empty, towards Pevensey'. When transport was captured by the Customs officers, it was impounded and sold along with the contraband. The officer at Seaford had an unfortunate experience in 1821 when he took a cart. He heard firing on the beach at 3 a.m. and following various clues (smuggling often seems to parallel the customs of the Wild West — gangs were often tracked by the marks of the horses) he came up with a cart containing six casks at Jevington at 5 a.m. The driver leapt out and made his escape 'across hedges etc.'. The cart, according to its inscription on the side, belonged to James Sharwell of Herstmonceaux. Horse and cart together were sold for £5 5s., but the officer had to show a deficit of £1 10s. 6d. in his books, as the expenses came to £6 15s. 6d. Contributing to the expenditure were such homely items as 'keep for horse for 22 days at 1–9d = £1–18–6d,' while the ostlers at Newhaven and Hailsham and 'the driver of horse and cart to warehouse' all had to be paid. There is a certain amount of evidence that people who lost their property like this often bought it back again at the sale. Occasionally one sees references to the smugglers resting and feeding their horse, and these domestic details make

* See page 73 post.

a rather pleasant change from the bleak reports of wounding and slaying which were favoured by the newspapers of the period.

In 1826 a smuggling boat, being chased, ran ashore in Rye harbour. One of the smugglers was taken by a Blockade man, amidst fighting and firing when suddenly two hundred smugglers dashed out of the sandhills and joined the fight. They were driven off, carrying several wounded with them.

Despite the number of engagements which were recorded in official documents or local papers, it is clear that the great majority of runs were either undetected, or noted by officers who were so hopelessly outnumbered, that they could only stand helplessly by. For example, the Newhaven Customs Office had many reports similar to the following:

> 16 April 1823.
> A seizure was made by Lt. Sankey, Chief Officer stationed at the Tide Mill, and there is every reason to suppose that about three hundred casks were landed, but we have no proof that such was the case. The boat from appearance would carry upwards of that quantity.
>
> 14 February 1822.
> On duty with Mr. Allwork from Seaford to Cliff End, from thence to Cuckmere, and Corporal Allen and William Wattery, 10th Hussars. 2 a.m. at Blatchington Battery, saw a company of smugglers return light.

At this period, as noted above, sunken casks were quite often washed ashore after gales, to the great delight of fishermen and beachcombers, who tried to get hold of them before the customs men did. Visitors to Brighton on occasions witnessed more than elegant holidaymakers strolling on the Steyne. In 1803,

> fisherman picked up at sea and brought to shore — upwards of 500 casks of contraband spirits, of which the Revenue soon got scent and proceeded very actively to unburden the fishermen. This landing and seizing continued with little intermission from six to ten, to the great amusement of upwards of 2,000 people who had become spectators of the scene. When the officers had loaded themselves with as many tubs as they could carry, the fishermen, in spite of their assiduity, found means to convey away as many more, and by that means seemed to make a pretty equal division.

It quite often happened that third parties freely sampled the fruits of the smuggler's labours. A Newhaven Customs officer's report mentioned a ship's carpenter on a Revenue cutter who was drunk for a week at a time on 'gallons of gin', which had been seized. A similar occurrence had a tragic ending when some soldiers stationed in Brighton, hearing a 'bustle' on the beach, fetched some comrades and dispersed the smugglers and seized the tubs. However,

> the two soldiers who were first supposed to have discovered the above mentioned tubs took such immoderate draughts of the baleful spirit as rendered them incapable of getting far from the spot where the casks were deposited. They were both found early the next morning lying dead drunk below high water mark. One of them, belonging to the artillery, never survived the shameful fit of intoxication in which he was taken up — he was generally estimated to be a sober man, and was to have been married the day he died.

The blockade lasted for fifteen years, being superseded by the Coastguard in 1831. During its existence it did a great deal of useful work, but none the less can only be looked upon overall, as a failure since smuggling continued to prosper as an industry throughout this period. Two gangs in particular operated with great success in Kent although both were finally crushed. One was the North Kent Gang, the other was the Aldington Gang, both of which are dealt with later. For the moment suffice it to say that following the final defeat of these particularly vicious groups Kent ceased to play an important part in the smuggling story and Sussex became the principal area for the remaining years of the trade.

The founding of the Coastguard Service in 1831 was one of the reasons for the end of smuggling. They were better organised than any previous force, and far more incorruptible. Their arrival was generally approved by the local population.

> Lewes. The Coastguard Establishment, under the regulation of the Customs, has commenced its duties within the last fortnight here: and on Thursday twelve of the horse police arrived for the performance of the interior duty for the prevention of smuggling: they are rather well-looking men, and accoutred in a manner calculated for the service. Eight of them left today for other districts.

The new force immediately had a series of engagements with 'the enemy' all along the coast, and they in particular captured smugglers rather than concentrating on seizing goods as the other forces had done, and this was one of the reasons for their success. 'The preventive coast guard, a few days since, captured near Rye Harbour, 140 tubs of contraband spirits: four smugglers were taken at the same time.'

In July, at Hastings, more than twenty smugglers, armed with bludgeons and with blackened faces, made a run from the *Rose of June* of Newhaven, wounding James Rogers the Chief Boatman of the Coastguard service. A reward of £200 was offered for information about the offenders. In several of the engagements of this period the smugglers had blackened faces.

Runs now were frequently made in broad daylight and with large numbers of men. In February 1832 the *Sussex Weekly Advertiser* gave an account of a Worthing run

> At three o'clock in the morning in question, in broad moonlight, a boat containing about 300 tubs of spirits was beached opposite to Stafford's Library and a party consisting of 200 men, succeeded in clearing nearly all the tubs, with which they proceeded along the Steyne and up the High Street, guarded in the rear by a

company of Bexhill batsmen, with a few firearms, and closely followed by a small party of the preventive men, who kept firing at intervals along the street to bring their party together. At the top of the High Street, Lieutenant Henderson and four of his men met, and immediately pressed upon the smugglers, who made their way over into the Brooks: here the parties had a skirmish: one of the preventive men was knocked down, another had his breast bone broken by a stone. The smugglers, with a man of the name of Cowardson as their leader, formed a line and came with many oaths, upon Lieutenant Henderson, who, maintaining the greatest coolness, warned them not to come any closer, and threatened to shoot the first person that advanced, but they still closed on him, when Cowardson, with his bat raised, being in the act of striking, Lieutenant Henderson shot him dead on the spot, and with his second pistol wounded another man in the thigh: the Lieutenant immediately afterwards had his left arm broken by a bludgeon, when, after striking another with a cutless in the neck, he was overpowered, struck down, and trampled on by the smugglers: at this time there were also three of his men on the ground, one of whom is in a dangerous state.

The following week a fight took place in Hastings against a large crowd of smugglers, and several of the newly formed Coastguard were badly hurt,

> ... one was killed by a gun shot on the spot ... a second wounded in the inferior part of the abdomen and expired on Wednesday evening ... a third has sustained a dangerous wound on the fleshy and muscular distribution of one of the arms, above the elbow, and it is expected, will die from the great degree of inflammatory excitement and irritability of the system which are produced: a fourth has escaped with several light injuries. There are no reports of any of the smugglers being injured.

The Coastguards were generally very brave men, their courage and steadfastness was instrumental in bringing the smugglers under control, despite the frantic last-ditch efforts of the smugglers, using overpowering numbers, or surprise daylight tactics, as in this raid in Brighton:

> many successful runs have been made, and one no longer ago than daylight on Saturday morning, when a boat came on shore on the beach opposite Burlington Street and ran a hundred and fifty tubs up a tunnel which passes under the Marine Parade from the sea, to the western corner house of that street. The policeman on duty there was surprised to see men emerge from the area of that house with half ankers on their shoulders, and gave notice of the event to the Coastguards men of the Black-Rock station. They ran over the Downs just as fast as they were able in pursuit of some light carts which were promptly laden with the crop ... many hair-breadth escapes ... among the places examined was a barn at The Bear near the Barracks, on the Lewes Road, where a swift horse was found harnessed to a light cart, bearing the name of 'Stephen Heather, Butcher, Brighton' and upon searching among the hay in the building, thirteen tubs were found, which with the horse and cart were seized by the officers, and three men who were there cutting potatoes were detained on suspicion of knowing how the hay became the positum of so foreign an article.

A subsidiary occurrence in this run in the heart of Brighton on the very dawn of the Victorian age was that two policemen who had been on duty, changed into plain clothes and were then seen carrying baskets. Their houses were searched and , 'Eight glass and three stone bottles of spirits of brandy were found'. This was a sad sliding from the path of duty, and Mr. Solomon, the new Police Chief for Brighton, took the matter in hand and they did not go unpunished. The creation of local police forces in the 1830's in the coastal towns was another reason for the demise of smuggling: there were now more official observers about both by day and by night, and the police force was, on the whole, incorruptible, as were the Coastguards. Lord Egremont, a public benefactor in many ways — it was he who urged the founding of Brighton's Sussex County Hospital — was one of those interested in the founding of Brighton's first police force. This I think has a significance: there was a greater desire abroad for public order and public utilities and for well-run institutions. This new mental outlook, together with the growth of non-conformist conscience in Victorian England, changed the spiritual and mental climate to one in which the smuggler was a criminal and not an 'honest thief'.

The smugglers, however, continued to fight for existence for a few years, despite the creation of the Coastguard and the police forces. In 1832, a Lieutenant Parry of Camber, on information received, tried to ambush an approaching boat by hiding behind the sea wall. When the boat landed, the two hundred smugglers who had been waiting to unload her, attacked Parry and his men. He received seven wounds, but survived. A well-known smuggler, Thomas Kent, was shot dead, and several smugglers badly wounded.

In January 1833 the Eastbourne smugglers ran a large cargo, and killed George Pett, the chief boatman, in the engagement. The last death in the cause of smuggling is generally held to be that of Thomas Monk, a fiddler from Winchelsea, who was shot at Camber by the Coastguard. Five years earlier, in November, a fierce engagement took place at Pevensey, and as it is a good example of the battle formation in which the opposing parties sometimes disposed themselves in the affrays of this period, the account in the *Sussex Weekly Advertiser* will be quoted:

> ... a boat laden with contraband goods came ashore ... perceived by one of the Coast Guard, who discharged his piece as a signal for assistance, when a great number of smugglers rushed down to the boat, and commenced unshipping her cargo of contraband spirits and tea: the boat was surrounded and protected by armed smugglers, who kept up a constant fire during the unloading of the boat. Having cleared the cargo, the smugglers proceeded with it towards the marsh, flanked and covered in the rear by their armed companions. When the Coast Guard ... came up with them ... the smugglers drew up in line, and upon the word 'fire' being given, some guns were discharged at the Coast Guard ... [smugglers] ... again retreated, when a sort of running fight was kept up for nearly two hours, covering a distance of six or seven miles.

One smuggler was killed and five captured, together with sixty-eight tubs and some tea. Two of the captured died later. In these last years the smugglers often used these tactics — protecting their cargo as it was unloaded by lines of smugglers, and then a skirmish in the rear as they took the load inland. An engagement of this nature did employ military tactics, and this affair could be called almost a military skirmish.

From this time on it is true to say that the golden age of English smuggling was well and truly over. Its decline was in no small measure due to the work of the blockade and of the Coastguard. The ultimate death blow, however, was from a cause much less dramatic.

CHAPTER IX

Breaking open Dover Gaol

As we have seen, once captured, smuggling men were frequently the subject of bold rescues by their friends and comrades. By the year 1820 this had become almost commonplace occurrence although it had, for many years, been in the best smuggling tradition. Almost one hundred years earlier a letter to William Carey, the Chief Gaoler at Maidstone referred to a group (probably members of the Hawkhurst Gang) who had broken into the prison and released some smugglers incarcerated there, seriously injuring guards in the course of the escape. It was Dover Gaol, however, which was to suffer most at the hands of the lawless Kent community.

On September 23rd, 1819 six men, Stephen Lusted, Richard Barker, John Bennet, James Easton, James Dooley and Henry Grigsby were committed to gaol, having been found with contraband aboard the *Anne* a smuggling vessel from Hastings. During the night of the 25th, however, someone from outside the building succeeded in making a hole in the wall with a crow-bar and so effected the prisoners' escape'

The following spring brought another, more daring, rescue at Folkestone. On April 11th, John Cook, Henry Laws and William Ridden were caught unloading a smuggled cargo near Folkestone and taken to the local gaol to await trial. All three were Folkestone men and feelings against the Revenue forces were running high in the town. Hostility simmered just below the surface for the next few days until it erupted on 17th April. A group of some forty or fifty townsfolk descended on the gaol after dark equipped with bludgeons, sledgehammers and ladders. The mob proceeded quite openly to break into the building and release their friends, dispersing before assistance could be summoned. A week later full descriptions of Cook, Laws and Ridden were issued together with an offer of £100 reward for information leading to their arrest. It goes almost without saying, however, that nothing further was heard with regard to these three.

The success of this bold venture was such that it was to be repeated in a still more spectacular incident only a few weeks later. Early on May 26th, eleven men from Folkestone and Sandgate were intercepted in the act of running an illegal cargo by a particularly zealous Revenue officer, Lieutenant Billy Hellfire Lilburn. The men, Richard Hart, Staphen Warman, John Stubbles, John Marshall, William West, Richard Grayland, Amos Cullen, William Fox, James Minter, Francis Roberts and Thomas Minter were brought ashore and taken to the gaol. Upon hearing the news a band of fellow smugglers wasted no time in proceeding to Dover for the purpose of securing their release. Just how many of the instigators of this attack were in fact active smugglers it is not possible to say. The newspaper notice reporting the event refers to 'a very numerous lawless and desparate gang of smugglers, disguised in round frocks, as Countrymen . . .'. It is clear, however, that as word got round of the attempt which was about to be made they were joined by a vast mob of Folkestone townsfolk, men, women and children all eager to give whatever assistance might be needed.

On reaching the gaol in the early afternoon they found their numbers swollen still further by locals from Dover. The assault began and by the time troops could be summoned from the castle to assist the beleaguered defenders of the prison, an entry had already been forced. The smugglers had, however, been removed to the least accessible place within the confines. By now the mob had worked themselves into a frenzy and set about the business of tearing down the building brick by brick using the rubble as projectiles to hurl and keep the military at bay. The Mayor attempted unsuccessfully to read the Riot Act, finally abandoning his efforts when set upon by a group of women and forced to beat a hasty retreat.

Lieutenant Lilburn, the Revenue officer whose action had brought about this whole episode had by now come on the scene and, true to his nickname endeavoured to pursuade the officer in charge of the military to fire into the crowd. According to one account the officer concerned was none other than 'Flogging Joey' McCullock. This seems unlikely, however, unless the forces turned out were marines (of which there is no mention made) since McCullock was, of course, a Naval Captain. Whatever his identity the officer refused to accede to Lilburn's demands suggesting that if the Revenue man wished to see bloodshed he should give the order himself. Bearing in mind that this was 1820 and only a few months after the 'Peterloo Massacre' the insurgents were indeed fortunate. Faced with only token resistance they continued to riot through the streets of Dover, causing local shopkeepers to close and barricade their premises.

In the meantime the instigators of the attack battered their way through the gaol and finally located their comrades. Postchaises had been obtained and the eleven smugglers were triumphantly bundled into these and whisked away whilst the infuriated Lilburn and the body of soldiers looked helplessly on.

Upon reaching Folkestone the liberated men dispersed and were taken to safe hiding places to wait while the hue and cry died down. One of the men, William West, was to have a further narrow escape. After returning home when he thought it was safe to do so he, and the other members of his household, were aroused in the dead of night by a heavy banging at the door of his cottage. The cause of the commotion turned out to be a party of Revenue men who, far from having forgotten the gaol-break, had heard of West's return and were intent upon his re-capture. West's father was quick to react to the crisis, declaring to the impatient officers that the women of the house were in their nightdresses and that he would shoot anyone who dared to enter the cottage before they were properly attired. In the breathing space gained William was concealed beneath some bedding and sat upon by his mother and wife who then proceeded to give a first rate impression of fear mixed with outrage and embarrassment. A search failed to reveal the whereabouts of the fugitive and the officers left empty handed and disappointed.

As things turned out West's escape was a mixed blessing. Some time later he was amongst the crew of a smuggling vessel, the *Jane* which traded between Folkestone and Flushing and which foundered in a gale with all hands lost.

But to return to Dover Gaol, the daring escape was duly commemorated in a folk song, much in the manner of the times:

We smuggling boys are merry boys
Sometimes here and sometimes there
No rent nor taxes do we pay,
But a man-of-war is all our fear.

'Twas on the 21st of May,
As you will understand,
We sailed out of Boulogne Bay,
Bound for the English land.

But to our sad misfortune,
And to our great surprise,
We were chased by two galleys,
Belonging to the excise.

Oh then my boys for liberty,
Was the cry of one and all,
But soon they overpowered us,
With powder and with ball.

They dragged us up to Dover Gaol,
In irons bound like thieves,
All for to serve great George our King,
and force us to the seas.

The wives for their husbands
Were in such sad distress,
For children round the gaol
Were crying fatherless.

And sure the sight was shocking
For any one to see,
But still the cry came from the mob,
For death or liberty.

Oh then a hole all in the wall,
Was everybody's cry.
And Lillburn and McCullock's men
were soon obliged to fly.

For bricks and tiles flew so fast,
From every point you see,
And these poor men from Dover gaol,
They gained their liberty.

And now they've gained their liberty
The long wide world to range,
Long life to the Dover women,
Likewise to the Folkestone men.

The final chapter in the story came on July 12th, 1820 when an advertisement appeared in the *Kentish Gazette*, issued by the Dover Corporation and inviting tenders for the construction of a new gaol for the town!

CHAPTER X

The North Kent Gang

That part of the coast extending from the South Foreland westwards across Romney Marsh and on into Sussex is a renowned area of smuggling activity and was worked by various great gangs such as those from Hawkhurst, Aldington and Alfriston from time to time during the heyday of the trade. The marshes of the Hoo peninsula on the Thames Estuary and the north Kent coast from Sheppey to the North Foreland, however, provided terrain and isolation equally well suited to smuggling. Like Romney Marsh, the Isle of Sheppey was once famed for its sheep (indeed its very name derives from this form of livestock) and no doubt the illegal export of wool occurred here as well as on the Marsh. The Hoo peninsula was a noted breeding ground for malaria-carrying mosquitoes and the disease was prevalent in the area which was consequently poor and sparsely populated. Ideal for landing contraband goods. This potential was fully exploited over many years in a manner just as ruthless as that employed elsewhere culminating in a series of forced runs and murders perpetrated by the so called 'North Kent Gang' in the early years of the nineteenth century.

The area was notorious as a hotbed of smuggling long before the gang brought it to real prominence. The reader will recall the venomous letter from the informer calling himself Goring concerning the affray at Bulverhithe in 1746. Prominent in this document are references to 'The Hoo company' clearly a well-organised and desperate group operating over a wide area. Not all the predecessors to the North Kent Gang however, were such large-scale operators. The Kent Records Office contains details of the activities of a number of comparative small fry working this part of the coast. In the mid 1720's several voyages were made by one Edward Rootes. He seems to have been the leading light in a small co-operative, undertaking the purchase of quantities of tea in Ostend. The amounts concerned were in the region of four hundred pounds at a time. Not much when compared with the kind of runs being undertaken by larger gangs elsewhere but still quite enough to realise a substantial profit. The second recorded run in February 1726, however, proved something of a minor disaster when, having successfully landed the tea and hidden it in woods near High Halstow, they were discovered by a Customs officer named Johnson and the tea seized. There is a strong indication that one of the gang, Matthew Holloway, had informed as part of the tea was returned to him by Johnson and no prosecutions were instigated as a result of the seizure.

Undeterred, Rootes and his team sailed to the continent on numerous occasions in the following months each time returning to the marshes of north Kent with tea. After several successful voyages trouble was encountered again off Herne Bay when they were chased by a Revenue cutter and forced to dump the contraband overboard. They did, however, manage to avoid capture. Following this incident, a system was adopted whereby Rootes' sloop the *Mermaid* anchored off Sheerness and transferred the tea to a rowing boat in which it was transported to the landing place some miles away. This change of pattern was necessitated by the unwanted attentions of Captain Clements the master of the Revenue cutter which had given chase on the previous trip. This officer had boarded the *Mermaid* on the outward voyage and attempted to seize her. Rootes with typical smuggler's determination had slipped the line from the cutter and sailed off leaving Clement's men to get back to their own vessel in the *Mermaid*'s dinghy. The team went onto Ostend and ultimately completed the voyage in the manner referred to. Nevertheless, Clements did seize the *Mermaid* shortly afterwards. Profits from the venture were such that Rootes was able to purchase another sloop and continue in business for some time after.

The activities of small operators such as Rootes and company may seem fairly harmless and certainly are more in keeping with the popular image of the smuggler. The records do refer, however, to the fact that members of this crew did carry firearms and presumably may have been prepared to use them if necessary. The blame for at least one murder is laid at the door of unknown smugglers in the Hoo area. This took place at Binney Farm, Allhallows in 1739. At that time the farm belonged to a family by the name of Boghurst. On the evening of the murder all except one of the family had gone to visit friends at nearby Stoke. Upon returning home they found the body of their unfortunate linesman lying in the avenue leading to the house. The victim had been bludgeoned to death. The culprit was never found but smugglers being active in the vicinity, the general opinion was held that one of them was responsible. There could be several motives for the killing; objections raised to possible borrowing of horses required for transport, discovery of a cache of contraband, possibly even double-cross.

The favourite landing place on Cliffe marshes was the spot known as Egypt Bay. Its appeal is still obvious, even today. Being a bay it provided sheltered water where boats could put in and lie unobserved by patrolling Revenue cutters or any other passing vessel. Unlike the neighbouring St. Mary's Bay, however, the contours of the surrounding terrain are such that it cannot be seen from any inland vantage points. Even the church tower at St. Mary's Hoo which stands on comparatively high ground does not command a direct view of the bay and any snooping busybodies would have to approach within a hundred yards before being able to observe any signs of activity. The nearby Shades House, an eerie isolated building standing alone on the marshes, was deeply involved in these goings on. The smugglers having landed their cargo and transported it inland to safe hides would then drive sheep, which could always be found grazing in the vicinity, across their tracks and thus conceal any signs of their operations.

Another much favoured haunt was the hamlet of Avery (otherwise Every) which once stood as part of the land now occupied by the Allhallows-on-Sea Holiday Estate much use being made of the old Lobster Inn, around which the hamlet was centred, as an initial hiding place. Avery has long since gone although the name is preserved in a local firm of which the Lobster Inn later became a part.

In the 1730's there were only two riding officers patrolling the Hoo peninsula, Francis Riggs and John Tomlin. These were based at Stoke and considering the size of the area there was clearly little chance of effective action by such a small force, particularly as Riggs was noted for his frequent absences from duty and general laziness. He was eventually moved inland to Chalk in an attempt to apprehend contraband consignments being transported along the turnpike road between Rochester and Gravesend. The move does not appear to have improved anything. In 1740 less than 17 lbs of tea were seized and this at a time when tea smuggling was at its very height. Sheppey at various times was even worse off, having no riding officers at all. This was a very serious deficiency. Considerable use was made of Warden Manor. This building is reputed to have been connected to the old church (now unfortunately vanished into the sea) and to the post office, which in those far off, lawless days was the 'Smack Aground' Inn, by underground tunnels. At another point in its history the Manor was occupied by the other side, being residence of the commander of the preventive forces in the area. Today there is a modern Coastguard station here — overlooking the estuary. The aforementioned 'Smack Aground' was incidentally, an inn with a particularly infamous history, the landlord's son being the leader of a gang of wreckers who lured unsuspecting ships ashore with false lights and plundered their cargoes. Like the Hawkhurst Gang, Sheppey smugglers extended their activities into other types of crime. In 1745 they are reported as having entered a farmhouse and stolen wool to the value of one thousand five hundred pounds. Despite such escapades they do not appear to have made the same mistake as the Hawkhurst company and gone so far that they eventually estranged themselves from popular public opinion. This is somewhat surprising as many of the survivors of that gang moved their operations to this area after the executions of 1749.

By the final quarter of the eighteenth century the rather haphazard operations of the various smuggling groups in this area had began to be formed into a more widespread if loosely knit organisation that was to become the North Kent Gang. The trend towards violence was also becoming more marked as the affray at Whitstable in 1780 for which John Knight was hanged plainly shows.

An ancient headstone in the burial ground of Minster Abbey in Sheppey bears testimony to such violence. The inscription on this monument shows the grave to be that of an unknown man found murdered on the morning of April 22nd, 1814, his head being nearly severed from his body. It further states that a public subscription was entered into to raise a reward of one hundred guineas for the conviction of the murderers who, none the less, went uncaptured. The dead man is believed locally to have come upon members of the gang in pursuit of their trade. This unfortunate individual was mistaken for a Customs informer and immediately received the treatment reserved for such. The subscription is said to have been instigated by the smugglers involved in order to divert attention from themselves. They are also alleged to have paid for the erection of the headstone.

The North Kent Gang smuggled all along the Kent coast from Chalk to Ramsgate, Reculver being another much favoured landing place. It was at Reculver that on one occasion the hazards of attempting a landing in rough weather were tragically illustrated, a small boat in which two smugglers were endeavouring to retrieve some tubs being capsized by a freak wave and both men drowned. If the legend referred to earlier concerning the Exciseman Anthony Gill and his fanatical pursuit of Smuggler Bill from Reculver into Thanet has any foundation in truth it is very likely that the latter was a member of this group.

The gang achieved real notoriety in 1820 and like other violent gangs it was this very infamy which led to their ultimate defeat and disbandment. At this time one of their main headquarters was Burntwick Island, a desolate spot at the mouth of the River Medway separated from the mainland by Stangate Creek. In March 1820 they landed a cargo in the creek but were surprised by two members of the Blockade forces. A skirmish followed in which one of the officers was seriously injured and the gang able to escape taking their cargo with them. When set against incidents such as the battle at Whitstable forty years earlier this seems to be a comparatively minor affray. It must be remembered, however, that with the formation of the Blockade in 1817 the whole climate had changed. This is the first recorded occurrence of direct confrontation between the gang and Blockade forces and it seems likely that after the establishment of those forces the gang had been exercising a great deal of discretion in their operations. Once contact had occurred, however, the gauntlet had in effect been thrown down and more violence was bound to follow.

The continuing success enjoyed by the group served to increase their boldness and make them willing to undertake still more desperate escapades. On June 16th, 1821 a Blockade force commanded by a Lieutenant Douglas encountered members of the gang at Bishopstone Gap near Reculver. In the ensuing battle two of the smugglers and several of the Blockade men were badly wounded. The gang made off with their contraband taking their wounded with them. No arrests were made on this occasion. Within a few days, however, another run was attempted at Whitstable and on this occasion the men of the Blockade were able to capture two of the gang, Daniel Harris and William Owens. These were taken to Faversham Gaol to await trial. Their comrades, however, were unwilling to brook such interference and on June 27th openly attacked the gaol, armed with bludgeons and pickaxes, broke it open and set the prisoners free. Despite full descriptions of Harris and Owens being issued, together with a reward of one hundred pounds for their capture, they do not appear to have been retaken. It should be added that daring as this escape was, those involved were, as we shall see, merely following the example of other smuggling bands further round the coast. In any event when five more members of the gang were arrested a month later during an attempt to force a run at Birchington Minnis, a further rescue does not seem to have been attempted. This may be because the authorities were mounting a more effective guard or more likely because no

Scenes from the 'Day of Syn' at Dymchurch.

Old Smugglers Inn, Alfriston, now demolished. Photographed in 1926 by Mrs J. S. Stevens.

Chimney corner at Market Cross House, Alfriston. Concealed chambers at the side of the chimney led to passages which ran right through the house, 1912.

A. H. C. Corder

Two scenes from the Walt Disney film 'Dr Syn Alias the Scarecrow'.
Above: 'In protective custody' — Squire Banks and his daughter Kate are protected by the Scarecrow.
Below: Dr Syn matches his wits against General Pugh in a courtroom battle.

A BRUSH WITH SMUGGLERS.

(From a Painting by Bernard F. Gribble)

By courtesy of H.M. Customs and Excise.

serious violence was used on the occasion of this arrest and consequently there was no danger of any death sentences. It certainly did not, however, indicate any softening of the gang's attitude towards interference by the Blockade.

In March 1821 members of the North Kent Gang attacked the sentry at the Blockade station at Herne Bay, bound him hand and foot and proceeded to land a cargo from a French galley before his eyes. Some fifty to sixty smugglers are reported to have been involved in this incident. In the following month was to come the most noteworthy of the gang's crimes — the murder of Sydenham Snow.

On Easter Monday, April 20th, members of the gang rendezvoused at the home of John Richardson at Hoath. The leader of this group was James West and he distributed pistols, blunderbusses and 'bats' to the twenty or so present who were to form the fighting responsible for the protection of the cargo. A further forty men were to undertake the unloading and transportation work. Working to a prearranged plan the smugglers split into a number of smaller groups and made their way by different routes to the Herne Bay turnpike (which was situated near the bottom of Mickleburgh Hill) Herne Bay being then little more than a few fisherman's cottages grouped near to 'The Ship Inn'. Proceeding to the beach the fighting men fanned out in the usual military style guard and the tub-carriers settled down to await the arrival of the boat carrying the contraband. The night was wet and dark, ideal for the business in hand and when about 2.45 a.m. the vehicles lights winked in answer to the signals from the beach, everything seemed to be going smoothly.

Unknown to West and his men, however, a Blockade party consisting of Midshipman Sydenham Snow, Quartermaster David North and Seaman Wilson and Barker had been put ashore shortly before and were even then proceeding on a routine patrol in the direction of the landing. Inevitably, they were attracted by the noise of the cargo being run ashore.

Snow as leader of the patrol took immediate action and, drawing his pistol, challenged the smugglers in the King's name. The reply, not surprisingly was a fusillade of shots. The young Midshipman, displaying extraordinary courage and determination, pressed forward. An attempt to fire his own pistol failed when the weapon misfired. Undeterred, he drew his knife and charged. Almost immediately he was brought down, wounded in the leg and shoulder. His companions were kept at bay by the firing and unable to offer any immediate assistance. It may be that they lacked something of Snow's heroism — or foolhardiness. Be that as it may, the record of the men of the Blockade throughout its existence is one of positive and determined action and it would be quite wrong at this distance in time and without a precise record of all the facts, to condemn their failure to follow their Midshipman's example. The landing completed, the smugglers coolly made off leaving Snow lying in a pool of blood and water on the shingle.

The coast being now clear, Seaman Barker appeared through the darkness and discovering Snow to be still alive, called to the others to assist in carrying him to The Ship Inn which stood only a few yards away. Here he was attended by a Naval surgeon from Birchington who ascertained that one pistol ball had lodged in his thigh, the other just below his shoulder blade. The *Kentish Gazette* of May 1st reported that he '... was conveyed ... to the Ship public house, with but little expectation of recovery, but subsequently the ball in the shoulder having been found, there are hopes of a more favourable issue'. Sadly, the account was out of date well before publication, poor Snow having surrendered up the ghost on April 21st complaining to a comrade 'that his life had not been yielded in open battle with the enemies of his country instead of being sacrificed in a vile midnight encounter with a gang of outlaws'.

He was laid to rest in the churchyard at Herne on April 30th with full military honours. His commanding officer, Captain McCullock and the other officers from H.M.S. *Severn* following his coffin. The cottages opposite to the church were much used by smugglers at that time and it may well be that members of the gang watched the grim cortege. The incident was far from closed however. Snow had made a statement to a local magistrate George May, providing information as a result of which arrests soon followed.

The trial took place at the Old Bailey on June 9th with Snow's companions as the fateful patrol giving full statements in addition to three of the smugglers concerned in the affray George Griffiths, James Smith and Edward Holman turning King's evidence. Those in the dock were James West, William Beer, John Richardson, Thomas Richardson and William Williams. Quartermaster North explained that he had been unable to go to the Midshipman's assistance because of the heavy fire coming from the ranks of the smugglers. Nevertheless, despite overwhelming evidence against the accused a 'Not Guilty' verdict was returned. The case against the smugglers was very strong but appears to have failed largely as a result of the considerable reliance placed by the Prosecution on the evidence of George Griffiths. Griffiths turned out to be a poor witness, easily broken down by the Defence in cross-examination. West and his comrades returned to North Kent to a hero's welcome.

It will doubtless be of interest to the reader to note that whilst these desperate men were stealing the limelight in the area at this time, numerous much smaller fish were being caught by the Revenue forces. The vicinity of Sheppey, Faversham and the surrounding area then formed the Petty Sessional Division of Upper Scray the minutes of which abound with such instances. On February 1st, 1821 John Warren of Minster-in-Sheppey was fined £100 for being found to have a half anker of smuggled Geneva on his premises. On March 2nd Robert Barker was convicted of running a 'blind pig' (or unlicensed establishment selling contraband liquor). On the same day Thomas Gooding was convicted of possessing smuggled tobacco. The catalogue of such offences would be almost endless but instances of convictions became less frequent after the breaking of the North Kent Gang. This was not far off.

A few short weeks after the Sydenham Snow affair, members of the gang led by Daniel Fagg, John Taylor and James Rolfe attempted to force a run at Marsh Bay near Margate. Approximately one hundred smugglers, many of them armed, were involved. Once again they were surprised by a small Blockade patrol this time led by

Midshipman Washington Carr. The battle which followed was both short and violent. Carr attacked and wounded several of the gang before Fagg managed to wrench his sword away from his grasp and use it to deal him a vicious blow to the head. By this time, however, the gang was in retreat. When one of Carr's party recognised James Taylor and called him by name the smugglers hastily broke off the encounter and left the beach, firing as they went but causing no further injury. The recognition of Taylor proved the gang's final undoing. The matter was passed to a local solicitor, John Boys, who pursued it with surprising (for those days) vigour. With the help of Bow Street Runners, Taylor was arrested and shortly after joined in Maidstone prison by a further seventeen members of the gang. In the spring of 1822 all eighteen were tried at Maidstone Assizes charged with armed assembly. Perhaps they had made the same mistake as the Hawkhurst Gang before them and gone too far down a violent road. In any event, a local jury did what their counterparts at the Old Bailey had failed to do and found the men guilty. All were sentenced to death although in the end only Fagg, Taylor and Rolfe danced the 'hempen jig' on Penenden Heath the remainder being transported for life. This episode marked the end of the North Kent Gang although small-scale smuggling continued in the area for several years. The main battle ground now switched back to the south of the county where the Aldington Gang had become the main antagonists. They were to prove a difficult nut for the Blockade to crack.

CHAPTER XI

The Aldington Gang

In his novel *The Further Adventures of Doctor Syn* Russell Thorndike includes an episode involving a gang of smugglers from the villages of Aldington and Bannington led by brothers by the name of Ransley. This misguided crew attempted to outwit the Dymchurch smugglers commanded by the Scarecrow and, naturally, came seriously unstuck. The Scarecrow is of course a fictitious character and the events depicted in the novel, being set at the end of the eighteenth century pre-date the real Aldington Gang by some twenty years or so. The gang did, however, exist and was indeed led by a man named Ransley, the father of the characters in Thorndike's story. Far from being the rabble so easily out-manoeuvred by the Scarecrow, Ransley's men were the most highly organised and infamous smugglers of their time, more dangerous and successful by far than the North Kent Gang and the worst thorn in the sides of the Preventive men in the years of the Blockade.

Thorndike's reference to the gang is not their only literary appearance. G. P. R. James's novel *The Smuggler* is set in and about Hythe and has among its central figures a group called 'the Ramley Gang' around whom most ot the smuggling incidents are woven. Many of the episodes depicted are taken straight from the exploits of Ransley and his men, although some of the doings of the Hawkhurst Gang (notably the Battle of Goudhurst) also turn up.

The Aldington Gang rose to prominence during the second decade of the nineteenth century. The Collins Gang, based on Alfriston, had taken the coast of east Sussex as their territory at this time, the North Kent Gang worked the estuary coast and the Aldington men in their turn claimed Romney Marsh and the Kent coast up to Dover. The gang's leader in the early years is uncertain although a man named Cephas Quested is usually accorded this honour. According to some accounts Quested was a particularly evil man, much in the same mould as Thomas Kingsmill. Charles Igglesden in his 'Saunter through Kent with pen and pencil' provides a much more sympathetic view of his character, crediting him with consideration for local country folk and a deep love for his own family. The suggestion of his leadership has been doubted, it being alleged that he was a stupid drunkard, incapable of the organisation necessary to command such a group.

Whether or not this is so it is Quested's name which survives. It should be noted by the reader that the great smuggling gangs were in any case rather loosely knit bodies, factions of which might undertake independent small runs under different leaders. When two hundred or more men had to be assembled for major operations it was inevitable that in those days of difficult communication the personnel involved would vary from one occasion to another. Whoever the leader, the gang certainly adopted increasingly violent tactics and made many successful runs. In 1818 a Preventive officer was murdered on the beach at Hythe, near where the Imperial Hotel now stands. The new attitude of determination to stamp out smuggling meant that their activities were not allowed to go unhindered as would have been possible in the preceding century. By 1820 the situation was getting out of hand and on November 8th of that year a particularly severe battle took place at Sandgate.

A cargo of spirits and tobacco was run ashore late that evening being met by a party of something like 250 men. These adapted the usual tactic of deploying two armed groups to guard the remaining men by whom the unloading was undertaken. They were challenged by two members of the local Blockade force and battle was immediately joined. One of the Blockade men was shot in the groin and the other seriously beaten. The sound of firing attracted two more Blockade men namely Lieutenant Peatt (of whom much more shortly) and John Green.

With the courage which so typified the new force Peatt and Green rushed the smugglers. They were soon surrounded and Peatt sustained a wound to the leg. Notwithstanding this he fought his way through the mob using both pistol and sword to advantage. The gang had by this time completed the unloading and made off in the usual orderly retreat, taking Green with them as a prisoner. He was released later and a comparatively small quantity of contraband was recovered next day. This appears to be the first major affray between the Aldington Gang and the Blockade.

Then, on February 11th, 1821 a detachment of Blockade men encountered a party of some 200 or more smugglers at Camber. The battle which ensued was typically violent, the Blockade men once again being far outnumbered by their adversaries. Unlike the incident involving Lieutenant Peatt the fighting continued inland across the marsh to Brookland the smugglers retreating in military style, forming up and firing in ranks as they went. Eight of the Blockade force were wounded and one, Midshipman McKenzie was killed. Four smugglers were reported as killed having been subjected to persistent firing and fierce close quarter fighting by their pursuers. Numerous others were wounded. Most of the gang escaped but two were captured. One was named Richard Wraight. The other was Quested.

The manner of his arrest is worthy of particular note. Clearly there was some prior inkling on the part of the Blockade forces that an affray with the gang was likely. A midshipman was disguised in a smock of the same style as those worn by the smugglers and, during the battle he took up a position amongst their ranks. Quested came up to this young officer, handed him a musket and commanded him to 'blow out the brains' of any soldier or sailor coming within range. Thereupon the midshipman rounded on Quested and covered him with the weapon so conveniently provided until assistance arrived. Quested and Wraight duly stood trial at the Old Bailey. Wraight was acquitted but Quested paid the inevitable price for his crimes on the gallows at Tyburn.

The trial was delayed for some months whilst abortive efforts were made to persuade the captive to turn King's evidence. Shortly before the execution he wrote to his wife:

Newgate Cell,
20 June, 1821.

Dear Loving Wife,

I am sorry to inform you that the report came down on Saturday night, and I was ordered for execution on Wednesday. I sent for Mr. Hughes on Sunday and he and the Sheriff came in the afternoon, and Dear Wife they told me that it was best for you not to come up. Dear loving wife, I am sorry that I cannot make you amends for the kindness you have done for me, and I hope that God will be a Father and a Husband to you and your children for ever; and Dear Wife, I hope that we shall be happy in the next world, and there we shall be happy. And, Dear Loving Wife, I hope that you will not fret, or as little as you can help. And Father and Mother, I send my kind love to you, and to all my kind Brothers and Sisters; and dear Brothers, I hope this will be a warning to you, and to all others about there. Dear Father and Mother, and Brothers and Sisters, I hope that you will not frown on my dear loving children. Dear Wife, I am happy in mind, thank God for it, and I hope you will keep up your spirits as well as you can. [Here followed a long quotation from poetry]. So no more, from your unfortunate husband.

CEPHAS QUESTED

His body was ordered to be hung in chains near Brookland but, as a result of intervention by the local magistrate, Sir Edward Knatchbull, Quested was spared this final indignity and buried at Aldington.

As a result of the furor caused by the battles and the trial the remaining gang members appear to have thought it wise to 'cease trading' and lie low for a while. The prospect of great profits was too great, however, and before long it was business as usual. The new leader of the gang was George Ransley. Ransley was a native of Aldington and although not possessing the psychopathic inclinations of Kingsmill was otherwise of a very similar character being unquestioned in his authority and willing to undertake the most daring of adventures. He has been variously described as a 'giant of a man, standing over six feet tall' or, more soberly as only five feet six and a quarter inches in height. Whatever his height his stature in the smuggling story is immense. Most counties from time to time had their master smugglers, men who were somewhat larger than life. Men such as Jack Rattenbury of Devon who combined smuggling with piracy; or Thomas Benson, also from Devon, who was both a successful smuggler and a Member of Parliament; or Thomas Johnson the famous Hampshire smuggler who later worked for the Revenue service and invented a submarine for the purpose of effecting the escape of Napoleon from St. Helena. Kent, however, despite being the most notorious smuggling county of all, is remarkable for its lack of such characters. Of the many hundreds who participated in the trade only two really fell into this category. One was Arthur Gray, the original leader of the Hawkhurst Gang who certainly outshone Thomas Kingsmill in terms of personality and financial success, if not in villiany. The other was George Ransley.

A tranter and farmer by day Ransley, or Captain Batts as he became known, used his profitable legitimate business as a front for his even more lucrative nocturnal activities. He came from a lawless family, two of his cousins, James and William (known as the Rascally brothers) having been hanged at Penenden Heath in 1800 for highway robbery. These two were also smugglers and George may well have been introduced to the trade by them. He seems to have started life in a fairly law abiding manner. He appears to have worked hard as a waggoner and been highly thought of. When caught once stealing a sack of grain his employer would not proceed with a prosecution declaring that he was a good man and expressing the opinion that he only stole for the sake of his horses. Ransley married a local girl, Elizabeth Bailey, and it was after this that he turned to smuggling. How or why we do not know — by one account he is said to have stumbled across a forgotten cache of contraband and as a result was able to finance future smuggling activities. However it happened, he quickly moved up the hierarchy of the gang and was ready to assume Quested's mantle when the opportunity presented itself. Under his leadership the 'Blues' as they are often styled became a highly organised body consisting of some twenty or so close associates each receiving a guinea a night and as many as eighty others, these being paid seven shillings for a night's work carrying tubs. The hard core group were deployed as fighting gangs and entrusted with the tasks of beating off any attempts by the Revenue forces to seize the cargoes being run. The system they adopted was to encircle the beach when the landing was taking place ready to shoot it out if necessary with anyone wishing to interfere. Once the cargo was on its way inland the armed element would bring up the rear in what was, in effect, an orderly military style retreat, forming and firing in ranks at any pursuers. Ransley's organisation extended to the retention of a firm of solicitors in Ashford and a surgeon, Ralph Papworth Hougham. At a time when the medical profession had not yet attained anything like its present standing, there can be no doubt that Hougham, a resident of Brookland, was very grateful for the fees earned in tending the wounded on both sides of the conflict.

Bloodshed was inevitable and the 'Blues' were soon involved in the same kind of violent incidents that were such an outstanding feature of organised smuggling. A particularly noteworthy occurrence was an extremely brutal attempt on the life of one of the Blockade's most outstanding officers, Lieutenant Peatt. To understand the reason for the animosity felt towards this man it is necessary to recount an event which had taken place some time earlier.

One of the gang, George Walker by name, had been taken in the act of running a cargo and convicted by a local magistrate. In order to forestall any attempts at the rescue of Walker, a decision was taken to have him taken aboard a King's ship which lay off Dungeness at the time. David Peatt was charged with the task of effecting Walker's safe transfer. Not surprisingly a mob of smuggling sympathisers assembled on the beach and a riot began. Peatt was supported only by a small detachment of marines and the convicting magistrate and it soon became clear that the chances of preventing a rescue were slight. The magistrate cried out 'Secure your prisoner sir, run the rascal through', upon which Peatt drew his sword and carried out the order without hesitation. Walker fell dead at the officer's feet and the mob dispersed rapidly. At an inquest into the happening held at New Romney a verdict of justifiable homicide was returned at the direction of the coroner — not it seems, without some resentment on the part of the jury — and a large detachment of dragoons had to be rushed from Hythe to protect Peatt from the anger of the local populace.

Peatt appears to have been a man of extraordinary courage, or arrogance, or both, since he ignored exhortations to accept a move to a different part of the coast and, in fact, moved deeper into danger by taking up residence in Folkestone — a veritable hotbed of smuggling activity at that time. The Ransley Gang were unable to countenance such defiance and an ambush was duly laid into which the unfortunate Peatt fell headlong. One dark night whilst patrolling the marsh accompanied by a Quartermaster the Lieutenant was attacked by a large body of smugglers. The Quartermaster was shot and killed and Peatt himself wounded. He fell to the ground and lay prostrate appearing to be also dead. The gang gathered over the 'corpse' and, to make certain of ridding themselves of the accursed officer fired a volley of fourteen shots into his body before making off. Unbelievably Peatt survived, recovered and returned to duty, continuing to plague the smuggling fraternity for many years. He ultimately attained the rank of Admiral.

Not all officers who crossed swords with the gang were treated with such ruthlessness. Ransley and his men did, it seems, have a well-developed, if somewhat cruel, sense of humour. A story is told of one Blockade man who had incurred the displeasure of the smugglers and was unlucky enough to fall into their hands. He was overpowered, blindfolded and had his legs bound. His assailants then announced their intention of throwing him to his death over the edge of a cliff. The distraught prisoner pleaded for his life but nevertheless found himself bundled over a precipice and left hanging on to tufts of grass along its edge whilst his bound feet dangled in space. For an hour or more the victim clung to life in this position before the blindfold slipped and he was able to realise that the 'cliff' was only seven feet high and his feet were only a matter of inches above the ground. The jibes to which the poor man was subjected by the local children over the next few weeks can only be imagined.

Ransley's leadership lasted from 1821 to 1826 the greater part of which period is remarkably short of documentary evidence of the gang's activities. This paucity is, of course, a testimony to the considerable success achieved. The last thing those involved in the trade wanted was the kind of large-scale fracas which make such gripping reading today but brought only undesired attention and inevitable loss of profit at the time. Trade did, however, continue throughout those years and occasional seizures were made, as the not infrequent advertisements for auctions of brandy, geneva silk etc., at the Customs House of Dover, Sandwich and Ramsgate clearly show. The Blockade force was maintained at a high level, it being reported in the *Kentish Gazette* in 1823 that forty-eight Lieutenants were employed in the Revenue service in Kent and Sussex alone. Incidents did occur which illustrate that whilst a more cautious approach was on the whole being adopted by the smugglers their audacity had not entirely been forgotten. On Friday, November 14th, 1823 one John Lawes managed to escape from Folkestone Gaol where he was being detained for a smuggling offence, a large hole having been made in the wall, presumbly by comrades on the outside. It is interesting to note that the description of Lawes refers to him as being clad in a blue frock and blue trousers. The nickname 'the Blues' does not appear in contemporary accounts of the gang's escapades and was probably not coined until after their demise. Opinions differ as to why the name should ever have been used at all, some saying that it derived from the working smocks worn, others maintaining that a blue flare was used to signal the arrival of contraband. Perhaps the description of Lawes clothes is mere coincidence but it does seem to point towards the first suggestion as having some truth in it.

On January 12th, 1824 William Carey a member of the company of H.M.S. *Ramillies* was on patrol at Aye Cliff Dover when he was set upon by a group of smugglers. His attackers beat him and held him down, threatening him with death if he tried to escape. Meanwhile the remainder of the party brought their cargo ashore and quickly dispersed leaving Carey to recover his pistols and cutlass and to report the incident. This attack bore the characteristic stamp of the Aldington Gang and needless to say no arrests were made. On November 26th in the same year, three Revenue men, George Hammond, John Baker and John Barns saw a suspicious boat come ashore at Dover. Barns went to investigate (the newspaper report makes no mention of what his companions were doing at the time) and was confronted with some thirty or more of the gang in the process of unloading a cargo. He too was attacked and beaten whilst the gang completed the unlaoding of the goods.

Numerous stories exist of the excesses practised by the gang. An article appeared in the *Folkestone Express* in the latter part of the last century in which an old man recounted how, like the Hawkhurst group before them, the gang took, as of right, whatever they felt would be of use to them and woe betide he who dared to oppose their wishes. An old woman is said to have been attacked for no reason than the warped pleasure of her assailants, stripped naked and left to find her way home. On a separate occasion another old woman is alleged to have encountered members of the gang and been killed by a blow to the head, the murderer declaring that she had lived long enough.

Stories such as these have been handed down by word of mouth and it is hard to say whether they are entirely true. There is strong evidence, however, that whatever acts of wanton cruelty and violence may have been perpetrated by gang members, Ransley himself remained aloof from such goings on.

At the end of the last century Commander Henry Shore (later Lord Teignmouth) had a hand in the production of two books, both of which remain amongst the leading works on smuggling. The first *Smuggling Days and Smuggling Ways* was the sole work of Shore; the second *The Smugglers* was co-written with Charles Harper. In researching these volumes he had many conversations with people living at that time who still remembered Ransley personally. The universal praise of Ransley by those interviewed is perhaps the most prominent feature of Shore's records. No one spoke ill of the old smuggler. With the profits from his illicit trade Ransley had a house built at Aldington — The Bourne Tap — and used this as a 'blind pig' or unlicensed outlet for some of the spirits brought over from the continent (brandy could be bought in France at this time for 12 shillings a gallon — in England the same quantity would fetch £3 12s.). This establishment was the scene of many a drunken orgy and became the scandal of the neighbourhood. George, however, is said not to gave taken part, preferring to sit thoughtfully outside — perhaps planning the next 'run'.

Just as Charles Igglesden's opinion of Cephas Quested was more charitable than that which seems to have been generally held so was his statement of Ransley's character at variance with the views expressed to Commander Shore. He describes him as leading the country folk a life of terror. It seems probable, however, that Igglesden in expressing this opinion is attributing to the master smuggler many of the crimes of his associates. But let us not forget that he was, after all, a criminal and a man of his times. He looked after his men, retaining the services of both a surgeon and a solicitor and care was always taken of the families of any who was killed or injured. The opposite side of this coin was the harsh treatment meted out to any who did not satisfy his demands or show complete loyalty to the gang.

The gang flourished until 1826 by which time the increasing ruthlessness of their methods was beginning to lose them some of the public sympathy which was, as ever, their greatest advantage over the Revenue forces. The final straw came on July 30th, 1826 when during a run at Dover the smugglers encountered two members of the Blockade. It was at about one o'clock in the morning and the Blockade men were Michael Pickett, a seaman and Richard Morgan, a Midshipman and Quartermaster, the same officer who had killed Charles Keely at Dymchurch some months previously as described earlier. They saw a boat coming ashore to where the bathing machines then stood. Morgan fired his pistol to sound the alarm. It may be that he was recognised and that revenge was in the air. In any event, a number of the smugglers let fly a volley of shots in return and Morgan was hit in the head, dying instantly. Pickett was wounded but survived. The gang made off and thirty-three tubs of spirits were later recovered. Morgan was buried in St. Martin's churchyard on August 2nd with full honours. A reward of £500 was offered for information leading to the apprehension of any of those responsible. Edward Horne (alias Spratford) turned King's evidence. In October 1826, on a storm-lashed night, a strong party of Blockade men, commanded by Lieutenant Samuel Hellard, Richard Morgan's superior officer, together with two Bow Street Runners marched on Aldington. The night chosen was one when no run was planned. The Bourne Tap was encircled and the throats of the watchdogs were cut as Hellard and his men closed in. Ransley was asleep in bed when the doors of his home were burst open and, despite having frequently boasted that he would never be taken alive, he was unable to offer any resistance.

In the same raid a further seven gang members were rounded up and within the next few weeks the total number of captives was brought to nineteen. In order to prevent any of the attempts at rescue which had become such a feature of the gang's operations, they were moved to Newgate prison. Their trial was set for Maidstone Assizes the following January. Richard Wire a man of only nineteen was charged with Morgan's murder. The others were charged with various offences ranging from aiding in the murder to carrying unauthorised firearms, all crimes for which the penalty was death. During the trial the more serious charges were dropped and pleas of guilty entered on the lesser offences. Death sentences were duly passed. The executions were set for February 5th, 1827 on Penenden Heath and there can be little doubt that a huge crowd would have attended to see Ransley and his friends turned off. However, the dropping of charges and the guilty pleas had all been part of a deal aimed at bringing a speedy conclusion to the affair. All the condemned were reprieved and sentenced to transportation for life to Tasmania — then Van Dieman's Land.

George Ransley left Portsmouth on April 3rd, 1827 and although he never returned to England he did become a prosperous and respectable farmer being joined by his wife some years later.

Both the Bourne Tap and the gang's main headquarters, the Walnut Tree Inn can still be seen today the latter remaining a popular pub which changed little with the passage of time. The inn sign depicts a smuggler carrying a tub of spirit in the moonlight.

The Aldington Gang was the last group in Kent to successfully practise the forced run in open defiance of the Customs service. During the years of the Blockade preventive measures became more successful and it was necessary for the smuggler, ever resourceful and adaptable, to adopt more subtle and artful measures in order to continue with his business.

CHAPTER XII

Tricks of the trade and strange hiding places

The patchwork forces established by the authorities in their desire to curtail smuggling activity resulted in a triple line of defence (Revenue cutters, Coastguard and riding officers) which had to be breached whenever a 'run' of contraband was attempted. This fact coupled with the particular difficulties arising from the shallowness of the waters around the South East coast, made efficiency and precision timing essential to the smuggling trade. Detailed information as to the numbers and deployment of the preventive forces was of course an incalculable advantage and this the smugglers went to great pains to obtain. It was not difficult. Poor pay and conditions among the preventive men made many of them susceptible to bribery and even recruitment to the smuggler's ranks.

One particular advantage possessed by the Kent and Sussex coast was its proximity to mainland Europe from which the vast majority of smuggled goods came. This enabled straight runs to be undertaken; that is to say the whole thing from departure from a foreign port to storage of the contraband in smugglers' hides on this side of the Channel could be achieved in a single, uninterrupted series of operations. A smugglers' galley — a specially constructed craft rowed by ten or twelve oars — could make the crossing in about five hours. Circumstances did arise occasionally, however, which necessitated sinking of the goods off shore to await collection by local men at a convenient time. On such occasions the sinking took place, if possible, in oyster beds, crabbing grounds or some similar type of location where the contraband could be retrieved without arousing suspicion. If a crabbing or lobster ground could be used in this way it had the added advantage of enabling the sunken goods to be buoyed in the same way as crab and lobster pots, thus making retrieval simple. Where this was not possible the technique of creeping was adopted. This entailed trailing a multi-hooked grappling iron along the seabed in an attempt to hook the tubs and casks. Visitors to Britanny may still see similar hooks being used in this way to catch crabs.

Direct landing was the favoured approach of Kent smugglers and to enable such landings to be achieved successfully it was necessary that all parties should be in the right place at the right time without fail. This was comparatively easy for the 'landsmen' employed in meeting the smugglers' craft and transporting the goods inland. For the men engaged in making the crossing it was not so simple and seamanship of the highest quality was necessary. Signalling from the shore was achieved by the use of 'flashers'. These were flintlock pistols with the barrels sawn off which were primed but not charged so that they went off silently but produced a bright flash visible for half a mile on a clear night. A small enough beacon at the best of times but unfortunately runs could not usually take place in clear weather, the need for secrecy making dirty weather more favourable to smuggling activities. Accordingly a sailor (or 'spotsman' as he was known) who could guide his boat accurately to the rendezvous was invaluable and when such men were caught they would usually escape the gallows, being pressed instead into the Royal Navy where their considerable talents could be put to good use.

The shallow waters created an additional hazard in the form of the possibility of grounding. A boat lying at anchor close to the shore might easily be caught by a falling tide and then be unable to do anything but wait for daylight and inevitable capture. Furthermore, if cargoes could only be landed when the tide was right, the preventive forces job became much easier since they could work out in advance the likely dates for possible runs. It was necessary, therefore, to develop methods of coping with this problem. One trick was for the smugglers' vessel to stand off in deeper water and run a circular rope ashore along which tubs could be passed in the style of a conveyer belt. Another method was the use of what might in twentieth-century parlance be termed disposable boats. These 'tub boats' were made of very cheap materials and would make the crossing by being towed by Deal Luggers or galleys. After the run the boats being of little value could be broken up or abandoned. Their advantage was that the whole consignment of illicit goods could be landed at once, irrespective of the state of the tide, and then run inshore once the lugger had departed in safety.

Goods were not always landed on beaches and in coves. Sometimes they were taken through gaps in the cliffs such as those at Birling or Crowlink in Sussex. At other times they were actually run up the cliff face. One is constantly amazed at the skill and daring of these men. John Banks, whose Father was a blacksmith who sometimes helped the smugglers, wrote of an incident in his youth:

> Jack and another (one Whittaker) were fortunate enough to find 5 tubs, which had been laid by, intending to be scamped . . . they were strolling along the top of East Cliff one forenoon, hoping to pick up a rabbit, having a ferret and a dog with them. Jack had been the previous day assisting his father at the Custome Warehouse, and his long blue frock had a spiritous scent about it. Whittaker kept sniffing and said he 'smelt sommat'. Jack told him it was his frock and explained the cause. 'No, No' said Whittaker 'It's too strong for that'. Looking about they saw a mark where a rock had been cut by a rope; they knew at once that some goods had been hauled up the cliff the previous night. They managed to descend onto a ledge a little way down, and here to their surprise they found 5 tubs of spirit. They very quickly took them away to a cottage near the Rocklands, and were paid by the owner 6s. a tub, not bad for a forenoon's work.

Burn marks of a rope on a cliff edge were a complete give away and the smugglers generally took good care to avoid making them.

The wooded gaps in the cliffs near Hastings afforded opportunities to smugglers, but even the cliff faces themselves were scaled. As the water in many places came to the foot of the cliffs at high tide, the Revenue men could no longer patrol the beaches and had to climb to the top of the cliffs to continue their duties. In the interval, while they were climbing the cliffs, it was possible for the smugglers to rush to the cliff tops, secure a portable derrick by a crowbar to the ground on the cliff edge, drop a rope through the pulley of the derrick, attach a basket to one end and a horse to the other, and they were ready for action. A boat could load up to a dozen tubs in the baskets, which was raised by causing the horse to gallop away from the cliff edge. The derrick was hinged, and could be swung round until the basket touched the grass; it was tipped up and the tubs tumbled out in seconds. The whole operation was so well timed that it took less than ten minutes, and there would be time for several loads to be secured before the watch had laboriously climbed from the bottom to the top of the cliff for his patrol.

An old Revenue man told Banks of such an arrangement as this that went wrong. Smugglers were operating a derrick near Birling Gap and had set the machinery up, when those down below realised that they had been a little premature and one of the Customs men was still on the beach; they therefore pushed their boat off and rowed away at speed, in their haste forgetting to signal to their colleagues on top. In the meantime, the officer had come up to the basket which he collided with in the dark. Not being quite sure what it was, he pulled it towards him to investigate. This movement of the rope was taken by the smugglers on top to be the signal for which they were waiting, as they were completely unaware of what was happening on the beach below. Consequently the unfortunate Revenue man found himself, without warning, hurtling upwards at great speed. Considering it more prudent to hold on than to let go, he ascended three hundred feet in a few minutes and then was unceremoniously dumped on the grass, together with a dozen tubs of brandy, at the feet of a group of astonished smugglers. The smugglers disappeared into thin air leaving the watchman with the half ankers of brandy and a derrick. Banks asked the man what his feelings were and he replied, 'Well Sir, I held on like grim death, and wasn't long a-travelling to the top'.

In February 1823 another officer, Thomas Furneaux had an adventure with smugglers who were hauling tubs up the cliffs near Newhaven, and suffered not only violence but an attempt at bribery (for once unsuccessful). He wrote in his report:

> I had but one dragoon with me when I fell in with a large gang of desperate smugglers in the very act of hoisting the goods up the cliff in defiance of a boatman who was among them, but on advancing up to them the rope was let go so that the goods fell with a crash to the foot of the cliff. I found them very obstinate and one came to me who appeared to be a person of respectability and said it was hard to loose all and persuaded me to take half. I presented him with a loaded pistol and ordered him to stand back or I would shoot him. At the same time my dragoon was hemmed in by part of the company when I advanced and told them I would fire among them if they did not let the dragoon out. They then fell back and after a severe scuffle and firing many rounds of ball over their heads we succeeded in repelling them and drove them from one part of the cliff to another as they endeavoured to haul the goods up at difference places.
>
> Your Honour will be pleased to observe that this gang is the same that is nomated the Desperate or Pinionia gang and have been the fatal instruments of many poor Boatman being dismissed the service for want of resolution to cope with them. I then proceeded towards the Watch House and went under the cliffs and found one of the Newhaven crew had seized 18 tubs, and a little further on the tide waiter Hoad had seized 45 tubs and 2 bags of tea. I still persevered and about a quarter of a mile further on I fell in with and seized 94 casks and 3 bags of tea. A preventive man came from Bearshide Gap and assisted me in collecting this number but I was the absolute seizing officer of this crop.

The reward for the seizure was £200, divided among the officers, and Hoad received £30. Not all official reports are as packed with human interest as this one. The fact the the leader was a person of respectability confirms the widespread belief that many of the principals and also the backers, were respectable citizens. The officer was a brave man to take on a large gang, and his anxiety that he should not lose any portion of his just reward reminds us that the service was not well paid and reward was part of their remuneration. There are comic overtones in his account, of the running fight at the bottom of the cliff, to the accompaniment of crashing casks and flying bullets. The use of derricks for unloading on the cliffs was not confined to smugglers; some were used quite innocently in the normal course of unloading goods. One remained at Rottingdean for many years.

Even more daring than the use of derricks was the ascent of the cliff face by rope ladders. These were about forty feet long, and were held at the top of the cliff by a crowbar. Several ladders were joined together until the required length was reached. The rungs, which were of wood, were usually about a foot apart, but some times a greater distance. One must admire the hardiness of a man who could climb such a ladder in the dark, on a stormy night, with two heavy casks on his shoulders, the boiling sea beneath him and the blank cliff face before. It was particularly difficult when the cliff top projected and these places were avoided if possible, as the man swung free, with his body inclined outwards. One unfortunate man did fall and became stranded, badly wounded on a ledge. He was taken by the Coastguards, but pardoned, as Nature had punished him, far more severely than any judge, by imprisoning him in his bed for life.

Revenue men too, suffered accidents on cliff tops, and their shattered bodies were sometimes found on the beaches. There are persistent traditions that in fact they were often pushed over by the smugglers. A particularly nasty story involving the Alfriston smugglers illustrates this. It was customary for some patrolling Customs men to place blocks of chalk at intervals along the cliff top. These could be seen by their whiteness on even the darkest night, and served as a marker for the cliff edge and the dangerous crumbling places. One night when the Alfriston men were waiting for a consignment at Cuckmere, an officer appeared on the cliff top just as the smugglers' lugger came beneath. Some of the gang moved the position of the stones, so that they guided the unhappy man over the cliff top. One of the smugglers looked down to see if he was dead: to his amazement, he had not fallen, but was clinging on with his finger tips. For a second the two men's eyes met, then without further hesitation, the smuggler stamped on the officer's hands with his sea boots, until he let go and crashed to the beach beneath.

The speed and efficiency with which runs were made was outdone only by the ingenuity of the smugglers in concealing cargoes both aboard ship and after landing. A novel idea employed by one smuggler involved encasing kegs of brandy in plaster of Paris to make them look like blocks of chalk. They were then deposited at the base of the Dover cliffs to await collection at the convenience of his associates. Hams and loaves were sometimes hallowed out and packed with tightly rolled silk or lace (up to sixty-eight yards of silk could be concealed in a large ham). A gang from Folkstone had a boat fitted with hollow masts in which tobacco and other contraband could be concealed. When the boat docked the masts could be unshipped (a common practice) and taken away, tobacco and all, while the Revenue men looked on.

Deception, however, did not stop at these relatively small items. Concealment on a truly mind boggling scale took place by means of hiding places in the ships themselves. Secret hiding places in cabins, under benches, behind cupboards and chests, hollow masts, false bottoms, false forecastles, in some enterprising cases complete double boats, abound in the annals of smuggling. It is impossible in a short study to present more than a few of the most notable examples. It is interesting to think of the Customs officer probing, tapping, sniffing, testing pitting his wits against the smuggler. There must have been many great trials of nerve and courage between the two sets of men when these inspections were taking place. There were of course, many give away signs — a hollow sound on tapping, a disparate measurement of proportions inside and outside the boat (this is where false bottoms were so clever as the boat was usually in the water and not beached) a lack of normal leakage through the outside hull: unexplained dowell ends that did not agree with the constructions of the boat: these and other significant details were the clues that set the Customs men on a trail that often revealed quite astonishing caches of smuggled goods.

On August 26th, 1823 the *Sally* of Hastings was discovered to be a whole double boat, with a five-inch gap between the outer and inner hull. The officers removed from her 180 parcels containing: '290 lb. tobacco, 91½ lb. tea in 51 parcels, 136½ gallons of spirits in 78 flat casks, 2 small parcels with silk shawls, waistcoat pieces and straw platting'. The crew of this boat behaved with magnificent nonchalence, saying, when the Customs officers started their search, that they would go off for a while for a beer. As a result, only the Master, a man called Noakes, was taken. In the event he was released, as the Board would not prosecute as they did not consider they had a sufficient case as they could not prove the goods were foreign.

A fishing smack, the *Flower* of Rye, had a false bow that would take forty to fifty half anker casks. The *Lavant* of Chichester had an entire additional bottom. The lugger *Fox* of Rye (John Soudon, Master), had concealments in the cabins in each of which fifty to sixty pieces of bandannas could be hidden. The smack *Asp* of Rye (John Clark, Master), had a false bow containing fifty flat tubs. Other ploys included a hollow tin-lined mast containing several gallons of loose spirits.

In March 1838 the fishing boat *Mary Anne* of Rye was discovered to have a false keel and in April 1823 the *St. Antoine* (a French boat) was found at Shoreham to have a false stern. A boat that was discovered to be smuggling by means of hiding places was stripped by the authorities and sawn in half. This probably accounts for the many boat-huts on the coast made of half boats. They often appear in Regency and Victorian engravings.

Tobacco was smuggled in disguised as rope. The great smugglers' warehouses at such towns as Roscoff and Boulogne thoughtfully supplied this disguise ready made. The rope contained some strands of hemp and some of tobacco. The tobacco was stained with rum to make it look like tarred rope. Readers who have seen the short twists of chewing tobacco sold in the mining districts of the North of England will know that a piece of solid, rounded tobacco, black and oily, looks uncommonly like a tarred rope. A coil of this rope, innocently stowed on deck, could bring in many pounds of tobacco. Many people think that our expression 'money for old rope' comes from this particular smuggling technique. A double wall, making a cell between bedrooms at the Red Lion at Hove, is supposed to have been a place where such ropes were hidden and unravelled. Many inns had small hiding places too small for tubs but probably for tobacco. Places of this nature were in the Lamb Inn at Sedlescombe, the Crow and Gate inn at Crowborough and the Gun Cottage at Sedlescombe.

During the Georgian period a great many English people travelled abroad, taking their own coaches with

A SMUGGLER.

THE PREVENTIVE SERVICE.

By courtesy of H.M. Customs and Excise.

A View near Shoreham with Smuglers Landing a Cargo.

CUSTOM-HOUSE, LONDON,

28th April, 1820.

WHEREAS it has been represented to the Commissioners of his Majesty's Customs that in the night of Monday the 17th instant, JOHN COOK, HENRY LAWS, and WILLIAM RIDDEN, who had been committed to the Gaol of Folkstone, in the County of Kent, for having on the 11th instant, within the liberties of the said town, feloniously assembled with divers other persons to the number of three or more, armed with fire-arms, in order to be aiding and assisting in the illegal landing, running, and carrying away certain goods liable to pay duties, which had not been paid or secured, made their escape from the said Gaol by forcing the doors with iron crows, in which they were assisted by forty or fifty persons dressed in round frocks, as countrymen; and that two large sledge hammers, together with two ladders which had been used for the purpose of effecting their escape had been found in the said Gaol.

The said Commissioners, in order to bring to justice the three persons who escaped, and also those who assisted them therein, are hereby pleased to offer a Reward of

ONE HUNDED POUNDS

to any person or persons who shall cause the said JOHN COOK, HENRY LAWS, and WILLIAM RIDDEN, or either of them to be retaken and safely lodged in the said Gaol of Folkstone, or some other of his Majesty's Gaols in Great Britain, and the like Reward to any person or persons who shall discover, or cause to be discovered, any one or more of the persons who aided the escape of the said three persons, so that such person or persons may be apprehended and dealt with according to law, to be paid by the Collector of his Majesty's Customs at the Port of Dover.

The said JOHN COOK is about 30 years of age, is of a dark complexion, has dark hair, rather crooked legs and is about 5 feet 8 inches high, and had on when he broke Gaol a light grey frock coat, was a journeyman butcher and lived in the Town of Folkstone.

The said HENRY LAWS is about 27 years of age, is of a dark complexion, has brown hair, is stout made and about 5 feet 7 inches high, had on when he broke Gaol a short brown gabardine, was a waggoner, and lived in the town of Folkstone.

The said WILLIAM RIDDEN is about 25 years of age, is of a dark complexion, has brown hair, is of an athletic make, and is about 5 feet 11 inches high, had on when he broke Gaol a long dark gabardine.

By Order of the Commissioners,

G. DELAVAUD, Secretary.

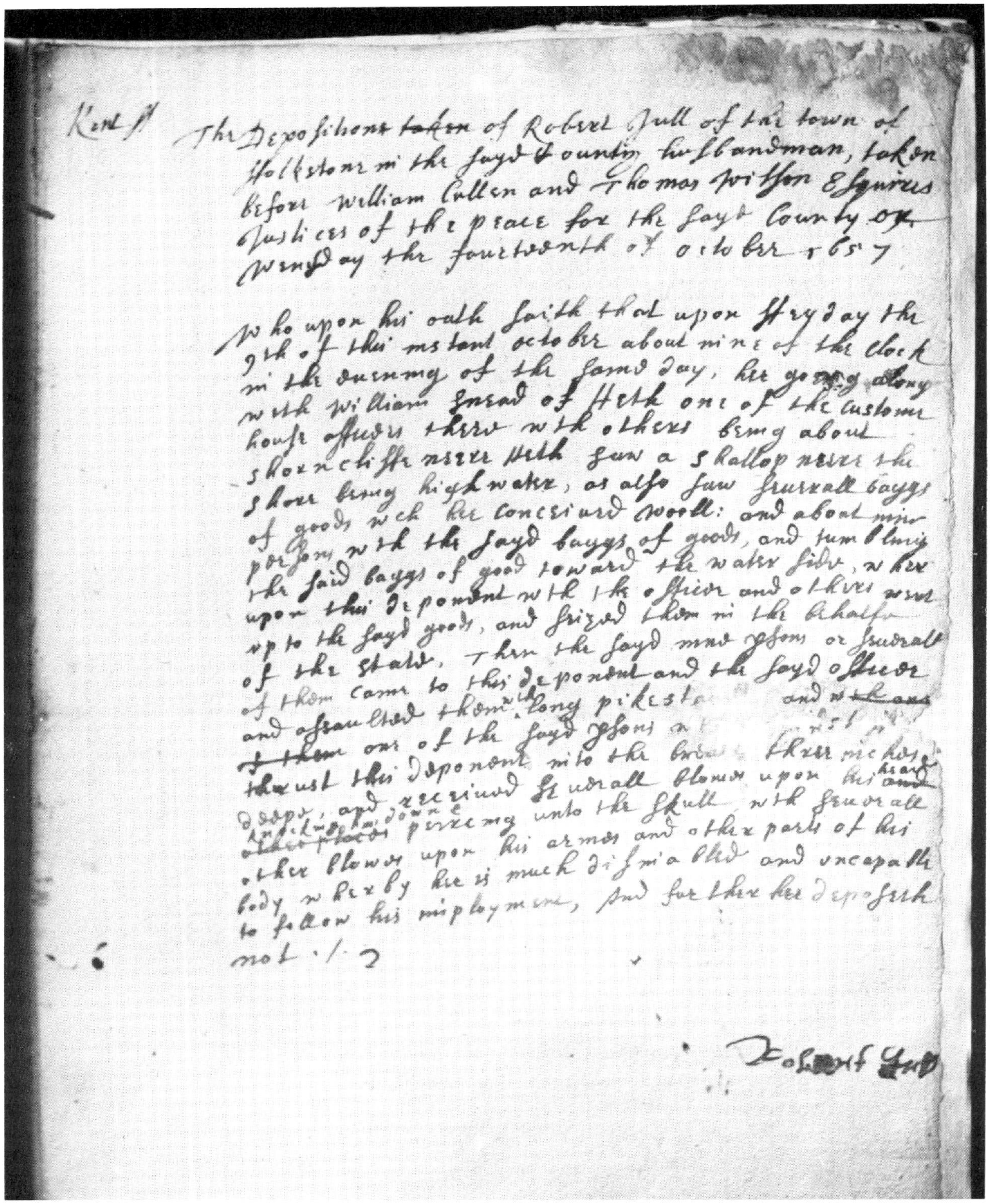

Kent ss. The Deposition taken of Robert Jull of the town of Folkstone in the sayd County husbandman, taken before William Cullen and Thomas Wilson Esquires Justices of the peace for the sayd County on Wensday the fourteenth of october 1657

Who upon his oath saith that upon Fryday the 9th of this instant october about nine of the clock in the evening of the same day, hee going along with William Snead of Heth one of the custome house officers there with others being about Shorncliffe neere Heth saw a Shallop neere the shore being high water, as also saw severall bagges of goods wch hee conceived wooll: and about nine persons wth the sayd bagges of goods, and tumbling the said bagges of good toward the water side, where upon this deponent wth the officer and others went up to the sayd goods, and seized them in the behalfe of the State, then the sayd nine persons or severall of them came to this deponent and the sayd officer and assaulted them with long pikestaves and wth one of them one of the sayd persons wth [illegible] thrust this deponent into the breast three inches deepe, and received severall blowes upon his head breaking downe other places piercing unto the skull wth severall other blowes upon his armes and other parts of his body whereby hee is much disabled and uncapable to follow his imployment, And further hee deposeth not. 1.2

Robert Jull

Deposition of Robert Jull.

them. The wheels were taken off for the journey across the Channel, and they were reassembled at the French port. This was so usual an occurrence that the parquets that sailed to and from the French coast had a published tarrif for the transport of carriages, as well as passengers. One such coach, on its return to this country, was found to have its cushions stuffed with over £1,000 worth of lace. One is reminded of the stories today of ingenious hiding places in the bodywork of cars coming into English ports, and must reflect that there is indeed nothing new under the sun.

But many runs still continued in the old way landing on deserted beaches and travelling inland at night on quiet roads. Cecile Woodford, in her *Portrait of Sussex* quotes an old lady who remembered files of smugglers' horses, heads low with exhaustion under their heavy loads, coming up Rock Hill, Waldron, when all was quiet. A farmer nearby would give a prearranged signal if Customs men were about.

There are tales of clever methods of warning the smugglers if there was danger, of windmill sweeps set at a certain angle; of shepherds' crooks held a certain way; of an ingenious signal system in a farmhouse chimney; of shawls placed on lamps in windows (a fire risk, one would have thought); of mysterious messages to servants to go and look after farm stock. There is no doubt that the smugglers did have a very good spy system, and that they had a great deal of help from the country people.

Once ashore the next problem was to get the goods away and safely stored. In places like Romney Marsh, tub carriers frequently took the most arduous route inland in order to avoid possible pursuers. Particularly dangerous dykes were crossed by planks which were carried for that purpose and could be taken away and hidden when the last carrier had passed. Caves and other natural 'hidey holes' were made use of to secrete smuggled goods. Churches were also highly favoured for storage purposes. The parish churches of Snargate, Brookland, Ivychurch, Hove and Fairfield are all known to have been used in this way as were the vaults of St. John's Churchyard, Margate. At Snargate, part of the North Aisle was sealed off and used for hiding goods. On one occasion tobacco was found in the belfry and a cask of spirit beneath the vestry table. At the same church Richard Barham, whilst Rector there in 1817, was turned away and forbidden to hold a service one Sunday morning. Why? because the pulpits and pews were fully occupied by casks of brandy! This same Vicar reports often noticing the smell of tobacco in his church tower. The parish church of Hove which was in a semi-ruinous condition until rebuilt by the Basevi in the 1830's had a sermon preached there on alternate Sundays by the Vicar of nearby Preston. One Sunday he arrived at Hove church to find the doors locked and no bells ringing and when he inquired the reason for this state of affairs the sexton calmly told him he was mistaken and it was Preston Sunday. The Vicar insisted that it was Hove Sunday but the sexton just as heatedly stuck to his guns. The Vicar held to his own opinion and finally ordered the sexton to ring the bells but the sexton replied: 'It's no use Sir, you can't preach today — the church is full of tubs, and the pulpit is full of tea.' So Preston Sunday it was!

The church is only five minutes' walk from the sea, and Hove Street, which leads to the beach was at that time the only village street. Hove consisted of a few cottages, a smithy, the Manor House and some barns, all clustered around this single street. At the bottom, by the sea was the Ship Inn, traditionally a haunt of smugglers. Nearby was a stretch of grass where village gatherings and fairs were held, and here was a bull baiting ring. Here in time, Coastguard cottages were built.

A Pevensey clergyman found he could not get into his coachhouse as the doors were jammed. With difficulty he climbed up the hayrack into the hay loft, and peered down into the coachhouse. To his utter amazement, he saw that it was entirely full of casks of brandy which must have been stored there during the night by smugglers. He returned to his house and decided to sleep on it before deciding what to do. It is as well that he did for the story goes that a smuggler had been posted to watch the house and he would have been stopped had he tried to inform the authorities. The next morning he cautiously walked over to his coachhouse; the doors swung open easily. Every cask had gone except one and that had been left as a thanks offering.

Village ponds were sometimes used to hide casks and the term 'Moonrakers' was applied to labourers in Wiltshire fishing in the water with a rake one night in order to retrieve some casks. When a suspicious Revenue man demanded to know what they were up to they adopted their best yokel manner and pointed to the reflection of the moon — 'Trying to catch the moon sir.' Another version of the same story exists in Sussex but in neither tale is there any indication of whether or not the officer was satisfied with the explanation. At Hurst Green in 1838 some unlabelled bottles containing fine brandy were found in a pond a possible smugglers' haul. Unfortunately not all such discoveries were so pleasant. The burials register at High Halden in Kent records the finding of a body, thought to be that of a smuggler, in the bottom of a pond, bound and weighted hand and foot with severe injuries to the head.

References frequently occur in official records to 'a private place in his barn', clearly referring to secret hiding places. Pig styes often had compartments under the floor, covered with boards, then with straw and dung. A barn at Blackness near Crowborough had a large hiding place in the floor.

Public houses too were frequently used by smugglers and many still boast the secret passages and cupboards that remain as relics of their more notorious pasts. The Ship at Dymchurch (of Doctor Syn fame) has a number of such passages whilst the Bull at Sissinghurst has an escape hatch disguised as a cupboard in a private room — more than likely used by both smugglers and highwaymen.

Not far from Gravesend, at the summit of Wrotham Hill stands the Vigo Inn. Some years ago a secret cupboard was discovered behind the taproom chimney and this is believed to have been used both as a smugglers' hide and as a bolt hole where locals could conceal themselves from the press gangs which frequently marauded out at Chatham. In Gravesend itself is the Three Daws an ancient tavern on the river front much used by the free traders. It is reputed to have no fewer than seven staircases designed to confuse would-be pursuers and three secret passages.

At Alfriston the George Inn had a bolt hole in the roof connecting with the next property. Stanton Collins, leader of the Alfriston smugglers, lived in Market Cross House, late Ye Olde Smugglers Inn. This has many hiding places and hidden passages. A ladder ran up inside the fireplace. There was reputedly a tunnel running as far as a cave near the Long Man at Wilmington. A room used by the smugglers when planning their runs had five doors, tunnels, one reputedly ending in a trap door at nearby Thorpe Cottage. There were many big operations in this area and in September 1783 about a dozen cutters had unloaded goods which were rapidly removed by two or three hundred of the Alfriston men. A week earlier over three hundred men had unloaded boats on one night despite mountainous seas. During the Napoleonic Wars troops were stationed at Blatchington, particularly The First or North Battalion of Hampshire Militia, and it was more difficult to carry out large operations.

At Rye, the Old Bell Inn had a cupboard with revolving doors that allowed one to step through into a passage. The cellars at Rottingdean and Jevington Vicarages are supposed to have housed contraband and certainly the cellars of Jevington Rectory are very large, and still bear the marks of crosses made by Customs men on the walls after searching for contraband. The Vicars from the time of William Carr in 1670 are supposed to have been at least tolerant of smuggling. Local memory also connects Doctor Hooker, Vicar of Rottingdean, with smuggling. He is supposed to have actively aided the smugglers by warning them of danger, depending on the speed of a particularly fine grey mare. There is, however, no proof of these traditions.

It would be too tedious to the reader to attempt to enumerate here all the 'pubs' connected with smuggling (but see Appendix 1) but it would be fair to say that if an establishment is around two hundred years old it has probably been involved or at least benefited from the trade.

One of the most bizarre hiding places in Sussex is reputed to be the tomb of John Olliver, a miller who lived at Highdown, a hill at Goring. There is an ideal landing place, with a quiet flat beach, and woods behind leading to the hill. Even today it is fairly quiet, and at that time there was no major road near. The hill is almost three hundred feet high, and a good place for watching a wide stretch of coast. Olliver's mill was at the top of the hill, and part of it was still there, in a ruinous condition, before the Second World War. The tomb, which Olliver built nearby still exists. He was an eccentric, and kept his coffin under his bed, and in about 1766 built his tomb on a plot of land about twelve feet square. It is a large stone edifice, a rectangular tomb of the altar type and did not receive John Olliver until he died at eighty-four in 1793. In the intervening twenty-seven years, according to local legend, it housed kegs of brandy. One would also think that a mill would afford plenty of scope for ingenious hiding places, especially for such a man as Olliver seems to have been. When his house still stood, it was surmounted by figures depicting a miller filling a sack, an Exciseman chasing a smuggler, the Exciseman in turn being chased by a woman brandishing a broom. One can presume that this was a fanciful representation of Olliver's own opinion. Pennant, in his *Tour of Sussex* wrote that Olliver 'carried on a very considerable trade in smuggled goods'. He was well known in Worthing, and when he died, hundreds of people came to his funeral, possibly in the hopes of at last getting a peep inside his tomb. The miller of Highdown's tomb was the most spectacular hiding place on record in Sussex, but tombs generally were often credited with being hiding places. Many family tombs are supposed to have had movable slabs in the sides so that smugglers could disappear into them, walk down a tunnel, and reappear elsewhere.

Another grave with a smuggling connection, albeit rather tenuous, is that of Edward Lakin in St. Leonard's Churchyard at Hythe. Lakin was the inventor of the lifeboat and the story goes that the first coxswain of the craft whilst carrying out preliminary trials succumbed to the temptation to indulge in a little contraband running. He was discovered and the vessel seized and destroyed — a sad beginning to the lifeboat story which was, happily, to recover to become so impressive in later years.

The sprawling outhouses and buildings of a farmyard were favourite hiding places and there are many records of ingenious deceptions, but one of the most imaginative was a hollowed out haystack at Sedlescombe.

Sometimes, in emergencies, smugglers made free with other people's property. Banks tells that his father's house was used one night to store about one hundred casks. One cask was leaking, and the smell of brandy pervaded the little house and wafted into the outside air, and a Customs man voiced suspicions. So John was awakened by his mother at night, and told to put on his Sunday boots, to help carry casks away. He put on his weekday boots, and the reason for his mother's words became clear as he clattered through the quiet streets in hobnailed boots : his Sunday boots had no nails in them. He and his mother carried a clothes basket with a cask covered with clothes on each journey. The kegs were put on the floor of a workshop nearby, where they were safe.

On another occasion, when John and his mother were sitting up late, a cargo being unloaded on Hastings East Parade was surprised by the Coastguard, the men in the boat pushed off hurriedly, whilst the three on the shore had to run for it, carrying their two kegs apiece round their shoulders. Seeing a light in the Banks house they burst in, and one said, 'Dont be frightened, Missus, but keep perfectly still.' When all danger was past they left, but first one of them asked for a gimlet, bored a hole in the side of the cask and poured a pint of brandy into a jug for Mrs. Banks.

Caves and recesses in the rocks were used for the temporary storing of casks; thirty-eight casks in a cave were found at Ovingdean in 1795. Sometimes platforms were hollowed out of the cliff face, so cleverly contrived that they could not be seen either from the cliff top or the beach below, and they were capable of taking dozens of casks.

Tunnels abound in smuggling tradition. At Rottingdean, the Rectory and the houses around the Green, and all supposed to have had tunnels. Also a West Worthing mansion, Courtlands, now a convalescent home, was supposed to have had a smugglers' tunnel. A mysterious tunnel called Huns Stables in Brighton, has been connected with the smugglers. It is, however, very difficult to pin these traditions down to actual fact. Many tunnels were used for legitimate purposes in Hastings, Eastbourne and Brighton. There are tunnels under the

Kings Road Brighton, for the passage of heavy goods from the beach to the houses on the other side of the road. Before the coming of the railways most heavy goods came by sea. At Brighton goods were unloaded on the beach and moved from there into the town. However, one tunnel in Brighton was used on one occasion by smugglers, and an account of it is given later. In Kent the numerous dene holes on the North Down were put to good use on many occasions.

There were many reputed underground passages in Sedlescombe, including ones to the Old Gun Cottage, The Manor and the churchyard. There is possible evidence of a passage from Beech House ending in a well, perhaps connected with a vault in the churchyard. Smugglers seem often to have arranged hiding places in churchyards; empty tombs made good entrances and they felt these places were avoided after dark.

They also liked and probably manufactured hauntings likely to discourage prying eyes. The Romney Marsh ghost with whom this book opens may well have been just such an invention. The headless lady at Old Erringham, the Dutchman at Copperas Gap, the Drummer at Herstmonsceux Castle are all ghosts that are alleged to appear in places that were noted smuggling centres in Sussex. Kent was not to be outdone. At Leysdown on the Isle of Sheppey a spectrial fisherman was supposed to rise out of the sea, shrouded in a net. The Aldington Gang were prolific in their stories. St. Bilsington Priory — a favoured storehouse — stories persist of a phantom monk with a red hat rosary and a bodyless head that floated down stairways. In more superstitious times than our own wonders could easily be done with a little phosphorus and weird masks especially if accompanied by a few carefully circulated rumours. Russell Thorndike makes full use of the idea with his demon scarecrow riders of Romney Marsh.

A lonely farmhouse at Fairlight had a tunnel leading down to the cliffs and hidden momentos of smugglers — a keg of brandy, changes of clothes for disguise, and decaying lace were found there. Certainly from the persistence of the many traditions, most smuggling centres had tunnels either leading to churchyards, or from house to house, so that a smuggler who had run into one house when being pursued could silently slip out of another one further down the village street.

The open countryside was often used as a hiding place, making use of natural dips in the ground and the growth of furze and bracken. Burwash Common was so used and there are many stories of caches in the bracken around Crowborough. One smuggler, taken as he was hiding his kegs in The Warren escaped as he was being taken to East Grinstead. Another, called Duke Read, whose strength and size were legendary also hid his goods in the heather here. Yet another, surprised by a Customs man, attacked the officer and left him for dead, covered in bracken along with his kegs. The officer, however, recovered and came later with twelve colleagues all in disguise to the local fair to catch his attacker. The smuggler's spy system was so good that the smuggler was warned and did not go to the fair and so escaped capture.

CHAPTER XIII

Decline

By 1840, smuggling had entered a decline: its great period was over, a period of activity that was part of the economic and social history of this country. Why did it begin, and why did it end? The prime reason was the search for profit, and it was possible to make that profit because during the eighteenth century England was almost continuously at war, and those wars had to be paid for. Therefore, taxes were placed on the luxuries that were now imported: it has been said, for example, that the tax on tobacco at the turn of seventeenth and eighteenth centuries paid for King William's Dutch wars, and after that there was an escalation of taxes on other goods to pay for the wars with France. Therefore, in the eighteenth century high taxes were placed on spirits, tea, laces and silks, and there were taxes on a huge range of commodities, and many items were forbidden to be imported or used at all. This combination of high prices and prohibition made an excellent climate for smuggling, and the proximity of the French coast allowed the smugglers to build up a very profitable trade importing luxuries. We have already looked at some of the prices paid for smuggled goods in early years, but even at the end of the period there were still good profits to be made. A smuggler told Lord Teignmouth that in the period 1815-40 he could buy brandy in France for £1 a tub, and £1 would cover all expenses. The fair trader, paying duty, had to lay out in all £6 for a tub.

There was, however, more to it than the simple urge to make a profit. This was a period when the entrepreneur spirit was gripping England, and the country was about to embark on a great surge of trading ventures. This spirit was felt by everybody, and there were many contemporary references to it. We need here quote only one notable example — the South Sea bubble. In 1711 — just at the time when smuggling was growing rapidly — Robert Harley, with the backing of the Bank of England and the East India Company founded the South Sea Company, to trade in the South Seas and South America. He took over the government's floating debt of £9,500,000 and got a monopoly trading right in return. All classes became obsessed with South Sea fever, and there were thousands of backers from every station in life. A little later the company took over £31,000,000 of the National Debt (and wished to take it all over). But trading faltered and the directors sold out, deserting their shareholders, the bubble burst and thousands were ruined absolutely. A member of Parliament collapsed and died after a row in the House of Commons, and the Hanoverian throne was shaken to its foundations, some doubting whether it could survive. This example will serve to show the attitude of mind, the boundless enthusiasm and optimism, the willingness to take on what we would consider to be the functions of government, which existed at that time. That these attitudes existed among the smugglers there is no doubt — when senior members of the gangs spoke it was often in terms of profit and loss.

The spirit of commercial enterprise was clearly shown in an old smuggler's conversation with Lord Teignmouth. Although a tub cost £1 in France, due to the exchange rates this amounted only to 18 shillings to the smuggler: furthermore the merchant selling the brandy always allowed one free tub in twenty as 'scorage'. All the backers of the run put two pounds each for the number of tubs they decided to run, £1 for purchase and £1 for expenses. This included a payment to the master and crew of the ship, 5 shillings a night for each porter and £1 a night for each batman. If the cargo was lost only the £1 purchase was paid, the ship's master only being paid on actual delivery. Some of the lesser organisers of the run would join in, pay for a few tubs and be happy with the smaller profit.

This commercial attitude to smuggling is doubly interesting when it is borne in mind that the age-old industries of Sussex — iron founding and fishing had withered away and there was little left but agriculture, which had its own difficulties. Iron founding diminished after the Restoration, and the last blast furnace in Sussex went out about 1810 — this is precisely the heyday of Sussex smuggling. Similarly fishing, which had been a flourishing industry in Tudor times, was badly affected from Stuart times onwards, as the fishing boats were often taken at sea by our enemies in the continual wars of the period, and also the actual coastline was altering by drift and erosion in a way that was not good for the beaching of boats and the fishing industry. Therefore, smuggling gave some employment to badly paid labourers who had only agricultural jobs to fall back on, and agriculture itself was going through a difficult period. The moderately prosperous yeoman farmers of previous years were having a difficult time for various reasons — prices, taxes, enclosures, and the painful introduction of farm machinery. It is no surprise, therefore, that a writer in *The Gentleman's Magazine* complained that local farmers could not get labour when the smugglers paid so much better for their twice weekly runs.

There was another reason for the growth of smuggling. The Far East was opening up to trade and enterprise and as a result new luxuries were coming into this country — fine furniture and porcelain, tea and coffee, silks and fine cloths. Even the taste for gin and brandy had been preceded by the opening up of the West Indies, with their rum exports, thus creating a taste for spirits. The middle and lower classes wished to participate in these wider horizons of material comforts, and to buy smuggled goods was one way of affording little luxuries.

Finally, there was a considerable element of rebellion in smuggling. Dr. Johnson, in his dictionary defined excise as 'a hateful tax levied on commodities . . . by . . . wretches hired by those to whom exise is paid'.

The dislike of the tax and the Exciseman was common in the smugglers' customers: in the smugglers themselves it extended to a willingness to flout the laws of the land and defy the government itself. We have already noted that some contemporary observers made a connection between the Swing riots of agricultural labourers and the habit of large crowds of men gathering together for smuggling. The Poor Law Commissioners noted, in their survey of Sussex in 1832, that Brede was a village noted for the fact that many of its farm labourers were also smugglers. The Commissioners went on to say that the farmers could not afford to pay the higher wages they had promised as a result of these riots, and went on to quote a Brede labourer. He said he knew the farmers could not afford higher wages, but, 'We shall now join together to get rid of tithes and taxes to enable them to do so.'

The men in the riots had often said it was not the farmers they blamed for their poor wages, but the taxes the farmers had to pay. It is very possible that many of the men who took part in the riots were even more actively withholding taxes from the government as part-time smugglers.

Having existed and thrived for centuries it seems odd that the smuggling trade should fade away as it did in such a comparatively short period. Why should this be? Not surprisingly it is not possible to point to a single cause for the decline — rather to a number of reasons which together made it unprofitable to continue on the old scale.

Towards the end of the eighteenth century the authorities began to show definite signs of real and intelligent determination to rid themselves of this drain on the revenues. In 1784, on the orders of William Pitt, the army occupied Deal and burnt the fishing boats on the beach whilst furious townsfolk were held at bayonet point and unable to prevent the destruction of their chief source of livelihood. The reason for this ruthless action was the open use of these 'Deal luggers' for smuggling. The burning must have been a great blow.

One of the few recorded occasions when the Revenue men had to struggle also comes from this period and is contained in the *Kentish Gazette*. The issue of June 8th, 1771 contains the following report:

> Last Tuesday a vessel appeared off Margate bound from Dunkirk to Chatham laden with rugs. An Excise Officer, having ignorantly boarded her, was informed by the Captain that he must bear him company during the performance of his quarantine, but the officer choosing to refer to a better authority, returned to shore and applied to the Customs-house Officer to know if the Act of Parliament remained still in force. The commendable mortification is better conceived than expressed when, we are informed, the officer and his

assistants were directed to return to the vessel and continue there during her quarantine! A number of the inhabitants assembled on the Pier, upon this occasion, to behalf the dejected quarantiners receiving from the sorrowful wives the necessary apparel, etc., for the time of their banishment. — The next morning the vessel sailed for Stangate Creek.

The paper published on July 6th contains the conclusion to the story:

> On Thursday last the excise officer and his assistants who went on board a vessel in Margate Roads from Dunkirk landed at Margate Pier the month for their performing quarantine being expired; they looked very shocking, having been forced to lay on nothing but the boards; but in searching the vessel they found three tubs of Geneva concealed, therefore, to revenge themselves on the Captain for his behaviour to them, they seized the vessel, and she is now ordered to Margate to be burned.

Notwithstanding these successes, as we have seen, the outbreak of the Napoleonic Wars worked very much to the advantage of the smuggling community and in the period that followed, the blockade forces took some considerable time to begin to get the situation under control. However, by the time of the establishment of the Coastguard in 1831, life for the smugglers was becoming very difficult indeed; those who would openly flout the law such as Ransley in Kent and Collins in Sussex having been successfully brought to justice. By 1848 the situation had improved to such a degree that it was felt that the Land Guard which had taken over the duties of the riding officers could be disbanded.

In addition to improved techniques on the part of the Coastguard, it has been suggested that the increase in the numbers of those who would inform for profit contributed greatly to the suppression of the trade. There can be little doubt that there is some truth in this. Nevertheless, smugglers had always been able to cope with new problems and we are forced to look for some other reason for the decline.

It is in changes in the law that the principal causes lie. The so called 'limit laws' added to the difficulties of those running contraband by making boats liable to detention or confiscation when found outside of their limits. A more important change, however, was the reduction in duties. The first half of the nineteenth century saw a steady movement towards official free trade and by 1860 it could be said that Britain was a free-trade country. Import duties had been completely repealed on most goods although fairly high rates still remained on tobacco and spirits.

Upon the outbreak of the Crimean War, 3,000 men of the Coastguard were enlisted into the Royal Navy and this move was followed by a complete transfer of the service to the Admiralty two years later. Despite this change, the chief function of the Coastguard remained the prevention of smuggling.

The retention of duties on spirits and tobacco meant that illegal import of these commodities continued to be widespread and the quantities, although not comparable with earlier times, were nevertheless considerable. In 1891, for instance, the Customs' return for the whole country shows that 16,756 pounds of tobacco and 239 gallons of spirits were seized. Kent no doubt contributed substantially to these figures. Tobacco was frequently smuggled into the country concealed inside 'free' goods. For example, in 1860, 1,000 lbs of tobacco was found hidden in tiercies of pickled port and 600 lbs concealed in six bales of hops. The engine rooms of the new fangled steam ships also provided numerous potential hiding places. In 1868, 630 lbs of tobacco was discovered stuffed in the pump casing of a ship from New York. Sinking and creeping however, continued to be the most favoured method for bringing in spirits.

In 1892 a specialist Waterguard service was re-introduced by the Board of Customs, its purpose being to deal with the new smuggling techniques. This new force was supported by a detective section, the terms of reference of which were to investigate conspiracies to defraud the Revenue and to endeavour to trace smuggled goods which had slipped through the net at the ports.

By the earlier twentieth century the nature of smuggling had changed little, although the quantities involved had diminished greatly. Tobacco continued to be a favoured item of contraband and was frequently brought in, concealed in the linings of suitcases or purpose-made waistcoats. We see clearly by this time the departure from the 'big business' approach and it might reasonably be said that the old trade was definitely a thing of the past. Indeed, between the wars the volume of incoming contraband appears to have reached its lowest point.

This, however, proved to be only a temporary lull and with the end of the Second World War, large-scale smuggling began again in earnest. The necessary restrictions imposed during the war resulted in great difficulty in obtaining some goods such as cosmetics, certain foodstuffs, jewellery and nylon stockings. Such goods became viable propositions for commercial smuggling. Old trickery such as false-bottomed suitcases and hollowed-out books were accompanied by new methods, like specially constructed compartments in motor vehicles, in the enthusiasm of latter day 'free traders' to make quick profits.

More striking, however, is the re-appearance of eighteenth century style 'runs', surplus naval motor torpedo boats becoming favoured craft for this purpose. One of these vessels, the *Dawn Approach* is known to have made twenty-three successful runs before being intercepted. On the occasion of her capture, her cargo was found to consist of some 13,000 watches. In addition to traditional seaboard landings such as these, the advent of air travel earlier this century had added a new dimension to the smuggling business. Kent of course holds a significant place in the history of international air travel, it being at Dover that Monsieur Louis Bleriot landed at the end of the first cross Channel flight in 1909. It is interesting to note that a Customs inspection of M. Bleriot's aeroplane was carried out on that historic occasion and the official concerned treated the aircraft as a yacht and issued a quarantine certificate.

The potential of the aircraft as a smuggling vehicle was not overlooked and the clandestine scenes that had taken place for so many centuries along the coast came to be re-enacted in out-of-the-way fields where pilots as skilled in their art as the seamen smugglers of yesteryear had been in theirs, guided their craft down to land on temporary air strips and the contraband hastily unloaded and whisked away to safe hides.

Relaxation of restrictions in the post-war period meant that this upsurge in smuggling activity on a wide scale was comparatively short lived. However, whilst import duties are retained, some smuggling will always be bound to occur. The present pattern involves most high value commodities such as cameras and watches being brought into the country through the airports and it follows that since Kent has no major international airport, such smuggling in the county is on a fairly small scale. Large quantities of tobacco and spirits continue to be smuggled through the sea-ports and this remains a problem for the Customs authorities.

Not all would-be smugglers are as successful or ingenious as their forerunners. On March 25th, 1969 the *Kent Messenger* carried the story of four men who had attempted to use a former Customs launch to try to smuggle 160,000 cigars via Faversham Creek. An earlier attempt had ended when the vessel being used had sunk. On the occasion reported they had run aground in the Creek. It got free but was boarded shortly afterwards by Customs officials and the illegal cargo seized.

By far the most sinister development in recent years, however, is the rise which has occurred in the smuggling of dangerous drugs. No matter how violent and ruthless the smugglers of earlier times, it cannot be doubted that the goods brought in to the country did no more than provide a little welcome luxury to what were in the main very austere lives. In contrast, modern drug smugglers deal in human misery and exploitation of those misguided enough to come within their web. Whatever view the reader may have formed of those old-time desperadoes it seems clear that should there in the future be written a retrospective look at the smugglers of the second half of the twentieth century, there will be no doubt as to the true nature of these criminals.

Whatever the trends of the future, it is certain that the Scarecrow's Legion will never again ride the Romney Marsh and whilst that is probably a good thing we cannot help but regret the passing of a romantic figure, undeserved as the romance for the most part was. Whatever his faults the smuggler has provided a wealth of stories, both exciting and amusing. In Lydd Churchyard is the grave of George Walker, the smuggler cut down so ruthlessly by Lieutenant Peatt. His epitaph reads thus:

Let it be known that I am clay,
A base man took my life away
Yet freely do I him forgive
And hope in heaven we both shall live.

May we not so freely forgive those old-time rogues. True, incidents such as the Chater and Galley murders plumbed the depths of human depravity and violence and bribery were rife. But this must be set against a century and a half of economic decline, continuous and damaging war and a brutal penal system. The real villain was the continuous stupidity of successive governments who put high taxes on goods everyone wanted and yet were too mean to support a good preventive force. So perhaps the smuggling phenomenon was just part of the growing pains of a nation.

Stay reader, before judging! What will the twenty-second century make of terrorism, vandalism or drunken driving! In an imperfect world there is perhaps little that really changes.

Glossary

Anker (or Anchor)	A small tub containing gallons of spirits
Bat	A long stave used by fighting parties to repel attack by Revenue forces
Blockade	Naval force established in 1817 to prevent smuggling
Carvel built	A vessel the hull of which was smooth being constructed of planks laid edge to edge
Clinker built	A vessel constructed of overlapping planks
Collector	The chief Customs officer in a major port
Comptroller	An official immediately subordinate to a Collector
Cutter	A single-masted ship rigged fore and aft with a bowsprit
Dragoon	A mounted soldier
Farmer	An early collector of Customs duties
Flasher	A flintlock pistol with the barrel swan off and used for signalling by smugglers
Frock	A countryman's smock
Galley	An undecked boat propelled by oarsmen (sometimes also equipped with sails)
Geneva	Dutch brandy introduced to England in the reign of William of Orange (gin)
Landguard	A branch of the Revenue force consisting of the riding officers
Landsman	A member of the Blockade based ashore who undertake a nightly foot patrol along a certain part of the coast
Lugger	Two- or three-masted vessel rigged with four-cornered sails laid fore and aft
Midshipman	A Royal Naval officer cadet
Owler	A wool smuggler
Riding officer	A mounted Customs official armed with a sword and pistols usualy patrolling alone
Rowing guard	A waterborne patrol sent out by the various Blockade stations
Sinking and creeping	A method of concealing contrabrand by sinking it in deep water and later recovering it by means of a kind of grappling hook
Sloop	Single-masted vessel rigged fore and aft
Surveyor	The chief officer of a Customs district
Tide-surveyor	The preventive officer in charge of a boarding crew
Tide-waiter	A Customs officer who boarded and searched vessels after they docked

APPENDIX I

In the steps of the smugglers (gazetteer of smuggling locations)

By the town pier at Gravesend stands THE THREE DAWES public house, the oldest 'pub' in the town and one much frequented by smugglers and seafaring men in its time. Formerly three subterranean tunnels are said to have led from here providing convenient escape routes for those wishing to escape the unwelcome attentions of the Revenue and press gangs. These tunnels have, however, been sealed off. At the rear is the old Pilots' House which boasts seven staircases constructed to confuse the Customs officials.

Leaving Gravesend and travelling east a short drive through country lanes will bring you to St. Mary's Hoo out on the Hoo peninsula. From here a walk along the public footpaths leading across the marshes will be rewarded with fine views of SHADES HOUSE used by the North Kent Gang and a sight of EGYPT BAY a favoured landing place of that notorious band.

Eight miles south of Gravesend and at the summit of Wrotham Hill stands THE VIGO INN where, during alterations a secret bolt hole was discovered where smugglers hid both themselves and their contraband. The Wrotham area was an important staging point for smuggled goods being run inland from the coast, the numerous dene holes being utilised for storage. Continue down the hill to Wrotham village and see THE BULL HOTEL, a coaching inn which was well used by a gang with a gentleman leader, one Lieutenant Colonel Shadwell who was shot by an army deserter on June 1st, 1799. Shadewell's smuggling associates wasted no time in capturing the murderer and his companion and duly beat them to death. A stone set into the wall alongside this hotel commemorates the incident.

From Wrotham it is only a short journey to West Peckham. On a hill close to the village are the ruins of DIAMONDS COTTAGE. This was the home of Jack Diamond a highwayman and member of the Hawkhurst Gang involved in the Poole raid. The cottage was destroyed by fire on a Friday the 13th and Diamond's ghost has been reported as appearing occasionally on this day.

Horsmonden is a picturesque village and was the home of William Fairall, a prominent member of the Hawkhurst Gang and here his body was hung in chains at one end of the road still known as GIBBET LANE although the gibbet has long since gone.

Four miles from Horsmonden is Goudhurst where one can see numerous reminders of the infamous Hawkhurst Gang. At the top of the High Street the PARISH CHURCH was used as a hiding place for smuggled goods and a tunnel is said to run from here to the nearby STAR AND EAGLE Inn, a favourite haunt of the gang. It was at this end of the High Street that the villagers led by William Sturt erected barricades and made their stand. George Kingsmill is buried in the churchyard where he was shot during the affray. A little way down the hill the attractive 'SPYWAYS' was the principal headquarters of the gang whilst under the command of Thomas Kingsmill. To Goudhurst Gore Kingsmill's body was brought to be hung in chains after his execution at Tyburn.

At Sissinghurst visit THE BULL, a pleasing hostelry with an escape hatch disguised as a cupboard in one of the rear rooms used by both smugglers and highwaymen.

At Hawkhurst still stands the OAK AND IVY the headquarters of the Hawkhurst Gang when Arthur Gray was captain. This inn was another key point for illicit goods being transported from Romney Marsh to London (and ultimately to Abingdon, near Oxford the main centre of distribution for organised smuggling throughout the golden era of Kentish free trade).

Along the A268 from Hawkhurst and just across the border between Kent and Sussex is the ancient town of Rye. Here the narrow cobbled streets and quaint old buildings retain the distinctive smack of the sea despite the fact that the watery element has retreated a considerable distance from the town. Much that was inevitably connected with smuggling survives but be sure to see the MERMAID INN in Mermaid Street which was another haunt of the Hawkhurst Gang and other members of the smuggling fraternity. WATCHBELL STREET figures prominently in one of the Doctor Syn stories.

From Rye travel back over the border into Kent to Dymchurch. On the way along the A259 one passes through BROOKLAND where the Aldington Gang fought a bloody battle with the Revenue forces in 1821. A short detour from the main road will take one through both SNARGATE where Barham was rector and IVYCHURCH. The parish churches of these villages were frequently used for concealing contraband. Standing by St. George's at Ivychurch is THE BELL which has a long smuggling tradition. At one time almost the only customers were owlers and free traders.

Dymchurch itself is, alas, much changed since the Doctor Syn days, being now a rather brash resort. There is still, however, much to interest the discerning visitor. THE SHIP HOTEL is well worth a look, for it figures prominently in the Syn stories and was in reality a smuggler's haunt. As the one time meeting place for the local coroner's court it saw many inquests into the cases of violent death caused by smuggling activity but it has been 'improved' in recent years and unfortunately the hidy hole behind one of the chimney breasts which was found at that time containing an old store of smuggled spirits has gone. There are, however, a number of interesting

'The Smugglers Leap.'

smuggling illustrations on the wall and a very pleasant atmosphere. Anyone staying upstairs will find things very little changed by time. The story that a tunnel links the hotel to the parish church opposite is, apparently, untrue. Incidentally the line of the Dymchurch to Hythe road had been changed and the 'back' of The Ship is really the front!

In the churchyard many of the old gravestones bear names of characters used by Russell Thorndike in the Doctor Syn books.

NEW HALL standing alongside the church houses a small prison cell. This again is mentioned in the Syn saga and in reality was used to accommodate captured smugglers pending trial and punishment. On the subject of punishment the gallows stood on the spot now occupied by the war memorial.

Along the coast road from Dymchurch is Hythe another ancient borough of the Cinque Ports and a place with much of interest. THE RED LION is a coaching inn mentioned occasionally in the Doctor Syn stories. THE BELL on the Folkestone Road is reputed to be the oldest pub in Hythe. There is the almost inevitable tunnel in the cellar and at one time a mill stream ran under the premises via which smuggled brandy and rum were floated in and the kegs could be hidden from sight by being hung from a hook in the ceiling.

Journeying inland from Hythe it is only a few miles to Woodchurch. Several members of the Ransley Gang lived here and a great battle between the Gang and the Revenue took place on the Green in 1826. THE SIX BELLS stood here then and has, of course, some concealed cellars. Almost next door is the interestingly named BONNY CRAVAT public house. This was used at one time by itinerant justices as a courtroom and some smugglers are said to have been sentenced to death here and duly executed on a gallows which apparently stood just outside. One explanation of the unusual name is that the pub was called after the smuggling vessel *Bonne Cravate*.

At nearby Aldington itself is THE WALNUT TREE the principal headquarters of the Ransley Gang in the 1820's. It retains its old world charm and has a tiny spyhole with a commanding view of Romney Marsh. The inn sign depicts a smuggler (George Ransley himself perhaps?) in pursuit of his business.

In the churchyard are the graves of Ransley's brothers, executed at Penenden Heath for highway robbery.

Leaving Romney Marsh and travelling north east to the Isle of Thanet the A253 takes one close to Acol and a deep quarry, the scene of Barham's poem 'The Smuggler's Leap'. The poem was based on a legend referred to in the following extract from the *History of Thanet* by the Rev. Samuel Pegge (published 1796):

> Near this hamlet is a long disused chalk-pit of formidable depth known by the name of 'The Smuggler's Leap'. The tradition of the parish runs that a riding officer from Sandwich, called Anthony Gill, lost his life in the early part of the present (18th) century, while in pursuit of a smuggler. A fog coming on both parties went over the precipice. The smuggler's horse only, it is said was found crushed beneath its rider. The spot has of course been haunted ever since.

Along the sea front at the very eastern end of Herne Bay is THE SHIP INN. Once again this was a regular retreat for smugglers and an establishment which benefited greatly from the 'trade'. It was here that Midshipman Snow was shot dead during a fight with the North Kent Gang in 1821, an incident which increased pressure on the gang and contributed in no small measure to their downfall. Snow is buried in the churchyard at nearby Herne. In addition to the grave of the unfortunate victim the reader will find interest in the SMUGGLERS INN situated in this pleasant village. Surprisingly, for a pub so blatently named this one does have real connections with the trade. Some sixty years ago the cellar was deepened and a cache of four casks of spirit was discovered. The Revenue made up for lost time and seized the lot! The pub has a distinctly nautical flavour.

If visiting the Isle of Sheppey a trip to WARDEN POINT (turn north of Eastchurch) is worthwhile, not only for the very fine views across the estuary but also for a look at the village Post Office which was notorious as the Smack Aground Inn, another base for the North Kent Gang. It was also used by a gang of wreckers led by a landlord's son who was eventually transported to Van Dieman's Land. At Warden there is also a modern Coastguard station.

Inland to Maidstone and take the A20 to Lenham and thence south to Grafty Green where THE KINGS HEAD has smuggling connections. By local tradition it was once the haunt of one Dover Bill. The Revenue are said to have surprised Bill and his crew in the pub. A running battle followed ending at Chiston Park where all the smugglers except Bill were captured. The gang were 'turned off' at Penenden Heath which Dover Bill watched from the crowd. None of his neighbours or friends ever spoke to him again.

APPENDIX 2

Chronology of significant dates in the smuggling story

742 Charter by King Ethelbald — first recorded grant of rights to collect customs duties.
1100 Reputed flooding of the Low Countries causing influx of Flemish Refugees to Kent the descendants of whom were to found the smuggling trade.
1203 Centralisation of Customs duty by King John and imposition of export duty on wool (tax known as the 'quindecima' at this time).
1275 Foundation of the true Customs service by Edward I with the introduction of the 'nova costuma' (new custom) and appointment of three tier system of collection, i.e. 'customers (collectors), controllers and chercheurs (searchers)'. Creation of 'farming' system.
1436 Certain wharves specified as having exclusive right to export wool.
1671 End of 'farming' system. Appointment of first Board of Commissioners.
1688 The Glorious Revolution — war with the Netherlands resulting in imposition of higher taxes on tea and spirits and giving impetus to smuggling.
Unsuccessful attempt by William Carter to bring certain smugglers to justice.
1735 Farmers forced to raise wages to entice farm labourers out of service with the smugglers and back to the land.
1736 Passing of the Smuggling Act.
1739 Murder (allegedly by North Kent Gang) at Binney Farm Allhallows.
1740 Rise to prominence of Hawkhurst Gang.
1746 Royal Commission on Smuggling.
1747 Defeat of Hawkhurst Gang by Goudhurst Militia.
Attack on Poole Customs House led by principal members of the Hawkhurst Gang and murder of William Galley and Daniel Chater.
1748 Reputed execution of Arthur Gray, original leader of the Hawkhurst Gang — unconfirmed.
1749 Execution of Thomas Kingsmill, William Fairall and other members of Hawkhurst Gang.
1784 Burning of Deal Luggers by army on orders of William Pitt.
1809 Introduction of Preventive Water Guard.
1814 Murder of Sheppey man (identity unknown) reputedly by members of North Kent Gang.
1815 End of Napoleonic Wars.
1817 Establishment of Kent Coast Blockade.
1820 Skirmish between North Kent Gang and Blockade forces at Stangate Creek
Attack by Folkestone townsfolk on Dover Gaol to release smugglers.
Battle between Blockade forces and Aldington Gang at Sandgate.
1821 Murder of Midshipman Snow at Herne Bay by North Kent Gang.
Battle between Blockade forces and Aldington Gang at Brookland. Unsuccessful attempt by Aldington Gang to murder Lieutenant Peat.
1822 Execution of ringleaders of North Kent Gang at Penenden Heath — transportation of less important members.
1823 Capture of the *Four Brothers* smuggling vessel and unsuccessful attempt to convict crew of firing on a King's ship.
1826 Arrest of George Ransley — leader of the Aldington Gang.
1827 Transportation of Ransley.
1831 Blockade disbanded and replaced by Coastguard.
1848 Landguard disbanded.
1848–60 Move towards free trade.
1860 Waterguard officers (tidewaiters) merged with waterside officers (land waiters).
1892 Re-introduction of Waterguard service and introduction of Revenue detective section.
1905 Customs personnel undertake work of immigration control.
1909 Beginning of cross Channel aviation with consequent increase in scope for smuggling.
Amalgamation of Customs and Excise services.
1923 Coastguard disbanded as a Revenue force and replaced with the Coast Preventive Service.
1932 End of free trade.
1945 End of Second World War and increase in smuggling activity.
1952 Passing of Customs and Excise Act containing current law appertaining to the crime of smuggling.

APPENDIX 3

Doctor Syn

'Eyes deep, piercing and alive. Hair raven black. Tall, slim and weird, with a brooding melancholy that faded only when he smiled, and that because his smile conveyed a princely graciousness, and a pledge of loyal friendship to the fortunate recipient. . . . A Doctor of Divinity. A priest. But more than all a man of high romance.'

Thus described does Doctor Christopher Syn stride, or rather gallop, into the pages of English literature. The character first appeared in 1915 in a book entitled simply *Doctor Syn*. This was intended to be a single novel and the author Russell Thorndike killed the character off at the end. However, such was the public response to the smuggler parson with his demon nightriders that Thorndike had to delve into the character's earlier life to provide fresh adventures. A further six novels in the saga followed, these following Syn's career chronologically from shortly after his creation as a Doctor of Divinity at Oxford in about 1754 until the year 1793, the original novel being tacked on the end (taking place at about the turn of the eighteenth century) to round the whole story off.

What of the character, this famous son of Kent? Well son of Kent he certainly was, born and bred. The family of Syn (entirely Thorndike's creation) were it seems great land-owning lawyers originating from Lydd with a family history going back to at least Tudor times. They were also Jacobites, Christopher's father, Septimus Syn, together with three of his brothers, were killed upholding the Stewart cause at Culloden. Syn's mother died in the same year, 'of a broken heart, it was said'. From this short history we are able to see that Christopher, being just fifteen years old at the sudden demise of most of his family, was born in 1731. He was, however, well provided for and under the guardianship of his sole remaining uncle, Solomon Syn, soon achieved prominence as a scholar at Oxford.

From such dry beginnings, however, circumstances combine to send the young Doctor on a path along which he must fight duels, become a pirate (the infamous Clegg), live with Red Indians and finally, following his return to the village of Dymchurch, from which his journeyings had begun, to turn smuggler giving birth to the infamous Scarecrow. Through all this Syn emerges as a most complex character. A man of great accomplishments, indeed it is probably true to say, perhaps a little too good for the modern reader; an invincible swordsman, equally superb with pistol and knife, exceptional horseman, fine athlete, marvellous sailor, expert swimmer, scholar, wit and, of course — lover. It is, however, in this last that we find the first chink in his armour, it being an unhappy love that first sends him off a-pirating. As the character develops so does Syn appear more difficult to understand. A kind of Jeckyl and Hyde figure who as himself, Christopher Syn, is capable of writing a book entitled 'A Solemn Discourse of Religious Assemblies and the Public Service of God, According to Apostolical Rule and Practice' and who travels the marsh comforting the sick and wretched and yet, as the Scarecrow, will hang a man out of hand for treachery or order the murder of an over-zealous excise officer with no sign of remorse.

It is, however, all too easy to get carried away with an investigation of the psychology of the whole thing. What is more important is that the stories are themselves fast moving and ingenious, tales of romance, daring and high adventure. They are peopled by a number of unforgettable characters in addition to Syn himself. The notorious, yet gallant highwayman, Jimmie Bone, the blustery squire Anthony Cobtree, the dry old doctor Sennacherib Pepper and of course the wily Sexton Mipps.

It is uncertain now how the character of Syn came to be created by Thorndike. In the preface to *Doctor Syn* the author's sister, Sybil Thorndike, makes reference to a trip to Spartanburg, South Carolina, when a murder occurred outside the hotel where she and himself were staying and the two of them sat up all night 'too frightened to go to bed' and Russell began to unfold the doings of the widowed vicar. Of course, whether or not this was the first inkling of the character for Thorndike himself we will probably never know. What we do know is that although born in Rochester he had a great affection for Romney Marsh and an association with the area going back well before he settled there in the early 1920's. Thorndike made many friends amongst the locals of Dymchurch and would sit for hours in 'The Ship' drinking with them and hearing yarns about their parents and grandparents' exploits in outwitting the Revenue men. Many of these stories are undoubtedly woven into the Syn saga. References to the Ransleys of Aldington, although inaccurate in the context in which they appear do, of course, have a firm foundation in truth. The use of French ports by the smugglers at a time when war between Britain and France was the usual state of affairs also occurred much as illustrated by Thorndike. Furthermore there really was a ship called *The City of London* which was wrecked in Dymchurch Bay as described in *Doctor Syn Returns* and the figurehead did stand in Wraights building yard until quite recently.

As to the characters, some of the names are taken from tombstones and church burial records. Notably Sennacharib Pepper, the village doctor, appears to be inspired by an eighteenth century villager Soloman Pepper, whose grave occupies a prominent position in the churchyard. Henry, one of the three Upton brothers referred to in *Doctor Syn Returns* was one of Thorndike's drinking partners and one of the few still living who can recall hearing the old smuggling stories direct from the participants. Mipps it seems was based upon a local who doubled as sexton and school caretaker at the time when Thorndike was first becoming familiar with Dymchurch.

As for Syn himself, whether or not there was any original character is by no means certain. The clergy did, of course, have a long association with the smuggling trade. Barham notably appears to have been a sympathiser. Thorndike himself admitted also that there was a parallel between his character and Conan Doyle's Sherlock Holmes. 'The eyes deep and searching.... The nose high with an aquiline droop', a description of Syn which might equally fit the sleuth of Baker Street. In an interview given to the *Kent Messenger*, Thorndike said, 'In the first Dr. Syn book I killed him off at the end, just as Holmes was killed off. I remember comparing notes with Sir Arthur Conan Doyle later about our readers' pleas to bring our characters back to life.' No matter what the sources of the inspiration Doctor Syn remains the unique creation of his inventor.

Thorndike also drew inspiration from the locality itself, most of the action taking place in and around Dymchurch. At that time Dymchurch retained its old charm and quaintness although most (but happily not quite all) of this was destroyed as the village sought to cash in on the holiday trade. He was undoubtedly aware of the legend that the 'Ship Inn' was linked to the church by a tunnel and of the interesting history of New Hall.

The Doctor Syn Saga was completed by Thorndike by 1944. That was by no means the end of the character's growth however. In 1936 a film of the doings at Dymchurch was produced by London Films Ltd. Two further films followed in the mid 1960's, these being surrounded by a certain amount of controversy. Hammer Films had bought out the London Film Company and commenced a re-make of the original film version. Meanwhile, however, Walt Disney Productions had acquired the rights to the other books (and to a novel entitled *Christopher Syn* by William Buchanan which appeared in America in 1959) and were able to produce their version 'Doctor Syn Alias the Scarecrow' in advance of Hammer. Litigation followed with Hammer losing and having to re-dub the script and substitute the name 'Blyns' for 'Syn'. Thus was the character of Syn lost to America.

The renewed interest in the character caused by the films roughly coincided with Dymchurch's own tribute — an inclusion of a Syn pageant in their annual fete. Such was the success of this event that a bi-annual 'Day of Syn' now occurs regularly in which all the villagers dress in eighteenth-century costume and the part of the Scarecrow is taken by the current rector of the parish. The beach and the Hythe end of the village form the centre of the day's attractions and on the Sunday before the Bank Holiday the villagers dress up to take part in an eighteenth-century church service with Mipps sitting at the foot of the pulpit.

And so Syn and the Scarecrow still live in the hearts of those with a sense of romance and adventure and the dreaded song of Clegg is yet heard in Dymchurch-under-the-Wall:

> Here's to the feet wot have walked the plank—
> Yo-ho! for the dead man's throttle.
> And here's to the corpses afloat in the tank,
> And the dead man's teeth in the bottle.

[The author wishes to acknowledge the considerable assistance given by Barry Marsh in the preparation of these notes.]

APPENDIX 4

The following account appeared in the *Folkestone Express* in 1875 and is based on a verbal account by E. Dole, an old smuggler.

The cruise of The Four Brothers

by JOHN ENGLISH

The capture of the lugger *The Four Brothers*, by the *Badger* revenue cutter, after an obstinate resistance on the part of the crew of the lugger caused a great sensation throughout Great Britain, and the event has undoubtedly originated many of the stories about sea-fights with smugglers which have come from the pens of novel writers. The facts have been very much distorted, but the following version, coming from the lips of a recently deceased member of the crew, may be accepted as a truthful account. At the time of the occurrence, in January, 1823, the narrator was in his 23rd year, and at the time of the narration he was in his 80th year. His memory was singularly clear, even on the most minute details of the fight and the subsequent events. As nearly as possible he told me the story as follows:

'I was born in 1800, and went to sea when about 13 years old, in fishing boats. When about 20, I joined a crew of smugglers, which brought much better pay. We had a guinea a week standing money, and for every successful voyage we had ten guineas. I had made several trips to the coast of Ireland, without meeting with any remarkable adventure. We never had much difficulty in running our cargo ashore, and the Irish people very quickly got it out of the way. Our lugger was a smart craft, and a very fast sailer. She had been a privateer, but was captured by an English vessel, and sold at Southampton. An old Folkestoner bought her and after making some alterations, fitted her out for smuggling. She was manned principally by Folkestone men, and my uncle had command of her, the crew numbering in all 26. On the 12th January, 1823, we sailed from Flushing, with a cargo of leaf tobacco, upwards of a hundred tons, in half bales of 60lb. besides a few kegs of brandy, and I have heard the ship and cargo were valued at more than £10,000. It used to be the practice to have whole bales, but these were unwieldy, and so they were made up specially in smaller bundles. A very light wind was blowing; we had got a new mainmast, and were only about half rigged, so that we sailed slowly. Just before daylight on the 13th we were abreast of Dieppe. It was just before seven, and suddenly we found ourselves close to what we supposed were French fishing vessels. Without any suspicion of danger we held on our course, when suddenly one of the cutters, which we then knew was a revenue cutter, ran up her flag, and fired a gun to bring us to. We felt that we were in for it, but our captain determined to make every effort to beat the cutter off, and get away. If our rigging had been complete we should have had no difficulty, but the cutter outsailed us. We tacked, and the cutter did the same, and firing was kept up on both sides. We carried four guns, but the cutter had more, and they were bigger than ours, which of course gave her great advantage. As soon as the firing begun, we hoisted Dutch colours, and the fight was kept up, as far as I can remember, for a couple of hours. The fierceness of the battle may be gathered from the fact that out of our crew of 26, four were killed and six wounded; how many of the *Badger's* crew were hit, I cannot tell, but one was killed. To avoid our fire they kept below, but all our men were obliged to be on deck to work the vessel. But from the first we had no chance, and presently the cutter drove her bowsprit through our mainsail, effectually barring our escape. We determined to fight to the last, and to sink our vessel rather than be taken, for we knew what the consequences would be. While the two vessels were thus in contact, we thought the day had turned in our favour. Our biggest gun almost touched the cutter's bows, and we attempted to fire it. I have never known why it was, but all our efforts were unavailing, and the piece would not go off, or the cutters bows must have been blown in. Seeing the critical position of his ship, the commander of the cutter called out to us to surrender, and promised that we should have our boats and clothing, and go on shore. He was an English officer, and we trusted to his honour, but the mean hound was playing us a trick. We packed all our clothing, got into our boats with our bags, and rowed away, sorrowfully leaving behind one of our comrades dead. But when about a quarter of a mile away, the cutter's boats came after us to force us to return. We knew then what was meant, for without arms, what could we do against two boats full of armed men? Sadly enough, we rowed back again, and for more than an hour we parlayed with the cutter's officers. It was no good, however, and we were at last compelled to go on board. Our lugger was taken into Dover Harbour, and the killed were buried in the churchyard there. We had a sorry time of it for some days. The cutter put us aboard of the *Severn* man-o-war, where three others of our crew died, and the rest were kept in irons in the cockpit, the cold all the time being intense. After some days the cutter took us off again, and carried us up the Thames, where we were confined on the Tower tender for three of four days, and then, handcuffed and chained in an old barge, taken ashore, and lodged in the King's Bench Prison. Next day we were all taken to Bow Street, and committed for trial for wilful murder, but before our trial we laid for eleven weeks in the King's Bench.'

The old sailor told me several stories of different matters which occurred while they were confined in gaol, and spoke well of the kindly treatment they received at the hands of the gaolers. They were aware from the first that the defence would be that they were Dutchmen, and were warned to speak as little English as possible, which injunction they carried out. They were all confined in one ward, and allowed to have what they chose in the way of food, and the Governor of the Gaol had a pew constructed in the chapel adjoining his own for their accommodation. Nothing was allowed to be cooked, however, in the ward, and the old man related with great glee how on one occasion a leg of pork had been frizzled before a fierce fire by their friends outside to give it the appearance of being cooked, and then stowed away to be properly finished on Sunday. But while it was roasting, the chief warder paid them a visit, and they were afraid their savoury joint would be seized. Their uniform good behaviour, however, saved their dinner: in fact they seem to have been allowed to do pretty much as they liked, prison discipline not being then so rigidly enforced as it is now. Another remarkable incident, which they quite failed to account for, was this. During their long stay in the prison, they had never seen a single rat, although the place was known to be swarming, and the massive door, studded with iron bolts, left a space of two or three inches at the bottom. But during the last night of their stay, the smugglers were infested with rats to such an extent that they were obliged to their beds to protect themselves. Naturally enough the superstitious among them took this visit of the rats as an ill-omen. But to finish the story.

On Friday, the 25th of April, the twenty-two prisoners were arraigned before Lord Stowell (chief Judge of the High Court of Admiralty), Mr. Justice Park, and Mr. Baron Hullock, In the words of an informant, 'the Court was packed so full that there wasn't room to move. The dock wouldn't near hold us, so some had seats along the front outside, and we took turns at sitting. They didn't try us for murder, as it was expected they would, all our friends being afraid we should be hung. But they tried us for firing at a King's ship. We had two of the best men in England to defend us, Mr. Brougham and Mr. Lushington, and our solicitor told us beforehand they were sure of winning. Of course there was lying on both sides; there was a great number of witnesses, and the trial lasted two whole days. At six o'clock on Saturday evening we were discharged, the jury having decided that most of the crew were Dutchmen. If we hadn't been turned into Dutchmen we should all have been hung, but they couldn't hang one and not the others. There was tremendous cheering and excitement when we got into the street. The first thing to be done then was to get the news home to Folkestone. Accordingly a mounted messenger was engaged, and riding hard all the way, he reached here about one o'clock in the morning. Next day (Sunday) we all started for Folkestone, some by the Dover and the others by the Folkestone coach. People knew what time to expect us, and when we got to Sandgate it seemed as though all Folkestone turned out to meet us. The church bells were rang, I have heard, but cannot say whether it was so, our heads being completely turned at our reception.'

At the close of his narration, the old man said, 'I never went smuggling again after that. My father took the lugger out of Dover harbour, and sailed her back to Flushing, the *Badger* cutter having to escort her, and thousands of people were present to see them depart. What became of the cargo I can't say. But it may have been carried safely to Ireland after all.'

After the foregoing appeared, the editor of the *Folkestone Express* was requested by may old inhabitants of Folkestone to republish the report of the trial, which was so notable that the newspapers of those days reported it very fully. A visit to the British Museum was necessary for this purpose, and in the *Globe* the following account of the memorable trial was found.

On Friday , April 25th, 1823 the men who were engaged in the fight with the *Badger* revenue cutter in the previous January, were tried at the sessions for the trial of offences committed on the high seas within the jurisdiction of the High Court of Admiralty. The Court assembled at the Justice Hall in the Old Bailey, the judges being Lord Stowell (chief judge), Mr. Justices Park, and Mr. Baron Hullock.

The grand jury having returned a true bill against Marinel Krans (37), Carle Kulke (30), William Dangerfield (18), Yan Schmidt, otherwise John Smith (31), Jacob Bodileau, otherwise Jacob Peters (26), Yan Lampe, otherwise Jeremiah Watson (33), Martin Kappee (34), Yan Vannees, otherwise John Eastwicke, otherwise Essex (22), John Harrison (27), Yan Yenner, otherwise William Wills (22) — the old man referred to — Vollin Marree, otherwise Joseph Millon (32), Yan de Friere (26), Kiest Mollinaar (24), Henfric de Breyne, otherwise Thomas Feswicke (25), Yan de Frenchberg, otherwise John Greenland (32), Jonathan Vandyke, otherwise John Kallee (24), Yan Crat, otherwise John Mallee (55), Hendrick Allason, otherwise Richard Boxer, Yan de Frenark, otherwise Brenald Eastwicke, otherwise Essex, Cornelius Reymer, otherwise Joseph Wills (38), and Abraham de Mollinaar (24), the prisoners were immediately put to the bar, charged with wilfully and feloniously firing on the revenue cutter, the *Badger*, on the 13th of January, 1823, on the high seas, about eight miles off Dungeness, within the jurisdiction of the High Court of Admiralty of England.

The indictment contained nine counts charging the offence to have been differently committed.

Krans, Kulke, Brobileau, Kappee, and the two Mollinaars had the benefit of a Dutch interpreter, and all the prisoners pleaded not guilty.

The Attorney General, Mr. Bolland, Sir C. Robinson, Mr. Gurney, Mr. Jervis, and Mr. Shepherd, appeared for the Crown; Mr. Broughan (afterwards Lord Brougham), Dr. Lushington, Mr. Adolphus, and Mr. Platt for the prisoners.

(An affidavit was put in stating that a material witness in the case, Mary Jane Graves, had absented herself from the fear of being illtreated in consequence of the evidence she would give. An officer was accordingly sent to protect her; but there is no mention of any evidence having been given by this woman.)

Mr. Shepherd opened the case, and Sir C. Robinson then addressed the jury, and during his address the grand jury returned a true bill of indictment against all the prisoners for wilful murder.

The first witness called for the Crown was Lieut. Henry Nazer, who said he was a lieutenant in His Majesty's Navy, and on the 13th January had a commission from the excise and was commander of the *Badger* revenue cutter, and stationed off Dungeness on the coast of Kent to prevent smuggling. About half-past seven in the morning, in consequence of something said by the men on watch, he observed a suspicious sail, yawl rigged. She appeared to be from a foreign port, and was on the leeward tack. The *Badger* was about eight or nine leagues from the coast of France. On observing the strange sail, witness immediately made sail after her. She tacked, and witness seeing her on her beam, tacked also and came near her about nine o'clock in the morning, and hoisted the revenue pennant at the mast head. The flags had been hoisted before the unshotted gun was fired to bring her to. A shotted gun was then fired, and in about ten minutes a second gun, which was returned by the chase from one of her stern guns. She had no colours flying up to this time. Witness continued firing, and it was kept up on both sides until nearly half-past eleven, when witness ran her on board on the starboard quarter. The action was continued for about ten minutes, when quarter was called for in English by the greater part of the crew. Witness particularly noticed Cornelius Reymer, who asked forgiveness, and said he hoped witness would look over what had happened. He spoke in good English. Witness said he would, and the firing stopped for ten minutes or a quarter of an hour. Witness ordered a boat to be lowered, and while this was being done, the strange vessel commenced firing again. The cutter had not fired again before this. The consequence was that William Cullum, a reputed mariner, was killed as he was standing by the windlass. The crew of the strange vessel again called for quarter in plain English, which was again promised, and firing was not renewed. Witness then ordered the boat to be lowered, and sent the mate and some of the crew on board the strange vessel. The mate sent the prisoners on board the cutter in their own boat. Seven of them were wounded; one died the next morning. Witness put the prisoners on board the *Severn* on the following day. On board the strange vessel, witness found two of the crew dead. Her burthen was about 119 tons. Six or seven men would be the ordinary number of her crew. There were about 8000 bales of tobacco, marked 60lbs. each. There was also foreign gin and brandy on board, in small casks, commonly called half-ankers, holding about four gallons. There were about 50 of these. There were also 13 chests of tea, about 14lbs. weight in each. They were ready slung to carry over a person's shoulder. Witness found a great deal of beef, but very little bread on board, and no colours. The vessel had four six-pound carronades and a large quantity of small arms. There was a large quantity of gunpowder and cartridges lying about the deck; the swivel was gone. Witness heard at least a dozen of them speak in good English. Witness was wounded in the left shoulder by a musket ball. He did not know any of the prisoners.

In cross-examination, witness said he could not swear that he had not said the strange vessel was eight leagues off the English shore. When witness first saw her she was standing on the starboard tack for the French coast. The *Badger* was three or four miles distant from her at the time. The gaff-top-sail was hoisted and continued so during the chase. The name of the vessel was the *Vre Brodiers*. During the chase she endeavoured to get away. Witness had been twice examined relative to the transaction, and had said, when Cullum was killed, the action was general. The strange vessel fired first, which was returned, and then Cullum was killed. Witness did not find any papers on board. Knew that the vessel had been valued at £11,000.

Other witnesses gave corroborative evidence as to the facts deposed to by the lieutenant, and Dr. Lushington then rose for the defence. He said he had some objections to make to the present proceedings, which he relied on with the fullest confidence. The first was, the attack had been made by the *Badger* in their attempt to search the vessel, which was not authorised by any statue nor by the law of nations. His learned friends had not attempted to show that the vessel in question was a British ship. In fact not the slightest evidence had been offered to the effect. She was not said to have hoisted colours at any time. She was not, as he had before said, shown to be a British vessel, and therefore the cutter had no right to seize or examine her, for in doing so they were violating the law of nations. If such a doctrine was to be held up, as was contended for by his learned friends, and the judgment of the court should then, for the first time, go in unison with it, the consequences would make their lordships tremble for the issue. His second objection was that there existed no statute that authorised any act against the law of nations. During a time of peace, it was not competent for any cruiser, however authorised by the British Government, to detain any vessel but those of British subjects, with the exception of known and true pirates. The vessel was seized contrary to all law; she was on the high seas, and even nearer to the French coast than to the English. That was admitted; and if a British ship had a right to capture her, a French vessel possessed the same right. If the present prosecution was maintained, there was no pretence for saying that every merchant vessel, not only on the high seas, but even in harbours, might not be searched. He might detain their lordships with quotations from all the great writers on the law of nations for the previous 100 years, but he should after all return to where he set out from, namely, to the noble lord (Lord Stowell), who then presided on the bench. He would, however, content himself with calling their lordships attention to the judgment of his Lordship in the case of the ship *Louis* (captured in 1816 by the *Queen Charlotte*) in which eight men were killed and twelve wounded. The learned doctor then went at some length into the proceedings on that case, and concluded with observing that by the judgment of Lord Stowell, the vessel was restored, and up to the present day no one person had been tried for the lives that were lost. He then noticed the claim set up by the Danish Government to search English vessels, and eventually withdrawn, and asked what would be said if a British vessel was attempted to be searched by one belonging to France, and resistance ensued — would their country suffer their subjects to be taken to a French prison and sacrificed? The idea was preposterous. He would not argue that the legislature had not the right to regulate the conduct of British born subjects engaged as these individuals were, but under the very first clause — even under the preamble itself of the 45 George III, chap. 51, the customs were not empowered to search within 100 leagues of the British shore. The first words of the statute were 'Vessels coming to England? Was this vessel proved to have been doing so? No'; and consequently on the very first clause this prosecution must fail.

Mr. Justice Park intimated that they intended to leave the important points raised for the jury, and the Court having sat for twelve hours, it was decided to adjourn, the jury being sent to the London Tavern in charge of an officer of the Court, and notices sent to their friends of their detention.

On the following day, which was Saturday, Mr. Justice Park asked Mr. Brougham (in the absence of Dr. Lushington) whether he wished to have two papers put in by Dr. Lushington read, and he having replied in the affirmative, the papers were accordingly read. The first was a defence addressed to the Court by Reymer, stating that he was employed on board the *Four Brothers* as pilot on the day of the engagement, and took no part in it. The second was from Krans, master of the *Four Brothers*, stating that the *Four Brothers* belonged to Flushing, and that he was directed to land the cargo on the coast of Spain. It denied the right of England to bring a Dutch vessel to on the high seas in time of peace, or that any law made in this country could bind the subjects of another country, and suppoosing the French to have made a similar law, would the English submit to it? He solemnly denied that there was any cry for quarter on board of the *Four Brothers*, but said come overt statement was to be expected when it was considered that the *Four Brothers* and her cargo were worth £11,000, which, if forfeited, would almost all become the property of the master of the *Badger* and her crew. He also complained of the cruelty practised on him before he was taken to prison.

The following is transcribed from the minutes of evidence taken for the defence, given verbatim as it appeared:

John Belie, examined by Mr. Adolphus, said he was a shipbroker, well acquainted with the Dutch language and ship's papers; the papers produced (six in number) were the regular Dutch ship's papers; the clearance stated that the *Four Brothers* was bound to Ferrel; the names of the owners were never put in Dutch papers.

James Lowes, examined by Mr. Brougham: Witness was a shipbuilder at Flushing, was a native of Kent; he built the *Four Brothers*; she was launched in October; he sold her to Mr. Inglebert, a Dutchman, who lived with his family at Middleburg.

In his cross examination, he said he lived 35 years at Sandgate, and knew Joseph Wills, who was called Reymer, and was one of the prisoners; he was asked respecting his knowledge of all the other prisoners, but denied having seen any of them before except the Dutch master.

Bowing Dollering was examined through an interpreter. Witness was native of Middleburg, and merchant there. Mr. Inglebert was a merchant there, and a native. Knew the vessel called the *Four Brothers*. A cargo of tobacco, gin and tea was shipped on board her in January last by merchants of the firm of Minter and Co., one-third on account of witness. She cleared out for Feroe, a Danish island, but her real destination was Ferrol, Portugal. Orders were given to him to be delivered to the master to proceed to Portugal, and a letter was given to him to be delivered to a house there, which letter contained directions to sell the cargo and send the amount by the captain in cash. Directions were given to the master to take a pilot, as he was not sufficiently acquainted with the channel. Saw Mr. Inglebert on the 15th April at Middleburg. He was very ill; quite unable to come to this country. Witness produced the invoice of the cargo received from Minter and Co., by whom it was shipped. He paid for his one-third of the cargo to Inglebert.

On his cross-examination the witness said he had dealt in spirits and tobacco for years, shipped spirits in small casks and bottles, and tobacco in small parcels. The vessels in those cases were never sent to England or Ireland, nor the cargoes intended to be smuggled into England or Ireland.

Van Aldenberg, examined through the interpreter. 'Lived at Flushing, and kept a lodging house, and was a carpenter. Knew Cornelius Feymer as living at Flushing with his family for seven years. Was known there by the name of Joe Wills. Thought him an Englishman; he got his living as a seaman. Knew Cusing; he was a sail maker in Flushing and came from Ostend. Knew Cusing, the prisoner, for seven or eight years. Thought both Cusings were Englishmen. The register of Baptisms was kept in the town house of Flushing, which was burned to the ground by bombardment. Knew Abraham de Molinaar; the prisoner was a native of Flushing. The prisoner Bobileau was a Dutchman. Never heard his speak in any other language. Schmidt was also a Dutch sailor. His father was an Englishman and lived at Flushing. Knew Kreis de Molinaar; he was a native of Flushing. Knew one of the prisoners by the name of Wills seven or eight years. His father lived at Flushing 23 years ago, and had children living with him. He was an Englishman. He knew Joseph Sanders who was said to have been killed on board the *Four Brothers*.'

Mr. Brougham submitted that the proof respecting the country to which the men who were killed belonged lay with the prosecutors.

Mr. Justice Park said he should give no opinion on that point at present. The counsel for the defence would take their own course.

The examination of the witness proceeded: He was a Dutchman. Persons keeping lodging houses in Flushing were obliged to return an account of their lodgers every evening to the Commissary of Police. The other men who were said to be killed on board the *Four Brothers* had lodged in his house, and he always thought they were Americans, and returned them as such to the Commissary.

Contrad Conrad, examined by Mr. Brougham: Witness was a seaman living at Flushing, of which he was a native; he knew Joe Wills four years. He was a sailor and a burgher of Flushing, having a wife and family living there. Knew Thomas Cusing in Flushing eight or ten years. His grandfather was a sail maker living in Flushing.

Sarah Curtis, examined by Mr. Brougham: Was an Englishwoman and had lived in Flushing 29 years. Married Abraham de Molinaar, the father of Kreis Molinaar, the prisoner, who was her son. He was born at Flushing and brought up to the sea, and followed it ever since.

Richard Wills said he lived in Folkestone. Was son of Richard Wills, of Folkestone, a mariner. Remembered his mother going to Holland with his father. Witness was then eight years old. His mother brought a young son with her on her return. Witness identified the prisoner Reymer as his brother, who was then brought to England by his mother. William Wills, the witness's son, was born at Flushing. Witness was at Flushing on secret service for government. Was a burgher for Flushing 27 years. Witness identified the prisoner Yan Yenner as his son, William Wells, who was born at Flushing. Witness had been often there and lived there at that time for eighteen months. His brother, the prisoner, was about 47 years old.

Phillippa Lanbrasie examined, was 61 years old and had lived in Ostend 50 years. Knew a woman of the name of Elizabeth Wells, who came from England, and died at Ostend 30 years ago. She recollected another woman of the name of Wills having come to her husband at Ostend, and having a son there about the year 1776.

Eleanor Gates was an Engishwoman, living at Flushing, and other parts of the Netherlands thirty years. William Brice Wills was born in Flushing about 25 years before. The woman in whose house he was born was killed during the bombardment; she had known William Brice Wills ever since. Thomas Cusing was born in Flushing; she had known him ever since, living in Flushing when he was not at sea. Two years ago he was drafted into the Dutch Militia, and was liable to serve when called on.

Isabella Wills examined: George Wills, her husband, was an invalid on board the *Severn*; in January she attended him. The wounded men from the *Four Brothers* were brought on board. One of them, who had since died, raved very much; it was mostly in a foreign language.

Daniel Milton lived at Folkestone. The prisoner called Vollinmaree was his son, and was born in Flushing in the year 1789; witness lived there at the time for four years. Witness came home in the year 1790; after which England was the prisoner's home.

Ann Boxer lived at Folkestone. Hancock Allister, the prisoner, was her son, and was born at Ostend about forty years ago; her husband was a seaman, and she at that time stayed in Ostend for eighteen months, during which time her husband sailed from that port.

In her cross-examination she said she returned to England when her son was six months old, and had him baptised at Folkestone, where he had lived ever since, except when at sea.

William Boxer proved that he was master of a vessel in the year 1783; the father of the prisoner Boxer was one of the sailors; he took his wife to Ostend in that year, where she lived for some time.

Thomas Small was quarter-master on board the *Severn* in January; saw Vaness, who was deranged before he died, and raved sometimes in English and sometimes in Dutch.

Mr. Brougham mentioned to the Court that the counsel for the defence had now closed the evidence on national character.

After some conversation amongst the counsel for the prosecution, Mr. Nazer was called up and re-examined by Mr. Justice Park. They were nine or ten miles from the coast of France when they first saw the *Four Brothers* and thirteen or fourteen miles off the English coast when they came up with her; the *Four Brothers* was not at that time, while in his view, nearer the coast of France than nine or ten miles.

Pepplewell stated that when the *Four Brothers* was first seen she was about three or four leagues from the French coast; she was at no time nearer.

James Harper and Charles Brett corroborated this evidence.

M. Fouche examined: Was a Lieutenant of the French customs at Marlemont; he saw the engagement between the two vessels on the evening of the 13th of January, about eight o'clock; they were about one league from the shore; he made a report to his chief the day after.

Marce de Mouton saw two vessels near the French coast on the morning of the 13th January. They fired at each other. He could not see whether they had colours flying.

James Lorce, a Captain in the West India trade, was called and asked whether the *Four Brothers*, in the situation she was said to be at the time, could see the *Badger*'s colours, but it was ruled that the question could not be put.

This closed the case for the defence.

Mr. Justice Park charged the jury. He said that the crime for which the prisoners were tried was not murder, but was a capital offence under the 53rd of the late King. There were two things which, if found, would acquit the prisoners. The first was that no part of the vessel which the prisoners navigated belonged to any subject of his Majesty; the other that one half the crew were not his Majesty's subjects. For if neither of these facts existed, his Majesty's ship had no right to fire at their vessel. But if the jury believed that either any part of the vessel was British property, or that one half her crew were British subjects, then his Majesty's ship the *Badger*, under the circumstances that had been proved, being on her duty, and having her proper colours flying, was justified in boarding their vessel, and their making resistance by firing at the *Badger*, was a capital offence. The reason for which the evidence respecting the distance of the vessels from the French coast had been given, was, because by the law of nations, ships of war of any power were not permitted to attack in a hostile manner any vessel within one league of the coast of any other power in time of peace, but the evidence given on that point could not leave any doubt in the minds of the jury that the vessels were more than a league distant from the French coast at the time the *Badger* required the *Four Brothers* to come to; and could not form any justification of the conduct of the prisoners. His Lordship made several observations on the evidence given to prove that a majority of the prisoners were English subjects, which he appeared to think greatly preponderated over that which had been produced to prove the converse of that fact. The first question for the consideration of the jury was whether the ship, either wholly or in part, was British property, and the next, which of the prisoners were British and which were foreign subjects, for upon this hereafter would arise a most weighty consideration of law, which was new; and must be decided by the judges of the land. It was not because a person was born locally abroad, his parents being British, that therefore he ceased to be a British subject, and entitled to the privileges and bound by the allegiance of such within the realm of the King. But it might so happen that a person born abroad, possessed as it were a double character — his foreign character being that of a merchantile person, and yet subject to the British law when here upon any of his occasions. The learned judge then read over the names of the six prisoners who had pleaded in Dutch, and also of five others, on behalf of whom evidence was offered of foreign birth. There were then the thirteen others, who were, if the evidence for the prosecution was sustained, to all intents and purposes clearly British subjects. He concluded by directing the jury to find a special verdict upon the points he had mentioned, so as to raise the ultimate consideration upon the law of the case.

At five o'clock the jury retired, and having deliberated for two hours, returned a verdict of Not Guilty for all the prisoners, finding that the ship and cargo were wholly foreign property, and that more than one half of the crew were foreigners. The announcement of the verdict was received with shouts of approbation by the crowd assembled in the court yard.

The prisoners were then given a charge on an indictment for murder, for which a bill had been found in consequence of one of the *Badger*'s crew (Cullum) having been killed, and no evidence being offered, they were immediately acquitted.

Bibliography

W. Carter	*England's Interest in Trade Asserted*, 1671.
B. F. Richards	Smuggling in Sussex a Hundred Years Ago (*Sussex County Magazine*, Vol. 4).
W. S. Grant	*The Golden Fleece*, 1656.
	First Report into illicit practices used in defrauding the Revenue, 1743.
	Committee to Inquire into the Most Infamous Practice of Smuggling (*House of Commons Journal*, 19, George II).
J. Treves	An Essay to the Restoring of Our Decayed Trade.
J. Manwaring-Baines	*Historic Hastings*.
Majendie	*The Administration of the Poor Law in East Sussex*, 1833.
K. M. Clarke	*Smuggling in Rye and District*.
W. Cooper	*Smuggling in Sussex*.
John Smith	*Memoirs of Wool*, 1747.
	The Sayer Manuscripts (East Sussex Records Office)
	Sussex Weekly Advertiser.
	State Papers Domestic 1672 and following Report to Inquire into Frauds and Abuses in the Customs, 1733.
George Bishop	*Remarks and Means to Prevent Smuggling*, 1783.
A Gentleman of Chichester	*The Genuine History of the Murders of Mr William Galley and Mr Daniel Chater*, 1749.
Elizabeth Melling (ed.)	Kentish Sources (*Crime and Punishment*, Vol. VI).
Margaret Brentnall	*The Cinque Ports and Romney Marsh*.
Brian Matthews	*A History of Strood Rural District*.
Robert H. Goodsall	*A Kentish Patchwork*.
Charles Igglesden	*A Saunter Through Kent with Pen and Pencil*.
F. F. Nicholls	*Honest Thieves*.
H. N. Shore	*Smuggling Days and Smuggling Ways*.
Charles Harper and Lord Teignmouth	*The Smugglers* (2 volumes).
An Old Folkestone Smuggler	*Smugglers and Smuggling Days*.
John Banks	*Smugglers and Smuggling*.
	The Kentish Gazette.

Acknowledgments

East Sussex County Library
Kent County Library
Kent County Archives Department
The Kentish Gazette
The Kent Messenger
H.M. Customs and Excise
Mr Barry Marsh
Mr Godfrey George

And all others too numerous to mention who have assisted in any way.
Cover illustration courtesy of Mary Evans Picture Library.

Index